P9-BIU-622

Handbook for Business Writing

L. Sue Baugh/Maridell Fryar/David Thomas

NTC Business Books
NTC a division of *NTC Publishing Group* • Lincolnwood, Illinois USA

Acknowledgments

Several people gave their support and assistance in preparing this handbook. For the chapters on business letters, we would like to express our appreciation for the valuable assistance of Patricia A. McDonough, corporate communications consultant. She made many excellent suggestions for sample letters and provided numerous tips on creating effective business communications for various audiences.

Special thanks also to Booz·Allen & Hamilton Inc. and Mitchell Bros. Realtors for their kind permission to use their letterheads for our sample letters.

For the chapter covering employment letters and resume writing, we drew on materials developed by the University of Houston Career Planning and Placement Center for its *Placement Manual.* Thanks are due to David B. Small, Director of the Center, for permission to use that material. Thanks also go to TOPS Business Forms, Division of Wallace Computer Services, Inc. for permission to use their Employment Application Form.

Section Seven, The Electronic Office, is unique in its future orientation. We are indebted to Mr. Jules Vieux of the Public Relations Department of Computerland's Houston area headquarters for his assistance in obtaining current information about office technology. In addition, special thanks go to Linda Montgomery of Digital Equipment Corp., Jack Ciak of Dictaphone Corp., Edward F. Clough of Wang Laboratories, Inc., Don Mathias of National Cash Register, and Bobbie Bethel of Xerox Corp.

Our sincere gratitude goes to our editor, Gay Menges, and copyeditor, John Stec, for their patience, tireless work, and many valuable suggestions.

1991 Printing

Published by NTC Business Books, a division of NTC Publishing Group.

Manufactured in the United States of America.
Library of Congress Catalog Card Number: 85-71592

1 2 3 4 5 6 7 8 9 ML 9 8 7

Contents

How To Use This Handbook

Whether you are a beginning or experienced writer, this handbook is designed to help you find answers to your specific business writing problems quickly and efficiently.

Finding What You Need

To get the greatest benefit from this handbook, you should be familiar with four ways you can locate the guidelines, information, and examples you need.

1. Read through Chapter 1. The first chapter, Three Steps to Effective Writing, summarizes a step-by-step approach to good writing you can use for any type of business communication. The approach breaks down the writing process into three stages: prewriting (preparation and background research); writing (outlining and writing first drafts); and revision (rewriting and proofreading). These three steps will help you prepare, plan, and write your letters, memos, reports, and other types of communication.

2. Use Specific Sections. Sections Two through Five cover specific types of business writing. Beginners will appreciate the detailed guidelines and examples in section chapters that show how to create effective business messages. Experienced writers can use the chapters' quick reviews, checklists, and samples to strengthen writing skills they have already developed.

3. Use Specific Chapters. You can select the particular business communication you need—letter, memo, proposal—and turn to the chapter(s) covering that topic. For example, you may need guidelines for writing a press release. Chapter 11 contains brief tips and complete examples for creating press releases commonly used in business.

4. Use the Index. The Index is cross-referenced to help you find related topics or locate a subject when you are not sure what to call it. For example, you may want to know how many dots to put in a quotation to show you have omitted part of the quote. Under the heading "Quotations" you will find an entry "ellipses" and a page number. You will also find the same entry under "Period."

Special Features of This Handbook

As a business writer—beginning or experienced—you will find several features of this book particularly valuable.

1. ***Review of Business Style.*** While there is no special language for business writing, certain points of style—tone, clarity, accuracy, brevity—are important to your message. Chapter 2: Choosing the Right Word; Chapter 4: Style in Business Letters; Chapter 10: Business Report Writing; and Chapter 11: Proposals and Press Releases provide brief, vivid reviews of major points in business style. These guidelines can help you write messages that will influence your readers and get results.

2. ***Finding Business Information.*** In the Information Age, locating the data you need can cost considerable time and money. Chapter 12: Finding Business Information shows you how to locate data sources and use the computer to save time gathering information. Advances in electronic communications technology have brought vast quantities of data within the reach of individuals as well as companies.

3. ***Finding the Right Job.*** Section Five: Business Writing and the Job Search covers resumes, job applications, and various employment letters you will need to find the job you want. You will learn how to create an attention-getting resume; fill out job applications; and write letters of application, acknowledgment, acceptance or refusal of a job offer, recommendation, and resignation. A well-written letter can be one of the best ways to introduce yourself to a prospective employer.

4. ***Review of Business Grammar and Style.*** Section Six provides a practical and thorough review of grammar, style, and spelling questions that plague most business writers. Chapters 14 through 18 cover parts of speech, sentence structure, punctuation, capitalization, abbreviations, numbers and spelling guidelines. You can review an entire chapter or look up specific topics in the Index to locate the exact information you need.

Good writing is no accident; it's the result of planning, practice, and revision. The guidelines and examples in this handbook can help you become the effective business writer you would like to be. We hope you enjoy the process!

Section 1
Business Writing Today

Chapter 1 Three Steps to Effective Writing

Many competent, articulate business people experience a moment of panic when they are asked to write a report, memo, or letter. Faced with putting their thoughts in writing, they become confused about what to say, how to say it, and how to manage the mechanics of grammar, spelling, and format.

If you are one of these people—and many of us are—relax! Like any business task, writing is manageable once you break it down into a series of smaller steps. Good writing is the result of good planning and clear thinking. The steps outlined in this handbook will help you identify your purpose in writing any type of business communication, clarify your thinking about what you want to say, and show you how to go about the actual process of getting your message to the reader.

This chapter presents an overview of the three basic steps to effective writing. You will see how to apply these steps in more detail in the chapters on business letters, memos, proposals and press releases, and special writing projects. Once you have a grasp of the principles of good writing, you will be able to use them for any written message, regardless of its length or complexity. The three steps to effective writing are:

Step One: Prewriting—preparation, planning, background research

Step Two: Writing—organizing and outlining material, writing the first draft

Step Three: Revising—reworking and editing the draft, final typing and printing, proofreading

Step One: Prewriting

Before you begin any project, you must decide what you want to accomplish and how you wish to accomplish it. You begin with a *concept*: a question, a problem, a new situation. You gather *facts* to flesh out the concept. What type of problem is it? What is the question? How much can you learn about the situation? Finally, you end up with a *finished product*: a letter, a report, a memo.

In step one, prewriting, you are defining the concept and gathering the facts that will serve as material for step two, writing.

Preparation

All your written communications in business should seek to answer these questions:

1. What is the purpose of this message? Why am I writing it?
2. Who is the audience? Whom do I want to influence?
3. What do I want to say? What is the scope of my subject?

You will first decide on a *purpose*. Do you want to sell a new product or replace an old one? Do you want to supply information or ask for a favor? In one or two sentences or a brief paragraph, state the purpose of your message. If necessary, talk the subject over with others until you have a clear idea of your objective.

Second, think about your *audience*. What should readers know or be able to do after reading your message? What is their level of understanding or expertise regarding the subject? Do you want to persuade them to do or to accept something? What are their interests and motivations—profit, comfort, health, convenience, savings?

Put yourself in the readers' place as much as you can and look at your subject from their perspective. For example, when reporting on company year-end performance, you would write different reports to the vice president of sales, the marketing manager, the president of the company, and the stockholders. Each reader would want to know different types of information and would have different levels of expertise. You need to tailor your message to the level and interests of the audience.

Answers to the first and second questions will help you answer the third—what do you want to say and what is the *scope* of your subject? You must distinguish between information the reader *needs* to know and information that is merely nice to know. For example, in your year-end performance report you would include product sales figures but not a history of the product in American culture—unless the reader specifically had requested it. You must limit your subject and focus on specific topics.

Background Research

By answering the first three questions, you determine what types of information you will need for your writing. The amount of research required can vary greatly, depending on the subject and purpose. In general, you have four basic sources of information:

1. Libraries—public, specialized, and industry libraries
2. Other people—interviews with experts and others, questionnaires, surveys
3. Industry and government—industry associations and groups, government agencies and officials
4. Your own knowledge—experience, training, education

Your research may be as brief as jotting down sales figures from memory or as lengthy as several weeks or months of gathering data for a report on new site locations. Replying to customer inquiries or complaints can also vary from a few minutes to several days or weeks. If your job requires research, learn how to use the various research tools available through libraries and other reference sources. Chapter 13: Finding Business Information provides a list of resources for locating data quickly.

When gathering information, remember the three cardinal rules of journalism: accuracy, accuracy, and accuracy. Make sure you copy or quote information correctly and have the data to support your statements. Nothing loses a reader's confidence in a writer's work more quickly than discovering errors in the material. Two or three careless mistakes can cast doubt on the credibility of the entire document. Check your facts from sales figures to the correct spelling of the company name and name of the addressee.

Step Two: Writing

You have established your purpose, identified your audience, defined your topic, and gathered your data. Now you are ready for the second step—organizing and writing the first draft.

Organizing

How you organize your material depends on your subject and your purpose for writing. For example, if you are giving instructions on machine assembly, you would choose a step-by-step approach to explain how the machine is put together. If you are making a special offer to a customer or breaking bad news to a client, you would put the most important information first, then fill in the details. Each type of letter or report has a specific purpose that will determine how you organize and arrange the material for the most effective presentation.

Outlining

Once you have chosen the format, the next step is outlining what you want to say and the order in which you want to say it. An outline breaks down a large topic into manageable bits and helps ensure that your writing flows logically from one part to another. The outline corresponds to a blueprint for a building. The more complete the blueprint, the easier it is to construct the building. Likewise, the more detailed the outline, the easier it will be to write the letter, report, or memo. Developing the outline enables you to see the process of your thinking at an early stage. You can spot gaps in data or logic quickly and fill them in before you get to the writing stage.

Outlining is also a good time to think about illustrations or graphics. Will your sales figures mean more to the reader if they are shown in a bar chart or colored pie chart? With the graphics capabilities of many computers, creating illustrations for text can be relatively easy. Check through your outline to determine where illustrations could make your presentation more effective.

Writing the First Draft

Your outline is complete, and you are ready to write your first draft. Many writers make a common mistake at this point. They try to "get it right" the first time. They may work on a paragraph for hours, fine-tuning the words until they are perfect. Writers thus shut off their creativity by insisting on perfection.

Remember: *The first draft is a working draft*. It should be written quickly without too much thought to elegant expressions or final order and paragraphing. Your object is to get the material on paper to flesh out the structure of your outline. Let the words flow. Start wherever you can—in the middle, even near the end. The opening or introduction can be completed later. Any weaknesses in logic or gaps in information, any points that are out of place can be corrected in the final version.

As you write the first draft, keep your audience in mind. Doing so will help you stay focused on the purpose of your work. Keep writing until you have completed the first draft.

Step Three: Revising

When you begin to revise your material, you are reading it primarily from the *reader's* point of view, not the writer's. If possible, give the draft to others and ask for their comments and suggestions. Let a few hours or days go by before you read your draft again. By allowing the material to "cool off," you can spot inconsistencies and errors more easily.

Read the draft several times. Don't try to correct everything the first time through. Check the facts and data in your draft. If you change a set of figures in one place, be sure you change the same set of figures when they appear again. Make sure your ideas are unified and transitions smooth from paragraph to paragraph, leading the reader from one step to the next. The lead sentence or "topic" sentence in the paragraph should give the reader the substance of what is discussed. Following sentences should elaborate on the idea and develop it fully.

Ask yourself, Is the text clear? Do you need to define special terms or phrases? Are your explanations complete or do they skip steps? Have you packed too many ideas into one paragraph? Have you fully developed your argument or explained your proposal so the basic objectives are clear to the reader?

Check your work for errors in style and grammar. Perhaps you can eliminate overused words and phrases. Make sure you write in the active voice rather than the passive voice. Vary your sentence structure to avoid a series of short, choppy sentences or long, complex ones. Read your draft for errors in spelling and punctuation. Section Six provides a review of grammar and style used in business communication.

Finally, revise your work for awkward phrases and lapses in tone. Awkward writing will sound clumsy and over-written, as though the words were stumbling over one another. For example, "We would like you, if you could, to look into the delay and readvise us of certain aspects of the situation which we have not been able, at this end, to ascertain." The writer meant to say, "Please investigate the delay and let us know why it happened. We have not been able to discover the reason ourselves."

Tone is the relationship you wish to establish with the reader. It may be formal, informal, academic, casual, or humorous, depending on the subject and the situation. For example, in a letter to a financial institution, company officer, or board of directors, you would adopt a formal, conservative tone. In a sales letter, you may want to use a more casual, humorous tone to engage the reader at a more familiar and friendly level. You can recognize lapses in tone by the appearance of inappropriate words or phrases in your material. For instance, you would not want to use slang or jargon in the letter to your conservative client. Nor would you insert a formal discussion of product specifications in a casual, light-hearted promotional piece. Consistency of tone will help you establish and maintain the appropriate relationship with your reader.

After your revised draft has been retyped in final form, be sure to proofread the material carefully. It's your last opportunity to catch any errors that have slipped through or that the typist has inadvertently overlooked. You don't want the reader to catch your mistakes. Proofreading your work carefully can save you considerable embarrassment.

Summary

Below is a brief checklist for the three basic steps to effective writing.

Step One: Prewriting

1. Identify and state your purpose.
2. Know your audience.
3. Define the scope of your subject.
4. Conduct background research and gather data.

Step Two: Writing

5. Organize the data and devise a rough plan.
6. Outline your writing project.
7. Write the first draft.

Step Three: Revising

8. Edit and rewrite the draft for clarity, tone, accuracy, brevity.
9. Check for grammar and spelling errors and other careless mistakes.
10. Make sure the final typed copy is neat and free from erasures, strikeovers, smudges, and other marks.

The three steps of effective writing—prewriting, writing, and revising—can be used for any type of business communication. As you practice them and become more skilled in the writing process, you will be able to work through each step more quickly. Throughout the handbook, you will see how these steps are used to develop the various types of letters, reports, memos, and proposals in business.

Chapter 2 Choosing the Right Word

Throughout much of your business career, you will use the written word to communicate with co-workers, managers, customers, suppliers, and creditors. Your messages must speak for you; you cannot stand at the reader's shoulder and explain what you mean. In addition, your letters, memos, reports, and other communications represent not only you but your company. As a result, you must choose your words with care.

In this chapter, we look at some of the guidelines used in business style, including business vocabulary, words frequently confused, and gender-inclusive language. We provide only an overview here. More detailed discussions of style are taken up in the chapters on writing various business communications. For specific grammar questions, see the chapters in Section Six reviewing business grammar and spelling.

Business Vocabulary

Business vocabulary is more than simply knowing some of the special terms used in various professions and industries. It is understanding the difference between everyday language and the language we adopt for more formal communication. Our casual conversational style is generally too vague and imprecise for most business writing.

Avoid the use of slang in your writing. It not only weakens your message but often leaves the reader wondering what you meant to say.

Avoid: The Purchasing Department considered the price from Allied a rip-off.

Better: The Purchasing Department considered the price from Allied much too high. (Explains more precisely what is wrong with the price.)

Avoid: I think Carla's analysis is a little far out in this case.

Better: I think Carla's analysis doesn't take into consideration the long-term impact of the problem. (Explains in specific terms the speaker's objections to Carla's evaluation.)

Avoid: The requirements for this job are unreal!

Better: The requirements for this job include having a Ph.D!

Avoid using overly technical terms, unfamiliar abbreviations, or terms that relate to a particular profession or specialty when you are writing to someone who may not be familiar with such terms. Jargon, like slang, can confuse the reader and obscure your message.

Avoid: We place a great deal of emphasis on employee participation through our QWL and MBO programs.

Better: We place a great deal of emphasis on employee participation through our quality of worklife and management by objectives programs.

Avoid: After analyzing your software program, we found an error that produced an infinite do-loop in the run.

Better: After analyzing your software program, we found an error that instructed the computer to repeat a step endlessly.

In general, avoid the use of clichés, that is, worn-out phrases such as "big as a house," "nose to the grindstone," and the like. Instead, choose words that convey more precisely the particular condition or situation you are describing.

Avoid: To reduce costs, we've got to keep our eye on the ball.

Better: To reduce costs, we've got to keep accurate records of all expenditures and look for ways to cut our overhead.

Avoid: Richard has heard from only one of two clients and is waiting for the other shoe to drop.

Better: Richard has heard from only one of two clients but is expecting a reply shortly from the second.

A good dictionary and a complete thesaurus (a reference book for locating synonyms and opposites) are your best sources for finding the right word. Use these reference works often. They can enhance your business vocabulary and help you express yourself clearly and accurately in your writing.

Words Frequently Confused

The meaning and spelling of the following words are commonly confused. Practice using them until they become familiar to you.

accept **except**	accept—to take, agree. I accept the offer. except—to exclude, omit. It's OK, except for this.
advice **advise**	advice—opinion, counsel. He needs your advice. advise—to counsel. Please advise him.
affect **effect**	affect—influence, change. Inflation always affects our level of income. effect—impression, results; to cause. The computer has had a profound effect on communications. It has effected a real change in office procedures.
already **all ready**	already—even now. They are already here. all ready—all prepared. We're all ready to leave.
assent **ascent**	assent—to agree; permission. Did you assent to the request? She gave her assent to the project. ascent—advancement. He made the ascent up the corporate ladder.
capital **capitol**	capital—seat of government; wealth. Our sales force is in the capital city. We need more capital. capitol—government building. We are in the capitol.
cite **site** **sight**	cite—refer to. He cited new sales figures. site—location. The new building site is in Dallas. sight—scene. The skyline is a beautiful sight.

consul
council
counsel

consul—foreign embassy official. Check these trade arrangements with the West German consul.

council—official body. The city council met.

counsel—legal advisor. The corporate lawyer will act as counsel in this matter.

counsel—to advise. Older employees often counsel younger workers about their new job duties.

continuous
continual

continuous—uninterrupted, unbroken. A continuous water supply is essential.

continual—repeatedly. The printer typed the same letter continually.

dissent
descent
descend

dissent—disagreement. Voice your dissent at the meeting tonight.

descent—a decline, fall. Sales made a steep descent.

descend—to come down. Commands descend from the top management.

fewer
less

fewer—used for numbers, individual units. We require fewer salespeople.

less—used for quantities. Net income was less than last year.

formerly
formally

formerly—previously. She was formerly at IBM.

formally—officially. She joined formally today.

later
latter

later—after a time. I'll deal with that later.

latter—last mentioned of the two. If I'm offered a raise or a promotion, I'll take the latter.

lie
lay

lie—to rest or recline. I lie down. I lay down this morning. I should have lain down earlier.

lay—to put or place something. I lay the book on your desk. I laid it there a minute ago. I have laid it there many times and never lost it.

lose **loose**	lose—misplace. Don't lose that address. loose—not fastened down; release. The pressure plate seems loose. Turn loose your imagination.
past **passed**	past—preceding. Our past record is good. passed—to go by. Production this year passed last year's high. We passed the factory this morning.
personal **personnel**	personal—individual. I jog for personal reasons. personnel—workers; a department. The personnel office knows what motivates company personnel.
precede **proceed**	precede—to come before. Hard work precedes recognition. proceed—to go ahead. We can proceed with the talk.
principle **principal**	principle—rule, standard. Values are principles that guide our lives. principal—main, chief; superintendent. His principal goal is quality. The principal taught us well.
quiet **quite**	quiet—silence. The office is quiet after five. quite—completely; to a considerable degree. I am quite sure she'll come. He's quite a person!
rise **raise**	rise—to go up, to get up. I rise early each day. I rose a little late yesterday. However, I have risen on time today. raise—to lift, bring up. If you need help, raise your hand. I am raising this issue for a good reason. No one raised an objection before. You have raised your hand three times in the past half hour.
sit **set**	sit—to assume an upright position. I sit at my desk. I sat here yesterday. I have sat here for years, it seems. set—put or place something down. I set your lunch on the table. I set the coffee there a minute ago. I have set it all in front of you.

stationary
stationery

stationary—still, fixed. The chair is stationary.

stationery—letter paper. The company stationery is printed on gray paper.

than
then

than—after a comparison; when. I'm taller than Ted. The copier no sooner started than it broke down.

then—next; in that case. She spoke, then left. If you want more pens, then I'll order some.

weather
whether

weather—climate. The crop needs good weather.

whether—if; regardless. I'm going whether you're coming or not. Do you know whether she's at home?

Gender-Inclusive Language

In today's business world, you will find both men and women in all types of occupations and at all levels in an organization. As a result, it is important not to assume that your readers are all male or all female. Increasingly, business firms are phasing out the use of *he, his, man, mankind,* and other exclusively masculine terms to refer to both sexes. The modern business writer uses language and references that are gender-inclusive, that is, not biased toward either sex but include both. Below are some practical guidelines for using gender-inclusive language in your business communication.

Avoid thinking in stereotypes—the manager is male, the secretary female—in your writing.

Avoid: Our course is designed to help your assistant or secretary reach her potential. (The person could be a man.)

Revised: Our course is designed to develop the full potential of your secretary or assistant.

Avoid: The prudent executive needs to know where his money goes. (More women are reaching the top of their professions, and companies and advertisers are recognizing them as a new market.)

Revised: Prudent executives need to know where their money goes. *Or:* As a prudent executive, you need to know where your money goes.

Rephrase sentences to avoid awkward constructions. The constant repetition of *his or her, he or she, him or her* can call attention to gender rather than subordinate it to the message. When possible, rephrase the sentence by using the plural form, changing word order, using *I, we, you, they,* and the like.

Avoid: If the employee is late, give him one warning.

Revised: An employee who is late receives one warning.

Avoid: If the manager files his or her report by Wednesday, he or she will have the revised copy returned to him or her on Friday.

Revised: Managers who file their reports on Monday will have a revised copy returned to them by Friday.

Avoid: Don't judge someone simply on the basis of his sex or color.

Revised: Don't judge someone simply on the basis of sex or color.

Or: Don't judge people simply on the basis of their sex or color.

Or: One shouldn't be judged simply on the basis of sex or color.

Titles, names of positions or occupations, and common references can also be made gender-inclusive. The U.S. Department of Labor in its *Occupational Outlook Handbook* lists nonbiased titles for all occupations and positions, such as the following:

Avoid:	*Revised:*
salesman	salesperson
chairman	chair, chairperson
craftsman	craftworker
draftsman	drafter
fireman	firefighter
watchman	guard, security officer
newsman	reporter, newspeople
foreman	supervisor
repairman	repairer
mailman	mail carrier, letter carrier
policeman	police officer

man-hours	staff-hours
man-made	artificial, synthetic
mankind	humanity, people, human race
man the office	staff the office
saleslady	clerk
gal Friday	assistant

Salutations in business letters should also be gender-inclusive when the name of the person addressed is not known. Many companies use the following salutations.

Dear Supervisor:
Dear Executive:
Dear Manager:
Dear Colleague:
(to those of the same rank or occupation)

Dear Customer:
Dear Subscriber:
Dear Investor:
Dear Friend:
(letter written as an appeal or to inform)

Section 2
Effective Business Letters

Chapter 3 Business Letter Format

In this chapter we take a look at the functions of business letters, the different parts of a letter, and various formats used to create professional, attractive communications.

Functions of Business Letters

Business letters are an indispensible part of business communication. Without them, much of the ordinary activities of business would not be possible. They are used to sell products or services, request material or information, answer customer inquiries, maintain good public relations, and serve a variety of other business functions.

In this age of rapid communications, you may ask if many of these activities couldn't be handled over the phone or in person. In some cases, these two methods may be the best way to get your message across. But few business people have the time to visit clients personally, and long-distance telephone calls can be time-consuming and expensive. More importantly, most people retain only about *25 percent* of what they hear. The chances of your message being forgotten or misunderstood greatly increase if you rely on oral communication.

As a result, "putting it in writing" remains one of the best ways to ensure that your message is accurately received, particularly if you are discussing technical or highly detailed information.

Business letters also serve as part of a company's permanent record. They can be used to verify bookkeeping and inventory entries. If you have a question about a customer order, whether someone's query was answered, or about the details in an agreement, you can check your file copy of the letter. You cannot do the same with a phone conversation unless you record every outgoing and incoming call!

Letters also function as written contracts, fully recognized by the courts. *Letters of agreement* are often drawn up between companies and independent suppliers or consultants. Job offers made through the mail are regarded as legally binding on the sender. If you accept in writing, your letter is a binding contract of employment.

Letters can act as formal or informal public relations material. They can help build goodwill between you and your clients, creditors, suppliers, and other public groups. Your letter represents you and your firm to people you may never meet personally or call on the phone. How you express yourself and the appearance of your letter forms an impression in the reader's mind of you and your business.

Every letter that leaves your office fulfills several purposes. As a result, your business letters deserve considerable care and attention.

Parts of a Business Letter

Most business letters, regardless of their purpose, have the following basic parts:

1. Heading or Letterhead
2. Dateline
3. Inside Address
4. Reference Lines (Attention, Personal and Confidential, Subject)
5. Salutation
6. Body
7. Complimentary Close
8. Signature
9. Stenographic Reference
10. Enclosures or Copies

Heading or Letterhead

In most cases, the heading of a letter is simply the printed letterhead on the company stationery giving the company name, address(es), phone number(s), and perhaps the name of an officer or correspondent. If the stationery you are using does not have a printed letterhead, type the company name, address, and phone number in the upper right-hand corner of the paper about one and one-half inches from the top and flush with the right margin.

Dateline

All business letters should have the correct date typed under the letterhead. The date records when the letter was written and may serve as an important reference. For example, if there is a question about an order or shipment, a contract, or a reply to customer complaints, you will have the dated copy of a letter in your files to verify when you wrote the message and what you said. Try to mail the letter on or close to the date typed under the letterhead. The postmark on the envelope and the date in your letter should correspond as closely as possible.

Inside Address

The inside address is typed below the dateline. It is single-spaced and placed flush against the left margin. The inside address contains the name, title, company division or department (if any), mailing address, and zip code of the receiver.

Mr. Alfred McKenna, Treasurer
Finance and Accounting Department
Warrne, Hanson & Associates
459 Third Avenue
New York, New York 10017

Reference Lines

In some cases you will want to call special attention to the subject of the letter or single out a particular person to whom the letter is addressed in a company. You would use a reference line for this purpose.

The reference "Personal and Confidential" is typed in initial capitals and underscored before the inside address as follows:

Personal and Confidential

Ms. Jane Purdy, Vice President
Trust Department
First National Bank of Atlanta
900 Grove Street
Atlanta, Georgia 30319

The other reference lines "Attention" and "Subject" are typed below the inside address. They are followed by a colon and are not underscored.

Mr. Earl Jacobs, Sales Manager
Merchant's Restaurant
633 South Dearborn
Leland, Kansas 67073

Subject: Delivery of red snapper catch

Personnel Department
Western Utilities, Inc.
817 West Main Street
Denver, Colorado 80061

Attention: Reena Culver, Data Processor

Salutation

After the inside address or reference line, the salutation is typed two lines down, flush with the left margin, and followed by a colon. The salutations for the above inside addresses are as follows:

Dear Ms. (or Miss or Mrs.) Culver:
Dear Mr. Jacobs:
Dear Ms. (or Miss or Mrs.) Purdy:
Dear Mr. McKenna:

If you do not know the name of the recipient but do know that you will be addressing a man or woman, your salutation would be:

Dear Sir:

Dear Madam:

If you do not know whom the receiver will be, use a title or some general greeting for the salutation:

To Our Friends at Royal:
Dear Manager:
Dear Executive:
Dear Members:
To the Sales Staff:

Various forms of address used in salutations are described in more detail in Chapter 6: Producing the Business Letter, pages 62-67. As a rule, use a formal salutation in your correspondence, even if you know the person to whom the letter is addressed.

Body of the Letter

The body of the business letter begins two lines down from the salutation. The body can be typed in block style with no paragraph indentations or semiblock style in which the paragraphs are indented. There is no "correct" style. Which one you use is a matter of personal or company preference. Paragraphs are typed single-space with double spaces between them.

It is best, even for a short letter, to divide the body into at least two or three paragraphs. This step makes your text easier to read and presents your message more clearly. A typical plan for a three-paragraph letter would look like the following:

1. Paragraph one—Begin with information that catches the reader's attention and refers to some need or interest of the reader. Put the "you" into the letter.

2. Paragraph two—Bring in your involvement, what role you are playing or what service or information you have to offer. Put "you and I" into the letter.

3. Paragraph three—End the body of the letter with the action or idea that you want the reader to consider or with the results you would like to have. Keep the "you and I" in the reader's mind, but emphasize "you."

The example below follows the basic plan of the business letter.

> In your October 10 letter, you mentioned that your company was purchasing an IBM office system with a main computer and several terminals and printers. You asked for a quote on our acoustical covers for microprinters.
>
> I am happy to report we can offer you a substantial discount on a lot order of 20-25 acoustical covers. These covers will fit any microprinter and can be adapted to fit printer options such as single-sheet feeders and track feeders. They will reduce printer noise levels by 80 percent. Studies have shown that lower levels of noise in the office increase productivity and worker efficiency.
>
> The discount offer will expire November 30. You can take advantage of our discount by phoning in your order, using our toll-free number. I would be happy to arrange for shipment directly to your home office or warehouse.

Notice that the writer states the reader's needs in the first sentence. The following paragraph describes how the writer can help satisfy that need. The closing paragraph outlines the desired actions for the recipient and the writer. The plan of the letter helps the writer be concise, specific, and direct.

Complimentary Close

The complimentary close is typed one double space after the body of the letter. It can be centered on the page or set flush with the left or right margin. The preferred complimentary close for most business letters is *Sincerely,* although many companies also use *Yours truly* or *Sincerely yours.*

The closing is followed by four lines and the typed name and title of the person sending the letter. In rare instances when the letter is not typed on letterhead stationery, the company name and address follow the name and title of the sender. A phone number or extension may also be included if the writer wishes to have a quick reply to the letter.

Sincerely,	Yours truly,
Frank W. Weston Vice President, Distribution	Caroline Roberts Admissions Office University of Arizona 445 Yellow Spring Road Tucson, Arizona 85725

Signature

The writer signs his or her name in ink in the space between the complimentary closing and the typed name. If you are signing for someone else or using a stamped signature, put your initials after the signature and on the same line.

Stenographic Reference

These reference initials refer to the person who is sending the letter and to the typist. The sender's initials are typed in all capitals, followed by a colon or a slash, then the initials of the typist in lowercase letters: FWW:tg or FWW/tg.

Stenographic reference initials appear one double space below the last line of the typed signature and are set flush with the left margin. In some companies, only the typist's initials, in lowercase letters, are used. If you type your own letters, omit the reference initials.

Enclosures or Copies

This designation is typed one single space below the stenographic initials. It alerts the reader to the fact that material has been enclosed with the letter or that copies of the letter have been sent to others. You may want to list the enclosures or simply indicate how many have been included. The reader can then check to make sure all the material is there. In general, you would list the names of those receiving copies of the letter.

Encl:	*or*	Enclosures: (5)	*or*	Enclosures: Map Brochure Car rentals Hotel list

cc: *or* Copies: R. Hanlin, Treasurer
M. McKenna, Secretary
T. Freund, Sales Manager

The parts of a business letter are discussed in more detail in Chapter 6: Producing the Business Letter.

Format for Business Letters

Format styles most often used in business letters include Full Block, Block, Semiblock, and Simplified. The main differences among them are the placement of the date, complimentary close, and signature block, and whether paragraph indentations are used.

Full Block is the easiest format to use, since all lines are flush with the left margin. However, some people prefer a more balanced appearance in which the date, complimentary close, and signature all begin near the center of the page, as in Block and Semiblock. Simplified, a newer format, is gaining popularity. It eliminates the problem of gender-specific salutations by doing away with the salutation line altogether. Pages 25-28 provide examples of Full Block, Block, Semiblock, and Simplified formats.

Whichever format you adopt, be consistent. Do not mix styles, that is, indenting your paragraphs while setting your complimentary close and signature flush with the left margin. The appearance of your letter on the page will influence the reader's perception of your message.

Full Block

NATIONAL TEXTBOOK COMPANY
4255 West Touhy Avenue • Lincolnwood Illinois 60646-1975 U.S.A.
Area 312/679-5500 Telex TWX 910 223 0736 (PATGROUP LCWD)

May 7, 19--

3-4 lines

Mr. Oscar Hamlin
Rightway Printers, Inc.
667 Oakton Road
Chicago, Illinois 60646

2 lines

Dear Mr. Hamlin:

2 lines

I received your quote for printing the book INTRODUCTION TO FILM. I am pleased to tell you we have accepted your bid and will be sending you copyboards by May 15.

We would like the job completed by June 25 as we have very tight deadlines to meet on this project.

We look forward to working with you on this book and others in the future. Your reputation among your clients for fast, reliable service is outstanding.

2 lines

Sincerely,

4 lines

Bruce C. Kaplan
Production Editor

2 lines

/rs

• All lines are set flush with the left margin. • No paragraphs are indented. • Signer's initials are not included in the stenographic reference.

Block

BOOZ·ALLEN & HAMILTON INC.

THREE FIRST NATIONAL PLAZA · CHICAGO, ILLINOIS 60602 · TELEPHONE: (312) 346-1900 · TELEX: 25-3312

October 11, 19--

Ms. Gail Fraser
Vice President, Planning
Carroll & Associates, Inc.
354 West Rydell Suite 3800
Tucson, Arizona 85713

2 lines

Dear Ms. Fraser:

2 lines

We have completed our preliminary study for Carroll & Associates, Inc. and have submitted our initial report under separate cover.

As I mentioned in our phone conversation of October 5, your distribution department is the primary cause of your firm's decline in sales volume. Serious thought must be given to replacing the head of this department.

If you would like to discuss this matter further, please call me at your earliest convenience.

2 lines

Sincerely yours,

4 lines

Frank G. Towers
Associate

2 lines

FGT/ehs

• Date line is flush with the right margin. • Inside address, salutation, reference lines, and paragraphs set flush with the left margin. • Complimentary close and signature are aligned with the date.

Semiblock

Mitchell
Bros.
Realtors
ERA
2528 Green Bay Road
Evanston, Illinois 60201
(312) 492-9660

March 18, 19--

2 lines

Ms. Roberta H. Quinn
Suburban Realty & Developers, Inc.
One Nogales Road
Northbrook, Illinois 60062

2 lines

Dear Ms. Quinn:

2 lines

We are about to sign a contract to develop Nogales Plaza, and we would like to know if you are still interested in managing the TGIF Lounge in the Alhambra Building. You mentioned that your firm would consider renovating the lounge if we secured the lease.

I am enclosing a copy of the lease agreement. I will call you next week to arrange a time for us to disuss the TGIF Lounge and Nogales Plaza.

2 lines

Yours truly,

4 lines

Marilynn C. Brighton
Realty Agent

2 lines

MCB: jh
Enclosure: Lease agreement

• Date is flush with the right margin. • Inside address and salutation are set flush with the left margin. • Paragraphs are indented. • Complimentary close and signature line are slightly to the right of the page's center.

Simplified

Edwards and Mason — Insurance Agency

1111 Fidder Blvd., East Chicago, IL 60010

6 lines

January 5, 19--

4 lines

Mr. Ryan R. Byrne
553 South Maple Avenue
Akron, Ohio 44330

3 lines

PROTECT YOUR COMPUTER INVESTMENT!

3 lines

For most of us, buying a personal computer represents a sizable investment—from $2000 to $5000. Yet that investment can be lost through fire, theft, or natural disaster.

For only $5 per month, you can purchase our complete HOME COMPUTER PROTECTION PLAN. Our coverage will give you 100% reimbursement on the list price of your computer should it be damaged or stolen while in your home.

To find out more about our PLAN, fill out the enclosed card and mail it today.

4-5 lines

BARBARA R. DEEBEN
CONSUMER PRODUCTS

• No salutation or complimentary close. • All lines begin flush with the left margin. • Date is six lines below the letterhead. • Inside address is four or more lines below the date line. • Subject line is typed in all caps, three lines below the inside address and above the body of the letter. • Writer's name and title are typed in caps, four or five lines below the body of the letter.

Chapter 4 Style in Business Letters

The style of a business letter has to do with the language and tone you use. Although there is no special language for business letters, the most effective letter is concise, vivid, and clear. It does not waste the reader's time. It uses active verbs and nouns and is free of clichés, jargon, and awkward phrases that confuse and complicate your message. Above all, an effective business letter speaks to the reader's needs and interests. (See also Chapter 2: Choosing the Right Word for guidelines on business style.)

Watch Your Language

You can learn to be more aware of your language and avoid outworn and stilted expression, wordy phrases, vague terms, and other lapses in style. As you read through the guidelines in this chapter, study letters you have written or received from others to see how they can be improved. You may find that your letters have an artificial style you would never use in conversation. You may write sentences like "The meeting necessitated my being out of town" instead of "I had to go out of town for the meeting." Through practice and attention to the language you use, you can develop a clear, concise "voice" in your business letters.

Pronouns

Whenever possible, begin the letter with a "you" reference, bringing in "I" or "we" after you have addressed the needs of the reader. Strike a balance in favor of "you." Check your letter to make sure you do not have too many "I's" and "we's" sprinkled throughout the text. A good use of personal pronouns can add warmth to your letter while at the same time letting readers know how you can meet their needs.

Active Language

Business letters do not have to be dull, stiff, or lifeless. You can use active verbs, nouns, adjectives, and adverbs to create vivid images in your readers' minds. Active language is particularly important in sales or promotional letters. You want to attract and hold the readers' attention. Remember that your letter is competing with countless other letters, phone calls, office duties, and personal visits. If your letter contains some emotional appeal or touches on pleasant memories or ties in to readers' fantasies or desires, it probably will hold their attention to the end.

In the sample letter below, the writer catches the readers' attention by piquing their curiosity.

> I have a job and a dream.
>
> The job is a challenging and exciting one: to create a Consumer Financial Association—the first one of its kind in the world. Through this Association, our bank will offer complete personal financial planning services to all its customers.
>
> The dream? To help people like you realize their fondest hopes. Now you can plan for that second home you've always wanted, for your children's college education, or for your retirement. You will have the help and advice of over 50 of the finest financial counselors in the country.
>
> You can help us create this Consumer Financial Association by filling out the application form below. The few minutes you take could be your most important step toward a new financial future.

Use active verbs and the active voice in your letters. They give your message vitality and immediacy, as if you were with the reader describing what is happening. The passive voice, on the other hand, slows down your message and leaves the reader with the impression everything is happening in the past. (See also Verbs, pages 202-210 in Chapter 14: Parts of Speech.)

> The location for the new plant will be discussed by the board at Wednesday's meeting.

Changing from the passive to the active voice and using a more descriptive verb improve the sentence.

> The board will debate the location for the new plant at Wednesday's meeting.

Diplomatic Passive Voice. The passive voice does have its uses. When you want to soften your statement, shift the emphasis from the writer to the reader, or be more objective or formal in a sensitive situation, the passive voice is the more diplomatic choice.

Active: We have reviewed your application and find that we cannot extend credit to your account at this time.

Passive: Your credit application has been reviewed carefully. Unfortunately, it did not meet the criteria established by our company for first-time credit accounts. For this reason, a charge account cannot be opened for you at this time.

In this example, emphasis has shifted from the writer's action to the reader's application. The writer has put the company in the background and highlighted the information most important to the reader. The passive voice also softens the refusal by avoiding a "we" versus "you" tone. The reason for the refusal is stated first, followed by the decision.

Clarity

Clear writing involves choosing the best words to express your ideas and arranging those words to help your readers understand your ideas. The more you practice "getting the words just right" the more skilled you will become in communicating your message to the reader.

It is important to remember that a word is not a "thing." It does not stand for something solid and unchanging. Rather, the meaning of a word depends on the context in which it is used and the understanding of the person who uses it. Each one of us has slightly—or even widely—different interpretations of what words mean. As a result, you cannot assume that what is clear to you is equally clear to your reader. For this reason, you must determine exactly what you want to say, and choose the simplest, clearest way to say it. The more abstract and vague your language, the less clear your message will be.

Keep Your Words Fresh

The best way to clarify your language is to edit ruthlessly. Challenge your sentences with the question, "Is there a simpler way to say this?" For example, the following paragraph may sound more "official," but it is also more confusing:

> Re your inquiry of October 30 please be advised that the item to which you refer (i.e., the 127-A Executive Model) has been removed from our catalog as of the present writing. The optimum solution would be to select the most appropriate substitute and resubmit your order.

What the writer meant was:

Thank you for your October 30 letter asking about our 127-A Executive Model. This item has been removed from our catalog as of November 22. However, the 128-A Trimline Model listed in our current catalog should do the job equally well. Just submit a new order for the 128-A Trimline Model, and we will ship it promptly to your address.

The first paragraph is not only less clear but gives the reader less information. The second paragraph uses simpler language and tells the reader how to solve the problem.

Make sure your letters are free of jargon and buzz words. Such words and phrases come easily to mind, a clue that they should be suspect and deleted. Some of today's buzz words include:

on line	interactive
input/output	bottom line
at this point in time	parameter
taxwise (or anything -wise)	viable
interface	

Some words and phrases from the legal field have been appropriated in business—usually inappropriately. Unless you work in a legal office, or are a lawyer, avoid using the following for everyday business letters.

aforementioned	per, as per
duly	pursuant to
herein	re
hereto	therein
herewith	whereas
notwithstanding the above	

Keep Your Words Concrete

Concrete words refer to something specific, often something we can see, hear, touch, taste, or smell. Vague or abstract words refer to concepts or generalities, philosophies, or ideologies. The more abstract the word or phrase, the more removed from our ordinary experience and the more likely we will misunderstand the term. The more concrete the word, the less room there is for misinterpreting the message.

Vague: Management has admitted the need for greater levels of productivity in the assembly area.

Concrete: Management agrees that assembly workers need to increase their productivity by 20 percent.

Vague: In view of the company's current economic situation . . .

Concrete: With company sales up 10 percent and inventory reduced by 12 percent . . .

Vague: Market conditions dictate that we take a more prudent course . . .

Concrete: Over forty firms currently are producing computer accessories. The risk for a new company is high, and we will need to target our products carefully.

Vague or abstract words leave the questions, *How much? What kind? Which one?* unanswered. For example, "greater levels of productivity" means little. How much greater? Read through your letters for abstract words and phrases that appear to say something but actually say little. By using concrete words, you answer readers' questions with specific information.

Abstractions and generalities, however, can be used for summarizing ideas and creating a framework for your discussion. Make sure you ground your framework with tangible, concrete details. Otherwise, you will find yourself writing a second letter to explain your first.

Keep Your References Clear

When you use words to modify or refer to other words, be sure your train of thought is clear. The reader should be able to tell easily which word or words are being modified. You may provide some unintended humor if you are careless about your references.

> You will be able to recognize the director. He is a tall, gray-haired man with a tan briefcase named Howard Guerson.
>
> If you cannot hang the sheet metal yourself, please ask for assistance in hanging them from the shop steward.

Here are some basic guidelines for keeping your references clear.

1. *Keep modifiers close to the words they modify.*

Poor: He visited over a period of six weeks each new plant the company had opened.

Better: Over a period of six weeks, he visited each new plant the company had opened.

2. *Place adverbs close to the words they modify.* The reader should not have to guess at your meaning.

Poor: An executive order she received recently managed to confuse the entire staff. (Is it recently received or recently managed?)

Better: An executive order she recently received managed to confuse the entire staff.

3. *Be careful about the placement of the adverb only.* Misplacing the word can distort your meaning.

Poor: He only walked four blocks to the store. (Perhaps he was supposed to run or take a cab. As used, only modifies the verb walked.)

Better: He walked only four blocks to the store. (He had only four blocks to walk, not six or eight.)

4. *Keep your subject and verb together.* This arrangement helps the reader follow your thought and understand the sentence more easily.

Poor: The merger of Apco and Sunnex, which was one of the largest and most bitterly contested in the history of the oil industry and which involved a staggering $250 billion in assets, was approved by the FTC on Friday, April 2.

Better: The merger of Apco and Sunnex was approved by the FTC on Friday, April 2. The $250 billion venture was one of the largest and most bitterly contested mergers in the history of the oil industry.

Often the best solution to this problem is to break the sentence into two or more shorter sentences that allow you to convey the information without separating the subject and verb.

5. *Make sure your references are correct.* Words such as *who, that, which,* and *it* refer to the preceding noun in the sentence. If your references are not clear, your sentences may be ambiguous or unintentionally humorous.

> We will paint any car, any make for only $59.95. Our offer is good for this week only. Have your car repainted before it expires!

The intention of the message is clear: "it" refers to the offer, not the car. But the image of a rusted car expiring adds an inadvertent comic twist to the message.

Study the following examples. Reread your own letters to see if you have committed any of the errors below.

Poor: The treasurer proposed an amendment to the bylaws, which the financial director opposed. (Did the director oppose the amendment or the bylaws?)

Better: The financial director opposed the treasurer's amendment to the bylaws.

Poor: The assistant to the sales manager, who was hired recently . . . (Who was hired recently?)

Better: We recently hired an assistant to the sales manager . . .

Poor: Several items in a customer's order were out of stock, and it delayed shipment by two weeks. (To what does it refer? Avoid vague pronouns that refer to an entire sentence or idea.)

Better: Several items in a customer's order were out of stock. The shortage delayed shipment by two weeks.

You can use a variety of methods to correct confusing references, breaking one sentence into two or more sentences, rearranging word order, restating the sentence, or filling in the missing reference. (See also Pronoun-Antecedent Agreement, pages 200-201, in Chapter 14: Parts of Speech.)

Keep Your Structures Parallel

Phrases and clauses in a series or sentence should be parallel, that is, they should have the same structure. In the following example, the writer began with prepositional phrases, then switched to a clause at the end of the sentence.

> We should aim for production levels that are above last year's rate, on par with industry norms, and should achieve our basic marketing objectives.

The reader is apt to be confused when structures in sentences are not parallel. You have established an expectation on the reader's part that each item in the series will be similar. The sentence above should read:

> We should aim for production levels that are above last year's rate, on par with industry norms, and in line with our marketing objectives.

Another common mistake writers commit is mixing verb forms within the same sentence. For example:

> Ted Roberts looked into the Morgan contract, talked with Hays and Ventura, and finds no conflict with the former client.

The verb "finds" is in the present tense while the other verbs are in the past tense. The sentence can be rewritten two ways as follows:

> Ted Roberts looked into the Morgan contract, talked with Hays and Ventura, and found no conflict with the former client.
>
> *OR*
>
> Ted Roberts looked into the Morgan contract and talked with Hays and Ventura. He finds no conflict of interest with the former client.

Making sure your series or sentences are parallel will help your readers understand the ideas you are communicating. Check over your writing to be certain you have not changed verb forms in the middle of a sentence or switched from one type of phrase or clause to another in a series.

Brevity

Brevity may be the soul of wit, but many of us have acquired wordy expressions that we use without thinking. They pad our messages and add nothing to the meaning or impact of what we have to say. Concise writing saves the reader time and effort in understanding your letter. A few guidelines can help keep your messages brief while communicating the necessary information to the reader.

Eliminate Unnecessary Words

We often use unnecessary words and phrases to give our writing a more "dignified, polite, or professional" tone. When such expressions are eliminated, the message comes through more concisely.

1. Avoid empty phrases such as:

    The desks are blue in color.
    The desks are blue.

    . . . thinking on a theoretical basis.
    . . . thinking theoretically.

In about a week's time . . .
In a week . . .

It is a matter of prime importance . . .
It is important . . .

The reason I take the train is that . . .
I take the train because . . .

2. In general, avoid the phrases *there is* and *there are*. Rewrite the sentences using more active verbs.

Poor: There are several flights that make the round trip from Newark to New York.

Better: Several flights make the round trip from Newark to New York.

Poor: Whenever we achieve a new goal, there is a rise in morale.

Better: Whenever we achieve a new goal, morale rises.

3. Try to condense clauses beginning with *which, that,* or *who* into fewer words. When you are revising your letters, look for these phrases and eliminate them wherever you can.

Poor: The consultant, who was hired from McKinsey, gave a speech that was long and boring.

Better: The McKinsey consultant gave a long, boring speech.

Poor: The Preston report, which was in two volumes, outlined the responsibilities that each executive was to assume.

Better: The two-volume Preston report outlined executive responsibilities for each officer.

4. Strike out the article *the* wherever you can to improve the flow and readability of your sentences.

~~The~~ staff recommendations from the Finance Department will eliminate the need for ~~the~~ outside consultants.

The October meeting will give us ~~the~~ two plans for ~~the~~ future office designs.

You can determine if *the* is needed by crossing it out and reading the sentence for meaning. If the sentence is less clear, restore the article.

5. Look over the list below of wordy phrases commonly used in business letters. Compare them to their more concise alternatives. Change the wordy phrases wherever you find them in your own writing.

Wordy	*Concise*
at this point in time	at this time
consensus of opinion	consensus
meet together	meet
during the course of	during
few in number	few
personal in manner	personal
in the vast majority of cases	in most cases
on a weekly basis	weekly
refer back to	refer to
square in shape	square
until such time as	until
due to the fact that	because
very necessary	necessary
in spite of the fact that	although
engaged in a study of	studying
depreciates in value	depreciates
opening gambit	gambit (a gambit is an opening move)

Use Adverbs and Adjectives Sparingly

When you need to use modifiers, make sure they work for you and do not simply add words to your sentences. A well-placed adverb or adjective can heighten the impact of your letter. Overused modifiers weaken your meaning and give the message a flat, shop-worn tone. (See Adjectives and Adverbs, pages 210-213 in Chapter 14.)

Poor: We will have to give the recommendation the acid test. It is extremely important that we find the best alternative, for in the final analysis, the very future of the company depends on our decision.

Better: We will have to test the recommendation against our own standards. Finding the best alternative is critical, since the future of the company depends on our decision.

Poor: She gave a quick and highly emphatic reply.

Better: She gave a quick, emphatic reply.

Avoid the following modifiers. They clutter your sentences and add little to the message.

absolutely necessary	final analysis
bitter end	acid test
perfectly clear	straightforward manner
incredibly	extremely
exceptionally	highly
very	greatly

Accuracy

Business letters must convey accurate information to the reader. Inaccurate information can be worse than no information at all, and it can be costly. Mistakes in ordering parts, purchasing supplies, billing customers, and answering inquiries cost businesses millions of dollars a year.

The guidelines below will help ensure that your facts are correct.

1. ***Double-check figures, dates, specifications, and other details.*** Being "pretty sure" or "fairly certain" that something is correct may be fine for your golf score, but not for policy numbers, dates of shipment, price lists, and the like. Do not rely on your memory—it is too easy to reverse numbers or remember the wrong sequence. Put this motto on your desk: *When in doubt, check it out.*

2. ***Make sure you have spelled all names correctly.*** Your letter will not impress readers favorably if you misspell their names or the names of their companies. Also verify the spelling of product names, titles of articles or books you may cite, or any other proper names that appear in your letter.

3. ***Check for clarity in presenting your ideas.*** Clarity is essential to accuracy. Learn to spot ambiguous statements, muddled expressions, and poor development of ideas. This step is particularly important when you are negotiating with a client. If you are to convey your terms accurately, you must state them in clear, unambiguous language.

4. ***Make sure your letter is neatly typed.*** Although it may sound strange, neatness is also part of accurate writing. If your letter is filled with strikeovers, erasures, or handwritten corrections, the reader may easily misread or misunderstand what you have written.

Inaccurate information costs time, money, and goodwill—three things no business can afford to lose. It is well worth the effort to ensure that your message is clear and accurate.

Tone

Tone refers to the emotional content of your letters. The tone can be formal, informal, positive, negative, persuasive, humorous, or argumentative. Each tone has its uses, although the negative and argumentative tones must be handled with sensitivity and care.

Tone is one way you adapt your letters to the needs and level of your readers. For example, you would use a formal tone in a letter to a prestigious institution, while an informal tone would be more appropriate when writing to a colleague.

Formal: Dear Dr. Hayden:

We have been informed that your institution has completed a study on the applications of artificial intelligence to forecasting. This subject is of special interest to us, and we would like to request a copy of the report.

Informal: Dear Bob:

I heard that your Computer Science group has just finished a study on the applications of artificial intelligence to forecasting. We have been looking at this idea for some time and would like to see a copy of your report. Could you send us one C.O.D.?

The following guidelines show how different tones can help you tailor your message to different readers.

1. Maintain a personal touch. In an age of computerized communications and conglomerates, people often have the feeling they are dealing with machines, not human beings. It is important to retain the personal touch in your business correspondence. You can be sympathetic and helpful in your letters. A conversational tone can offset the formal sphere of business dealings and add a warm, friendly touch to your message. If you have dealt with your reader over several years or developed a close relationship, it is appropriate to include personal references to shared interests, mutual friends, or activities of other family members.

> The FX-80 printer will be ready in July. I will be in Spain on vacation the following week, but I'll be back in time to help install your printers. We can trade vacation stories, since I understand you'll be back from Germany about the same time.

Please give my best to John Vail in purchasing. He has worked many hours to help close the sale. My warmest regards to your wife and two sons as well. I wish you an enjoyable trip to Europe.

2. ***When you must mention bad news—a refusal, rejection, or delay—use a positive tone.*** Do not mention the bad news in the first line. Establish some type of common ground with the reader first, explain the reason for the decision, and then state the decision. In your letters, develop the *you* attitude that puts the reader's interests first. Notice the difference between the examples below.

Poor: You claim that we did not enclose all the parts in your order . . .

Better: We regret any delays in your production caused by missing parts in your order . . .

Poor: We don't feel your qualifications match our job needs.

Better: Your qualifications are excellent and show that you have assumed greater levels of responsibility throughout your career. The candidate we are looking for, however, will have a stronger marketing background. For this reason . . .

Poor: This is to inform you that as of January 5, 19--, your job with Racal will be terminated . . .

Better: Even though your job performance rating was in the top ten percent, Racal's recent losses in earnings and revenue have forced us to lay off 20 percent of our staff . . .

Try to emphasize what is positive in the situation and suggest an alternative course of action. Instead of saying "I cannot mail your certificate until Friday," state the message from the reader's perspective: "Your certificate can be mailed on Friday. If that is not convenient, please let us know." You want to maintain a friendly, positive tone even when breaking bad news.

3. ***Never send a letter written in anger.*** This statement is one of the few *nevers* you will encounter in a handbook. Write several versions of the letter until you can compose one with a tactful tone. Sending off an angry letter may be satisfying for the moment, but you may have to deal with the consequences for a long time. Any loss of goodwill is difficult to recover.

Knowing how to use various tones for different situations is a valuable skill in business communication.

Sentences

Sentences in business writing tend to be short, about twenty words or fewer. In past centuries, the average sentence ran up to sixty words. Modern language experts state that shorter sentences are easier to understand and can communicate information more effectively. It seems we like to digest facts in small bits!

When we start putting thoughts on paper, however, we may end up with either one of two extremes: long, complex sentences or short, choppy ones. Part of the problem may stem from the rule that a sentence must represent a complete thought. As we add a qualifier here, a modifier there, or an incidental fact, our "complete thought" is likely to become a verbal maze for the reader. Or we may write our thoughts in brief, staccato sentences that leave the reader short of breath.

The following guidelines can help you write sentences that move the reader gracefully from one point to the next. (See also Chapter 15: Sentences and Sentence Patterns.)

1. *Focus on clarity and meaning rather than "complete thought" as your criteria for good sentences.* Each sentence must say *something* about the central idea without having to say *everything*. Build understanding step by step, with each sentence contributing to the main point of the paragraph.

2. *Include only one to two ideas in each sentence.* A series of ideas in one sentence rushes the reader too quickly through the material. Before one idea has time to settle, another crowds it out of the way. In the following example, one sentence contains several thoughts. The writer appears to be thinking out loud rather than writing to someone else.

> Our discussion of the new product division has given me a chance to reconsider obtaining the Baton Rouge plant which has always been an attractive prospect, even in the recession because of its location and local labor supply, and it might be a good time to bring the purchase proposal before the board when it meets on Thursday.

The conjunctions *and* and *but* often signal where a new sentence can be made. The paragraph above can be rewritten in shorter sentences as follows:

> Our discussion of the new product division has given me a chance to reconsider purchasing the Baton Rouge plant. I've always felt the plant was an attractive prospect, given its prime location and the local labor supply. I'd like to propose that we purchase the plant. Perhaps we can bring the idea before the board at its Thursday meeting.

3. Avoid short, choppy sentences that give a monotonous sound to your letters. Vary your sentence structure so that the reader is led easily from one sentence to the next. Read aloud the two versions below. Notice how the change in rhythm affects your perception of the material.

Choppy: I received your order for 25 office chairs on October 4. I regret to inform you that a labor strike has delayed production. We recently hired new workers. We expect to be back in production within one week. I apologize for the delay. We will offer a 10 percent discount on all back orders. Your patience is appreciated in this matter.

Varied: I received your order for 25 office chairs on October 4. Because of a labor strike in our factory, production on new chairs has been delayed. Recently, we hired new workers and expect to be back in production within one week. We sincerely apologize for the delay and would like to offer you a 10 percent discount on your back order. We appreciate your patience in this matter.

Short, choppy sentences tend to mimic a curt, unemotional tone. Varied sentences convey a more relaxed and friendly delivery. To vary your sentences, you may need to break one sentence into several, combine two or more sentences into one, or rearrange the word order within sentences.

Paragraphs

Paragraphs, like sentences, should lead the reader from one step in the message to another. The purpose of a paragraph is to develop each point in enough detail so the reader has a complete understanding of your message. Breaking the letter into paragraph form makes the various points easier to read and understand. A solid block of type is discouraging to someone who has only a few minutes to read, digest, and respond to your letter.

While there are few hard and fast rules about paragraph length, the guidelines below will help you write effective paragraphs to increase the impact of your message.

1. Use key sentences—called topic sentences—to introduce or summarize your paragraph. Topic sentences highlight the essential point in a paragraph. The remaining sentences support or elaborate that point. A topic sentence at the beginning introduces the subject being discussed, while at the end it summarizes the preceding information.

Topic sentence at beginning: Our survey indicates that a chain department store located in Eden's Plaza would be successful. Over 70 percent of plaza shoppers indicated they would shop at the store. All the adjacent and surrounding small businesses supported the location of such a store in the plaza.

Topic sentence at the end: Twenty percent of the retailers have responded using the business reply card. Fifteen percent replied by phone, 10 percent by postcard, 14 percent by personal note, and 7 percent by third parties. The remaining 34 percent have not yet responded. In all, the business reply card elicited the largest response from retailers.

In some cases, a paragraph may be too short to have a topic sentence. You will need to use your judgment about when a topic sentence is appropriate.

2. To determine where paragraph breaks should occur, notice how sentences group around your ideas. As you write your letter, you will be developing various ideas or points you want the reader to understand. You will find that, in general, sentences will fall into a natural grouping around these points. Proper paragraphing will help you draw attention to each topic and move the reader from one topic to the next. Short paragraphs can emphasize specific points more strongly. Longer paragraphs can explain an idea or give more detailed information.

3. Avoid extremes of lengthy or choppy paragraphs in your letters. One-sentence paragraphs, each covering a different point, give your letter a disjointed, staccato tone and appearance. You have not developed a central concept but provided a list of ideas. On the other hand, lengthy paragraphs are likely to be skimmed by the recipient, if they are read at all. Each paragraph should be about eight to ten lines long, covering only a few points and presenting the main point quickly.

4. Keep in mind that your primary concern in writing paragraphs is the overall organization of the letter. Paragraphs will follow the same basic order regardless of the type of letter you write: opening, body, and closing.

- *Openings.* The opening paragraph indicates the purpose and subject of the letter.

  > We received your report that the FX-100 printer manual was missing from your shipment. Our customer service department is looking into the matter.

  The reader needs to know immediately what the letter covers and your reason for writing.

- *Body.* Paragraphs in the body of the letter develop the main points and indicate the goal you would like to achieve through your letter. In the example given above, the body of the letter would detail the steps the customer service department is taking to locate the missing manual and what the company intends to do. These paragraphs can vary in length, depending on how much detail and information the reader needs.
- *Closing.* The closing paragraph should be no more than one or two sentences long. It indicates the action you wish the reader to take or expresses appreciation for the reader's understanding or patience. Make sure you restate any pertinent information or mention items by name that you refer to again. If you open with a statement of a need or problem, close with a statement of action or solution to the problem. In the example above, a closing paragraph might state:

  > We appreciate your patronage and wish to extend every support to our customers. A new manual for your FX-100 printer will be shipped to you at our expense within five days.

Format and style considerations focus on the presentation and appearance of your business letters. In the next two chapters we return to the three steps of effective writing and show how to organize, write, and produce the final version of your letters.

Chapter 5 Organizing and Writing Business Letters

Effective letters are the result of good thinking and careful planning. The three steps introduced in Chapter 1 will help you plan your letters, outline them, and write polished final versions.

Step One: Prewriting

As you begin to plan your letter, keep in mind the questions every letter must answer.

1. What is the purpose of this letter? Why am I writing it?
2. Who is the audience? Whom do I want to influence?
3. What do I want to say? What is the scope of my subject?

State Your Purpose

Clarify your reason for writing the letter by jotting down the purpose in one or two sentences. It may be as simple as granting or refusing a request or as complicated as trying to justify a company decision to support a certain piece of legislation in Congress.

If you cannot state your purpose in a brief sentence or paragraph, talk the letter over with another person or give yourself time to rethink your reasons. In a sales letter, for example, is your purpose simply to tell the customer a product is available or to solicit an order by providing a business reply card? In a collection letter, do you want to extend the payment date or let the reader know payment is due immediately?

You should be able to state the purpose of your letter clearly and concisely before you begin the planning stage.

Know Your Reader

Knowing your audience is as important as knowing your purpose for writing. You need to identify who they are and what motivates them.

You can gather facts about your readers fairly easily. A little research about their companies will tell you their positions, responsibilities, decision-making powers, as well as their budgets, types of business, and customers served. These facts will give you a good profile of your readers, a "snapshot" that will indicate their level of expertise and experience.

The art of writing effective letters, however, involves knowing something about what motivates people. Why do they decide to expand into a new market, develop a new line of products, cut back on services, move to a new location, upgrade or downgrade services? In business, people are driven basically by certain common concerns. You can probably add to the list.

Profit	improving it
Saving	spending less
Prestige	position and pride
Security	confidence in the future
Comfort	feeling of well-being
Convenience	saving time, boosting efficiency
Health	maintaining or improving it
Productivity	increasing it
Loyalty	fidelity to others and one's self
Curiosity	a sense of wonder, willingness to take risks

Knowing what motivates readers will bring that "snapshot" to life and help you decide what tone to adopt in your letters. For example, someone strongly motivated by saving would respond to a letter that promised to reduce the cost of office supplies by 20 percent. An executive motivated by prestige would be in the market for high-quality accessories or club memberships that offered special privileges to executives.

If you can identify your readers' motivations, you have a better chance of gaining their attention, cooperation, and compliance. You can establish goodwill and assure them that you are sensitive to their particular problems and interests. Each letter can be tailored to the individual recipient.

Determine the Scope of Your Letter

Once you have identified your purpose and your audience, you will need to decide what you should cover in the letter. How much of the subject will you need to include? Will you require background material or research? Even before you make an outline, you can begin planning the content of your letter.

For a short, simple letter, your plan may be nothing more than a brief list of items you wish to mention. You may want to make notes in the margin of a letter to be answered: "Request latest catalog from this company" or "Interested in products offered but not now." For more complex letters, you will need to do more planning. If you know the subject well, you can jot down a type of "laundry list" of topics that you want to cover. For example, suppose a client has asked you to explain your company's approach to convert a standard office to a computerized system. Your laundry list might look like the following:

Converting Client Office to Computer System

Survey office staff—attitudes, experience
Analyze work flow
Check on office color scheme
Research best computer system
Develop data forms for computer
Research history of office automation
Do cost analysis
Establish installation and training schedules

Such a list will help you determine what needs to be included in the letter and what can be eliminated. For example, "Check on office color scheme" and "Research history of office automation" are not necessarily appropriate topics to cover. However, you may want to add "Do follow-up study" to the list.

Research Your Subject

When you have identified the scope of your topic, you will know whether background research is required. Perhaps you can fill in the information from memory. On the other hand, you may need to check price lists, update your knowledge of suppliers, or investigate a customer's background.

Try to gather all the data you will need before you sit down to write your letter. You want to avoid having to stop in the middle of your first draft to check your facts or fill in missing information.

Step Two: Writing

By this time you have completed your preparation work and are ready to begin the actual writing. You will need to organize your material in the most logical and effective manner. Letter formulas and a good outline can help arrange your ideas and clarify your thinking.

Organizing with Letter Formulas

Over the years, people have developed formulas for organizing letters. You can use these formulas, along with outlining, to develop your ideas before you begin writing.

One widely used formula for sales letters is AIDA, an acronym for:

Attention: (getting the reader's eye)

Interest: (arousing the reader's curiosity or interest in what you have to say)

Desire: (making the reader want what you have to sell)

Action: (showing or telling the reader what to do)

IDCA is a variation on the AIDA theme and stresses conviction or the believability of your presentation. The object of this letter is to convince the reader to act on your message.

Interest: (catching the reader's eye)

Desire: (creating a need for your product or service)

Conviction: (convincing the reader of your message; some action is required on the reader's part)

Action: (showing or telling the reader what to do)

Another formula, OFAC, is used to inform a reader of a service or product you are offering, to solicit funds, or to convey information.

Occasion: (telling why you are writing to the person or company)

Facts: (giving information needed for action on the reader's part)

Action: (making a request, suggestion, statement, demand, appeal)

Closing: (offering additional help or information, mentioning how the reader benefits)

Formulas make it easy to keep your purpose in focus and to concentrate on essential information.

Outlining

Your outline may consist of a few main points you wish to cover or a more detailed breakdown of each point. For example, suppose an office manager from another firm asks you to explain how your company analyzes work flow among clerical workers. Your outline for a reply letter might look like the following:

I. On-site observation of work flow
II. Analysis of observation data
III. Recommendations
IV. Monitoring and follow-up

OR

I. Observation of work flow
 A. Conducting one-week, on-site study of workers
 B. Compiling detailed data
II. Analysis of observation data
 A. Identifying strengths/weaknesses
 B. Comparing data with similar office surveys
III. Recommendations
 A. Drawing up new work schedules
 B. Describing new work methods
IV. Monitoring and follow-up
 A. Checking on staff progress every two weeks
 B. Adjusting recommendations as needed

Your outline should be more detailed as your subject becomes more complex. Below are a few guidelines for developing effective outlines.

1. ***List the major topics in the order you feel they should appear.*** Assume for a moment that each major topic will be a paragraph. Take your time with this step. Write two or three lists if necessary. The major topics are the framework on which you will build your letter.

2. ***Arrange supporting ideas under each main topic in their order of importance.*** You may want to put the most important items at the beginning or end of each paragraph. If you find you are putting too many subtopics under each major topic, you should probably break each major point into two points.

3. ***Make sure everything in your outline needs to be there.*** Keep in mind the purpose of your letter as you check through your topics. Do you have any trivial or irrelevant information? Have you left out data that would support your topics?

4. Check the order of your topics again. In light of the complete outline, would you change the way the information is presented? Should you start your letter with a question and then build to your solution? In most cases, your letters will follow a simple chronological or narrative order, building up to the main points. But in special cases you may want to vary the order and present the main idea in the first paragraph and use succeeding paragraphs to support it.

Lengthy letters will call for an extensive outline. For example, to explain in detail how you would automate a standard office, you might write the following outline:

I. Survey office staff
   A. Poll attitudes toward computers, automation
   B. Determine skill level and experience
   C. Determine staff abilities to learn new procedures

II. Analyze work flow
   A. Conduct one-week, on-site observation
   B. Analyze individual job responsibilities
   C. Make detailed study of current work methods

III. Develop data-entry forms
   A. Devise new forms for each job
   B. Devise forms for general office procedures
   C. Compare with industry forms

IV. Research best computer system
   A. Determine software needs
   B. Survey plant outlets, power lines, electrical capacity, lighting, ventilation
   C. Determine best hardware for office

V. Do cost analysis
   A. Analyze costs of hardware/software
   B. Determine cost of maintenance, supplies
   C. Estimate insurance and service costs
   D. Estimate cost of training staff

VI. Establish installation and training schedule
   A. Determine set-up and installation time
   B. Establish training schedule for staff
   C. Estimate time for conversion from manual to computerized system

VII. Do monitoring and follow-up
   A. Debug hardware and software
   B. Evaluate worker progress and attitudes
   C. Monitor time and cost schedules

VIII. Reassure client
   A. Outline benefits of computerized office
   B. Assure client of continued support

Remember that your goal is not to develop the perfect outline but to organize your thoughts and data in the most effective way possible. The outline should be a guide to your writing, not a rigid structure. You may find as you write that you need to add or delete information or rearrange the order of your topics. Your goal is a letter that influences the reader. A good outline can help you achieve that end.

Writing the First Draft

No matter what type of letter you are writing—sales, credit, collection, acknowledgement, refusal—the opening paragraph, body, and closing paragraph must enhance your message. You may find it better to begin in the body of the letter and write the opening paragraph later. The best rule of thumb is simply to begin and complete the first draft without being too concerned about which paragraph you write first.

Each part—the opening, body, and closing—has a different purpose. The following guidelines will help you develop concise, attention-getting paragraphs.

The Opening. Your opening paragraph must catch the readers' interest and get them to read your entire message. Keep the opening concise and fresh. Avoid repeating information already known to the reader. If you need to refer to previous correspondence between you, do so unobtrusively.

Poor: I have before me your letter of July 16 in which you list your computer accessory requirements for a surge protector, serial cable, dust covers, copyboard, and printer table. You would like each of these shipped UPS by the 23rd and billed to your home office.

Better: The computer accessories you ordered July 16 will be shipped UPS and billed to your home office as requested in your letter. The shipping department has verified that your order will be mailed by July 23. An invoice listing the items you ordered is enclosed.

You might wish to open your letter with a question or bold statement.

> We'd like to build the best customer service record in the industry.
>
> How long has it been since you had a *real* vacation?
>
> Why buy from Tango when you can get Centrex for less?
>
> Ninety percent of American executives pay too much for their insurance. Do you?
>
> What do IRA, CD, and FICA have in common?

Not every reader will respond favorably to a bold or innovative opening. They may believe it is merely a gimmick to attract their attention. You must use your best judgment after analyzing your target audience.

Whether you adopt a conservative or innovative approach, make your opening paragraph an active one. Plunge right into your subject, whether it's providing information, expressing regret or pleasure, asking or answering a question. Your reader has little time and needs to know why you are writing.

Make sure your opening sets the tone appropriate to your subject and reader. In general, use a positive, direct tone. It will help the reader form a favorable impression of you and your letter.

> Most insurance companies won't cover businesses your size. We're the exception.
>
> We are pleased to inform you we have increased your credit limit from $1000 to $1500 as of April 25. Congratulations on your excellent credit record.
>
> We are offering a February "white sale" on all letter-sized bond paper for your office needs.

Avoid openings that restate the obvious, have a negative tone, begin with a participle, or contain clichés:

Restatement:	We have received your letter of March 30 in which you state . . .
Negative tone:	Your failure to comply with our request for payment has forced us to close your account . . .
Participle:	Regarding your order of June 24, we have . . .
Clichés:	Good banks are a dime a dozen, but finding a full-service bank is like looking for a needle in a haystack . . .

Look over letters you have written or received and study the opening paragraphs of each one. What makes them effective or ineffective? How can you improve your own opening paragraphs?

The Body. The body of the letter will develop your main points and move the reader toward the closing. The greatest consideration you can show your readers is to take only enough time to say what is important. Separate what they *need* to know from what is merely *nice* to know.

Poor: Our file cabinets come in four colors: blue, red, black, and beige. Beige is the most popular color among our customers, accounting for 45 percent of the file cabinets ordered.

Better: Our file cabinets come in red, blue, black, and beige. The colors are baked-on enamel, scratch-resistant, and easy to clean.

Your readers don't need to know that beige is the most popular choice; they do need to know the colors are durable.

Keep your paragraphs brief and to the point. Brevity is the result of using simple language and discussing only a few points at a time. Put yourself in your reader's place, and you will begin to streamline your letters almost automatically.

The Closing. In the closing paragraph you are bringing your letter to a courteous, businesslike conclusion and indicating what action you would like the reader to take. The specific action will vary according to the purpose of your letter. Here are a few guidelines for writing your closing paragraph.

1. Use positive words—when not if.

Poor: If you would like more information . . .

Better: I would be happy to provide more information . . .

Poor: I will call you next week to see if we can get together.

Better: I will call you next week to see when we can arrange a meeting.

2. Indicate what specific action you would like the reader to take. The amount of pressure you apply will depend on the nature of your letter. In the examples below, the closings range from a simple expression of goodwill to a high-pressure call for immediate action.

Please let us know when we can be of further assistance.

May we have our field representative Karla Shore call on you next week?

Just fill out and mail the enclosed postcard. We will send you our free 20-page booklet on tax tips that could save you hundreds of dollars.

Our sales offer ends in ten days. Send in your order today to secure this exceptionally low price. Hurry! Supplies are limited.

If you do not send in payment by the 25th we will be forced to turn your account over to a collection agency. Please send your check or money order in the enclosed envelope. Do not let such a small amount jeopardize your credit rating.

3. ***Avoid closing paragraphs that diminish the effect of your letter.*** A weak ending can ruin an otherwise well-written message. Your closing paragraph should not apologize unnecessarily, begin with a participle, add trivial afterthoughts, or use clichés.

Your final paragraph should leave the reader with a clear understanding of what you want done or what you have to offer.

Step Three: Revising

In revision you switch roles from writer to reader. Review what you have written as if you had never seen it before. If possible, let the first draft cool off for a while. Put it away overnight so that you can read it with a fresh eye in the morning. Use the following checklist in revising your letters.

1. What is the purpose of this letter? Have I made it clear?
2. Are the points developed logically and completely?
3. Have I used clear, simple language? Have I avoided clichés, jargon, overly complex technical terms, and abstract or vague nouns?
4. Have I used the active rather than the passive voice?
5. Are modifiers close to the words they modify?
6. Have I expressed myself in the fewest possible words?
7. Are the sentences an average of fifteen to twenty words long?
8. Are paragraphs no more than eight to ten lines long?
9. Do sentences and paragraphs flow smoothly from one to the next?
10. Do my nouns and verbs agree in number?

Pay particular attention to opening and closing paragraphs. As you revise, ask yourself the following questions:

1. Is my message tailored to the reader's interests and motivations?
2. Does my message begin with information important to the reader or in answer to the reader's request?
3. Did I adopt the correct tone?
4. Does the closing paragraph state specifically what action I want the reader to take?
5. Do I make it easy for the reader to act?
6. Have I given the reader one action to take rather than several?

Revision is essential to good writing. As you revise, remember three key terms—clarity, brevity, simplicity. Look over the following first draft and subsequent revision.

First draft

February 4, 19--

Mr. Colin Graham
Director, Human Resources
Tilston Cereals, Inc.
923 Victor Parkway
Michigan City, Michigan Zip

Dear Mr. Graham:

cliché

opening too wordy—what is the main point?

In this day and age, companies must focus on increasing the productivity of their employees. After all, productivity is the key to any company's survival in today's competitive environment. But to increase worker productivity, you must know what motivates people to work harder and take pride in their work.

As Director of Human Resources, you have been given the responsibility of discovering how to motivate workers and reward their efforts. I am sure that you find this a challenging task! In fact, 40 percent of the human resources managers in the country today stated that they felt their jobs were the most difficult and most underrated of any position in the company.

body is too long and not focused enough on reader's needs and writer's solution

Finding out what motivates people is our specialty. We have developed a range of seminars to help managers like yourself determine what needs drive employees and how they seek to fulfill them.

Our program—What Motivates You?—is a self-learning series that focuses on identifying individual needs and explores how to meet those needs on the job. There are four seminars in number, each one focusing on a different aspect of motivation and satisfaction. At the end, each employee will have a better understanding of his or her needs, and you will have a detailed map of employee motivations and how to satisfy them on the job.

language vague and abstract; need more specific facts about program

Our program is offered at a discount for companies with 200 or more employees. You can earn an additional discount by indicating whether you would like to take a special introductory course for managers only. We would enjoy talking to you about our program—What Motivates You?—in more detail.

closing is weak—what action does the writer want the reader to take?

Sincerely,

Maureen Houseman

Maureen Houseman
Program Director
University Learning Resources
766 South Petterson Avenue
Lansing, Michigan
(716) 364-5540

Revision

February 4, 19--

Mr. Colin Graham
Director, Human Resources
Tilston Cereal, Inc.
923 Victor Parkway
Michigan City, Michigan Zip

Dear Mr. Graham:

As Director of Human Resources, you know how difficult it is to discover what will motivate employees to work harder. Yet increased productivity, key to your company's survival, depends on worker motivation.

University Learning Resources specializes in helping managers discover employee needs and how those needs can be met on the job. Our program—What Motivates You?—is a four-part series of self-learning seminars. The four seminars cover the following topics:

Seminar 1. What Do You Really Want? Helps employees determine their own motivations.

Seminar 2. How Do You Get What You Want? Explores ways that people fulfill their needs.

Seminar 3. What Do You Get From Your Job? Identifies employee expectations and ambitions regarding their work.

Seminar 4. Get the Most Out of Your Work! Focuses on how employees can obtain the highest satisfaction from their jobs and fulfill company objectives.

At the end of the program, (1) employees will have a better understanding of their motivations and (2) you will have a better idea how to motivate them. You will know what rewards get results.

Our program—What Motivates You?—is offered at a discount for companies with 200 or more employees. We would enjoy talking with you about our seminars in more detail. Please fill out the enclosed reply card and mail it today. Or call us at (212) 364-5540 and ask for Maureen Houseman or Richard Teale.

Sincerely,

Maureen Houseman

Maureen Houseman
Program Director

Proofreading

Once you have revised your letter and had it typed in final form, proofread it carefully. Whether you sign the letter or have someone else sign it for you, you are responsible for the accuracy of its content. Check for spelling and grammatical errors, inversion of numbers, mistakes in format, and errors in paragraph breaks.

Proofreading marks listed below will tell the typist or word-processing operator how to correct the letter. Learn to use these symbols; they are universally accepted by typists and printers. (See Chapters 14 through 18 for grammar and spelling review.)

Mark	Meaning	Mark	Meaning
	Delete	^, or ,/	Insert comma
⁀	Close up space	’ or ’/	Insert apostrophe
	Delete and close up	“ / ”	Insert quotation marks
#	Leave space	⊙	Insert period
¶	Begin new paragraph	?/	Insert question mark
no ¶ run in	Run paragraphs together	;/	Insert semicolon
tr	Transpose	⊙ or :/	Insert colon
(SP)	Spell out	=/	Insert hyphen
stet	Let it stand	1/em	Insert dash
lc	Lowercase letter	[/]	Insert brackets
C (triple underline)	Capital letter		

Study the example below. Compare the proofread and corrected versions.

Original:

May 20, 19--

Mr. Foster F D'John
Reservations
Ambassador West Hotel
55 W. State Street
Chicago, IL 60614

Dear Mr. D'John;

I would like to reser ve Guild Hall for Friday, Novmeber 7, from 7:00 pM to 10:00 PM for our group, the northshore Executive Women's Club. Is the hall available on that date?

You mentioned that catering is provided (on a first-come first serve basis) and that We could receive a discount if we could guaranteed at least 100 paying guests.

We will have twice that number and would lik e to order the catering service as part of our our reservation for that evening.

Please list us on your activities roster as "Northshore Executive Womens Club. We thank you—and your staff for the help you have given us.

Sincerely yours,

Karen Christoffersen
Executive Director

Corrected:

May 20, 19--

Mr. Foster F. D'John
Reservations
Ambassador West Hotel
55 West State Street
Chicago, Illinois 60614

Dear Mr. D'John:

I would like to reserve Guild Hall for Friday, November 7, from 7:00 PM to 10:00 PM for our group, the Northshore Executive Women's Club. Is the hall available on that date?

You mentioned that catering is provided (on a first-come, first-serve basis) and that we would receive a discount if we guarantee at least 100 paying guests. We will have twice that number and would like to include the catering service as part of our reservation for that evening.

Please list us on your activities roster as "Northshore Executive Women's Club." We thank you—and your staff—for the help you have given us.

Sincerely,

Karen Christoffersen

Karen Christoffersen
Executive Director

Chapter 6 Producing the Business Letter

Whether you type the letter yourself or have it prepared by a word-processing pool, you should be familiar with the mechanics of producing a final typed version of a business letter. In this chapter we cover stationery used, forms of address, complimentary close, signature block, addressing envelopes, and mailing procedures.

Stationery

The first page of any letter is always typed on letterhead stationery. When the letter is more than one page, use blank sheets of paper that match the color and quality of the letterhead.

You should carry the recipient's name, the page number, and date on all pages after the letterhead. Type this information six lines below the top of the page. The line can be typed across the page or in block style:

Ms. Carroll Presnell, 2 June 4, 19--

OR

Ms. Carroll Presnell
Page 2
June 4, 19--

If more than one individual in the company is to receive the letter, type the line as shown below. The names are in alphabetical order.

Ms. Carroll Presnell June 4, 19--
Ms. April West
Franklin National Bank, 2

OR

Ms. Carroll Presnell
Ms. April West
Franklin National Bank
Page 2
June 4, 19--

Inside Address

The inside address is typed flush with the left margin regardless of the format you have chosen. The individual's name and title, the department or division, company name, address, and zip code are typed in the following order.

Ms. Patricia McDonough
Treasurer
Finance Department
Tristate Trucking Co.
1435 Elm Street
Oakdale, Ohio 45656

If you must carry over a long line, indent the second line at least two spaces.

Mr. Frank Senior
National Alliance for Radio, Television,
  and Movie Distributors

When you need to address more than one person in a company or institution, list their names in alphabetical order on separate lines.

Ms. Joan Sample
Mr. Norm Zuefle

You would then write the following salutation:

Dear Ms. Sample and Mr. Zuefle:

If you are addressing two or more men, use *Messrs.* (an abbreviation of *Messieurs*):

Mr. Donald Kahn
Mr. Barry Templeton

Dear Messrs. Kahn and Templeton:

For two or more women, you would use *Mesdames*, *Mmes.*, or *Mses.*:

Ms. Arlene Day Ms. Janet Stone	Miss Barbara Clark Miss Yvonne Ruez
Dear Mses. Day and Stone:	Dear Mmes. Clark and Ruez:

When the gender of the person you are addressing is not known and the name could be that of either a man or a woman, a new business practice suggests using the single letter *M*.

M. Jan Voyce
Direct Sales Department
CNA Insurance Co.

In a letter addressed to a department within a company, but not to any particular individual, you would place the company name on the first line and the department on the second.

Montgomery Ward
Customer Relations
414 North State Street
Los Angeles, California 90099

Street Addresses and P.O. Box Numbers

Business letter writers are often confused about how to deal with numbered street addresses and post office box numbers. The following guidelines should answer most of these questions. However, you should always check the preferred style used at your company. Few hard and fast rules exist for letter writing, and each company has developed its own style over the years.

1. Suite, room, or apartment numbers follow the street address. They appear on the same line, separated by a comma.

6571 Duluth, Suite 407
Michigan City, Michigan 49254

973 West Ontario, Apt. 14
Miami, Florida 33139

2. If the company stationery of a letter you receive contains both the post office box and street address, use the post office box, placing any postal station after the post office box number.

P.O. Box 1445, Central Station *OR* P.O. Box 1445
Central Station

If you need to list both the street address and the post office box, the post office will send the letter to whichever one is directly above the city and state line.

Ace Hardware	Ace Hardware
269 Central Avenue	P.O. Box 117
P.O. Box 117	269 Central Avenue
Rosemont, Illinois 60018	Rosemont, Illinois 60018

The post office takes longer to route mail to a street address. For faster delivery, put the P.O. number above the city and state line or use the P.O. number alone, without the street address.

3. The number *one* is always written out in the address.

One Washington Square

4. Numbered streets ten and below are written out. Above ten, they are typed as figures.

Sixth Avenue

33rd Street

Insert a hyphen between building and street numbers when both are written as figures. Put a space on each side of the hyphen.

40 Sixth Avenue

1435 - 33rd Street

5. When compass directions precede a numbered street, use cardinal numbers (1, 2, 3 . . .). When they follow the street, use ordinal numbers (1st, 2nd, 3rd . . .).

375 North 78 Street

622 - 104th Avenue NW

Notice that no comma is placed between the street and the compass abbreviation, and no periods are used in NW.

Abbreviations

Spell out all words within an inside address, except for compass directions that follow the street name.

459 West Crystal Lake Avenue

633 Lomax Street SE

The post office prefers the two-letter abbreviation for states. However, you may want to spell out the state name in the inside address to give your letters a more formal, professional look. The two-letter abbreviation is handy for envelopes when your word-processing program has a limit on the number of characters you can type in the address block.

Titles in the Inside Address

In business writing, as in other types of formal writing, a courtesy title is customarily used with a person's name: Mr., Mrs., Ms., Dr., Professor, and the like. If a title or degree follows the person's name, it is the practice in this country to omit the courtesy title. Business writers in other nations usually include it.

Look over the wrong and right ways to address individuals with titles or degrees following their names. *Esquire* (abbreviated *Esq.*) may be used when addressing a lawyer or diplomatic consul.

Wrong	*Right*
Ms. Jane Hardwick, Esq.	Jane Hardwick, Esq. or Esquire
Mr. Stanislaw Miloch, Esq.	Stanislaw Miloch, Esq.
Dr. Robert Block, M.D.	Robert Block, M.D.
Honorable James McKenna, Esq.	James McKenna, Esq.
Dr. Lenora Wright, Ph.D.	Lenora Wright, Ph.D.

Junior or Senior. When the abbreviation *Jr.* or *Sr.* follows a name, you can either use a comma or omit it. Follow the preference of the individual, if you know it.

George C. Hayes, Jr. *OR* George C. Hayes Jr.

The *Sr.* abbreviation is not generally used unless identical names are closely associated, as in a family business. Both titles are usually dropped when either the father or son dies.

Forms of Address for Women. The traditional forms of addressing married, single, divorced, and widowed women in business correspondence have changed considerably over the past twenty years. Letter writers must now ask themselves if they should use a married woman's husband's first name or her own? How should you address divorcees or widows? The only sure guide is to find out what the woman herself prefers. If that is not possible, the following guidelines can help you establish a style in your correspondence.

1. If marital status is unknown, use *Ms.*

2. Use a married woman's first name: Mrs. Susan Nightengale.

3. If your reader is widowed or divorced, use her first and married name unless she has chosen to return to her maiden name. The title *Mrs.* is generally used when addressing married, widowed, or divorced women who have kept their husband's name. However, if the woman prefers *Ms.*, then use that title.

Multiple Addressees. When using the abbreviation *Messrs.* (Messieurs) or *Mesdames, Mmes.*, or *Mses.* in the salutation, omit all first names.

Wrong: Messrs. Carl Stone, Frank Hubbard, and Timothy Nye:

Right: Messrs. Stone, Hubbard, and Nye:

Wrong: Mses. Laura Pilar, Sandra Copeland, and Alicia Ruby:

Right: Mses. Pilar, Copeland, and Ruby:

Couples. The question of addressing couples can be just as confusing as addressing women. While there are few set rules, customary forms of address do exist in business communication.

1. When the husband has a title, the traditional form of address is:

   Dr. and Mrs. Avery Brown

   OR

   Judge and Mrs. Bernard Snow

2. When only the wife has a title, the form of address is:

   Dr. Kelley Osborne and Mr. Fredrick Osborne

   OR

   Dr. Kelley and Mr. Fredrick Osborne

3. When both have a title, any of the following forms is acceptable:

   Drs. Janet and Douglas Green
   Drs. Janet Green and Douglas Green
   Drs. Douglas and Janet Green
   Dr. Douglas Green and Dr. Janet Green

Always use the form preferred by the people you are addressing, if it is known. People are sensitive about their names and will notice if you have spelled their name and used their title correctly.

Complimentary Close

Although *Sincerely* or *Sincerely yours* is generally the closing preferred by business writers, other closings can be used depending on the occasion.

1. Highly formal closings are used in diplomatic or ecclesiastic correspondence:

    Respectfully yours,

    Respectfully,

2. Polite, formal closings can be used in institutions or prestigious associations, government agencies, and the like:

    Very truly yours,

    Yours truly,

3. Less formal closings are used in general correspondence:

    Sincerely,

    Sincerely yours,

    Cordially,

4. Informal, friendly closings are used between long-standing business associates, friends, or colleagues:

    As ever,

    Best regards,

    Kindest (Warmest) regards,

Signature Block

The signature block contains the writer's name and title and, in some cases, the company name. In Full Block and Simplified format, the signature will be flush with the left margin. In Semiblock it will be slightly to the right of the center of the page. In Block format, the signature will be flush with the right margin. The writer's name in Simplified format is typed in all capitals, four lines below the body of the letter.

Simplified:	*Semiblock:*
LIONELL H. CEDRICK	Sincerely,
	(Mrs.) Ethyl Houseman

Block:	*Full Block:*
Sincerely yours,	Yours truly,
Leslie R. Taylor	Irene P. Ratner, M.D.

The only titles that precede the writer's typed name are *Mrs.*, *Miss*, or *Ms*. Since their use is optional, they are enclosed in parentheses, as shown above in the Semiblock style.

If you sign a letter for someone else, put your initials on the same line and to the right of the signature.

Respectfully yours,

(Ms.) Galena Thomas

Occasionally you may compose as well as type a letter for your employer or supervisor. You would then sign your own name above the typed title.

Sincerely,

Secretary to Mr. Richard Van Duyne

When the company name is part of the signature, as in contractual letters or letters of agreement, type the company name in capital letters two lines below the complimentary close. The writer's name goes four lines below the company name.

Very truly yours,

DELAWARE SAVINGS AND LOAN ASSOCIATION

Elizabeth Moore

Elizabeth Moore
Vice President

In some cases, as when a letter states a professional opinion or gives professional advice, the company name may be used as the signature rather than the writer's name. This style is common practice among lawyers, consultants, and accountants when they conclude a letter report for their clients. Usually the word *By* and a line for the writer's signature appears four lines below the company name.

Respectfully,

ARTHUR ANDERSEN & CO.

By Carol Walnum
Carol Walnum
Associate

Reference Lines

Reference lines include the Attention, Personal and Confidential, and Subject lines in a letter as well as optional reference lines listing documents and files.

Attention Line

The attention line guarantees that your letter will be opened even if the person to whom it is addressed is absent. The attention line is typed two lines below the inside address and may be centered on the page or typed flush with the left margin. The word "Attention" is typed with an initial capital letter only and followed by a colon. It is not underscored. When possible, use the recipient's full name.

Attention: Mr. Kaplan (flush left)

Attention: Ms. Ruth C. Kozinski (centered)

Personal and Confidential

A *Personal* or *Confidential* notation indicates that the letter is to be opened only by the recipient. Type Personal or Confidential four lines above the inside address and underscore them. This notation should be used only for matters that are strictly personal and not as an attention-getting device.

Personal

(4 lines)

Mr. Warren I. Pierce
Sales Department
Clayborn & Reston Furriers, Inc.
558 South Water Street
St. Louis, Missouri 64744

Subject Line

The subject line summarizes the topic of the letter in a few words. Since it is part of the body of the letter, it is centered about two lines below the salutation. In the Simplified format, which has no salutation, the subject line is typed three lines below the inside address. You can use the word "Subject" followed by a colon, typing the line in all capitals, or simply center the line and use upper and lower case letters, underscoring the line.

SUBJECT: PURCHASE OF NEW TELEPHONE SYSTEM

OR

Purchase of New Telephone System

Other Reference Lines

Some letters will have a reference line for use in further correspondence about the subject discussed in the letter. In your reply, type the reference number cited about four lines below the date and flush with the right margin. If your company also uses file reference numbers, type this number one line below the incoming reference. Such lines are often used to refer to documents, purchase orders, manufacturers' orders, and other numbered items.

Letterhead
(Semiblock)

February 4, 19--

Reference: P.O. #46-555-02
Our File Ref: Invoice #717

Stenographic Reference Line

This line is used primarily for the convenience of the issuing company. Generally, only the typist's initials are used. Many companies, however, like to show a more complete stenographic line with the initials of the person who wrote or dictated the letter plus those of the typist.

Sincerely,

Francis Jenks

Francis Jenks
Director

rs

Sincerely yours,

Francis Jenks

Francis Jenks
Director

FJ:rs (or FJ/rs)

When the person who dictated the letter is not the same as the person signing it, the signer's initials are typed in capital letters first, followed by those of the person who dictated the letter, then the typist. Either colons or slashes can be used to separate the sets of initials.

Yours truly,

Sylvia G. Ryder

Sylvia G. Ryder

SGR:FRG:rs (or SGR/FRG/rs)

The stenographic line is always typed flush with the left margin regardless of the letter format chosen.

Enclosure Line

The enclosure line is used as a reference check by both the recipient and sender to make sure everything included with the letter was actually sent. The word "Enclosure" or the abbreviation "Encl." is typed two lines below the signature or one line below the stenographic reference and flush with the left margin. If more than one item is enclosed, you can either list the items or type the number of items in parentheses. If you wish the reader to return any of the enclosures, type (please return) after the item.

(Block)

Sincerely,

Joseph T. Crane

JTC/gh
Enclosures: 1985 catalog
Prepaid reply card
Complimentary booklet "Saving Energy"

(Semiblock)

Sincerely yours,

Linda E. Verne
Manager

Encl: (3)

(Block)

Respectfully,

Karen Trout

(Ms.) Karen Trout
Director, Sales

KT:ds
Encls: Credit application
Office equipment catalog
Directory of dealers in SMSA (please return)

Spacing of the enclosure line can be varied to balance the appearance of the letter on the page. If the letter is short, the line can be dropped further down from the stenographic reference line or the typed signature. If spacing is tight, the enclosure line can be typed on the same line as the typed signature.

Copies Line

If you wish the reader to know who else is receiving a copy of the letter, type "Copy to", "Copies to," or "cc" and the name or names of the other recipients. The copy line is set flush left and two lines below all other notations.

Sincerely,

Matthew A. Townsend, Jr.

Matthew A. Townsend, Jr.

Enclosure

Copy to Ms. Alice Walker

Yours truly,

Helen C. LeFleur

Helen C. LeFleur
Manager

HCF/ds

cc: Ms. Alice Walker
Mr. Hanley Edwards
Mr. Rice T. Getty
Mrs. Judith Gallagher

The names can be listed either alphabetically or according to each person's rank in the company. If you do not want the recipient to know you have sent copies of the letter to others, enter a blind copy notation (bcc:) *on the copies only*. Type the abbreviation bcc: and names of the people who received the letter in the upper left corner of each copy.

Postscripts

In typical business letters, postscripts are not used. However, since they do catch the reader's eye, they can be an effective technique in sales letters. Postscripts can highlight special offers or urge the reader to take advantage of a special benefit. They are typed flush with the left margin and two lines below the signature block.

We know you will want to take advantage of our limited offer. You can mail your order or call us today using our toll-free number, 800-567-8334.

Sincerely,

Donna Fuller

Donna Fuller
Customer Service

P.S. First-time customers will receive an added bonus with each order of $25 or more—your choice of a pocket calculator or digital alarm clock free!

Addressing the Envelope

Your message should not be jeopardized by careless mistakes in addressing the envelope. By following a few guidelines, you can ensure the best service from the post office and guarantee that your letter will reach the right person on time.

All envelopes should include the following elements for both the sender and receiver.

Name of the individual or company
Department or division
Company name
Street address (with any apartment, suite, or
floor numbers on the same line)
Post office box number
City, state, and ZIP code
Country (if sent to another nation)

Some companies type the addresses using initial capitals and punctuation, while others type them in all capitals with no punctuation. Whichever style you use, be consistent. Do not mix the two. Avoid italic, script, or other unusual type faces that make it difficult to distinguish numbers or letters. Type the address single space and center it on the lower half of the envelope.

Mr. Jacob W. Andrews
Vice President
Telecommunications WorldWide, Inc.
4435 South Western Avenue
Boise, ID 83702

OR

MR JACOB W ANDREWS
VICE PRESIDENT
TELECOMMUNICATIONS WORLDWIDE INC
4435 SOUTH WESTERN AVENUE
BOISE ID 83702

Your letter should have a polished, professional look both inside and out. Other guidelines for addressing envelopes include the following:

1. For formal letters, do not abbreviate compass directions in the street address: 58 West Chicago Avenue

2. If you do use abbreviations, follow the style listed in the *ZIP Code Directory* (Ave, St, Apt, S, W, N, E, Rt, and the like): 718 N Taylor Blvd Apt 334

3. Use the two-letter abbreviation for state names (CT, NY, NJ, etc.). In formal letters, you may want to spell out the state name on the envelope as well as the inside address.

4. Put two spaces between word groups such as street address and suite or apartment number and two to five spaces between the state and ZIP code.

44 South State, Suite 409
Chicago, IL   60611

5. Type notations for special mailing methods (SPECIAL DELIVERY, EXPRESS MAIL, PRIORITY MAIL) in capitals two lines below where the stamps are placed.

6. Type the Attention line below the company name.

Johnson Sea Foods
Attention: Vera Casey
One Miami Drive
Jacksonville, FL 32244

7. Type the Personal or Confidential line two lines above and just to the left of the address.

Confidential

Ms. Jean Holen
First Illinois Bank of Evanston
800 Grove Street
Evanston, IL 60201

The following chapter provides guidelines and sample letters for a variety of everyday business situations.

Chapter 7 Sample Business Letters

During your business career, you will write various types of letters to respond to a customer's complaint, answer a request, sell products or services, grant or refuse credit. This chapter provides not only sample letters but brief, practical tips on how to compose letters that get results. The samples are typed in Full Block, Block, Semiblock, or Simplified format, with various reference lines. Models are included for the following:

1. Adjustment letters (responding to a claim)
2. Claim letters (making a claim)
3. Collection letters
4. Credit letters
5. Goodwill or public relations letters
6. Letters to government officials, agencies, the press
7. Inquiry letters (asking for information)
8. Request letters (replying to a request)
9. Refusal letters
10. Sales letters
11. Social business letters
12. Transmittal letters

Letters of transmittal are also discussed in Chapter 10: Business Report Writing. Letters relating to employment—application for a job, recommendation, resignation, and follow-up—are included in Chapter 13: Resumes, Applications, and Employment Letters.

Adjustment Letters

The primary purpose of adjustment letters is to handle customer complaints and problems while being fair to all parties involved. A reputation for handling customer claims quickly and fairly is a powerful public relations tool for any firm.

Most companies tend toward generous settlements whenever possible, giving the customer every benefit of the doubt. A company must walk the thin line between preserving a client's goodwill and maintaining the firm's integrity.

Customers should not feel shortchanged, yet at the same time they should not believe they can take advantage of a company's desire to maintain good customer relations.

In writing adjustment letters you should make the claimant feel that telling you about the problem was the right thing to do. Convey an understanding attitude, even if the customer is initially angry or hostile. By sympathizing with the client's problem, you establish the basis for a just settlement. Accept responsibility for the problem; doing so will reinforce your firm's integrity in the customer's eyes.

At times the claim may involve a third party, such as a distributor or carrier. Your company may have a policy that simply replaces the goods or services, then obtains an adjustment from the third party. In other cases, the customer may not know how to get an adjustment from the third party on their own. In such instances, you would act as go-between for the client. You may offer customers legal assistance to make their claim.

The format for an effective adjustment letter generally follows these steps.

1. ***Assure the customer that telling you about the problem is the right step to take.***

2. ***Explain your policy of handling customer claims.***

3. ***Describe the results of your investigation into the matter as clearly and concisely as possible.*** You can itemize your findings, particularly if they lead up to a refusal of the customer's claim.

4. ***State your decision on the basis of your investigation.*** Avoid giving the decision before you state the facts. The reader may become so irritated by the decision that the rest of the letter is ignored.

5. ***Close with a positive statement.*** If you have had to refuse the claim, offer an alternative solution: A new service or product, or a substitute, may solve the client's problem. If you are granting the adjustment, close with a statement expressing the hope that the customer will continue to enjoy the services and products of your firm.

6. ***Above all, do not judge or accuse the customer.*** Avoid negative terms that cast the customer in the role of complainer or troublemaker.

Poor: We received your complaint about the damaged shelves . . .

Better: We received your report about the damaged shelves . . .

Your objective in writing the letter is to grant any reasonable adjustment and maintain good customer relations.

ADJUSTMENT LETTER

(Block Format)

June 30, 19--

Ms. Dorothy Markle
37 Parke Road
Madison, Wisconsin 53711

Dear Ms. Markle:

We deeply regret that the bulbs and flowers you ordered in early March were received too late for spring planting.

We have enclosed a refund check for $43.56, which covers the purchase amount plus your shipping costs for returning the order.

You mentioned that you had to purchase your bulbs and flowers from a retail florist since you did not receive the order you placed with us. We understand that you spent $10 more for the retail order.

Unfortunately, we cannot reimburse you for the added expense you incurred by purchasing at retail. However, we are including two complimentary lilac bushes, perfect for fall planting.

Thank you for your patience in this matter. We hope you enjoy the lilac bushes and that you accept our sincere apologies for the delayed shipment.

Sincerely,

BLOSSOM GARDENS,
INC.

A. Jane Reading
Customer
Relations

AJR:iw
Enclosure

Claim Letters

Delayed shipments, damages to goods, misunderstandings, errors in filling orders, and other problems occur between the most well-run companies. When such problems arise you will need to make a claim against another firm. You have two objectives in writing a claim letter: to settle the claim to your satisfaction and to preserve the cordial relations between you and the other firm.

Make your claim accurately and tactfully. Assume in your letter that your claim will be granted and that the other firm will attempt to make a satisfactory adjustment. Avoid threats, accusations, or veiled hints about what you will do if the matter isn't settled promptly.

If possible, address your claim to a specific person in the company: the head of customer relations or customer service, the salesperson who took your order, the executive who heads the department where you bought the merchandise or service. You may even want to send your complaint directly to the president of the company. This tactic is often an effective strategy, particularly if the company is small. Go directly to the source that can provide the most help.

In reporting your claim, give the company accurate and complete information so they can investigate the matter and offer a fair adjustment. Make sure you include the following:

1. ***All pertinent dates.*** Indicate purchase and shipping dates and a record of any conversation or correspondence with the company about the item or items in dispute. Include copies of proof-of-purchase such as invoices or receipts.

2. ***A description of the problem.*** State your points one by one, giving all the details such as model number, type of service, and the like.

3. ***Explain the implications of the problem for you.*** Does it mean a loss of business, interruptions in service or operations, inconvenience, injuries, and so on?

4. ***State what adjustment you would like.*** Should the company replace the merchandise, perform the service again, refund your money, compensate you for your loss of business? Make your claim realistic in light of your injury and the other company's resources.

5. ***Close by stating your confidence that the company will respond favorably and fairly to your claim.***

Be open to negotiation. The company may not be able to grant everything you request. Decide which points can be negotiated and which points cannot. Always keep in mind your second objective—preserving cordial relations with the other firm. You may need to do business with them again.

CLAIM LETTER

(Full Block Format)

January 15, 19--

Mr. James Jordan
Jordan Productions
901 Avenue C
Stamford, Connecticut 06902

Dear Mr. Jordan:

After receiving 10,000 copies of our Summer '85 brochure from the printer, we discovered several typos and a major content error in the text.

We feel that these errors resulted from an oversight on both our parts. While we gave final approval to the graphic design and copy that your staff developed, careful proofreading of the text was included as part of your services.

The brochures must be corrected and reprinted at an estimated cost of $3,000. We believe that your firm and ours should share the cost of the correction. As a result, we will deduct one half of the printing charges ($1500) from the invoice you submitted to us.

Should you differ with our solution or have an alternative suggestion, please call me. I will be happy to discuss the matter with you.

We realize that mistakes can happen. This situation will not affect the fine relationship we have enjoyed in the past nor prevent us from using your excellent services in the future.

Sincerely yours,

Alice Davis
Creative Director

/lw

Collection Letters

Companies often use a series of collection letters that range from polite, friendly reminders for payment to stronger requests, to termination of credit accounts. You want to show your customers every consideration while letting them know that you are entitled to the same respect.

The tone of your initial letter should encourage a delinquent customer to say why payment has been delayed or to pay the overdue amount. Stronger messages are reserved for those times when all your friendly letters have failed to produce results. The guiding rule for collection letters is "Be firm but fair."

Polite Reminders for Overdue Payment. The first collection letter is sent to a customer after an account is 60 to 90 days overdue. It informs the customer of the overdue amount and suggests that perhaps payment has already been made. The letter is polite but seeks to jog the customer's conscience about the unpaid bill. You can remind the person of his or her excellent payment record of the past. Few customers will want to damage your good impression of them.

The following pattern can be used for your first polite reminder.

1. Appeal to customers' self-interest. Show how paying the amount due benefits them as well as you.
2. Show customers that you are confident they can and will respect their business obligations. Express your concern for their interests and situation without being overly sympathetic or patronizing.
3. End with an action statement for the reader. A collection letter is "selling" customers on the idea of paying an overdue amount promptly. Indicate whether you want clients to send in a check, notify you when you can expect payment, make a partial payment, or other action.

Stronger collection letter. If the first appeal does not work, send a second letter that is more pointed but still friendly. You are pressing the customer to take immediate action. Statements like, "We urge you to take care of this matter promptly" or "Please do not jeopardize your fine credit standing with our company" can help motivate readers to respond.

Often, second collection letters ask customers to explain why they haven't made payment or to suggest their own plan for paying the amount due. The tone of the letter is still polite, with the expectation that customers can and will pay. You have left the initiative up to them.

Final collection letter. For the final letter in the series, you assume a tougher tone. Your letter is courteous but more blunt and warns of actions that will be taken if payment is not made. You want to leave no doubt in the reader's mind that you intend to collect the amount due. This letter is a "no-nonsense" approach that states clearly what steps the reader needs to take to prevent further action on your part.

If the customer still refuses to pay, or even to notify you that your previous letters have been received, you can choose between two alternatives. You can send another tough letter, giving the reader the benefit of the doubt that the first letter did not arrive. Second, you can simply send a final notice stating what action you have been forced to take.

If you decide to send another tough letter, emphasize the following points:

1. Review past attempts to collect the amount.
2. Hold the customer responsible for damaging a good credit standing.
3. Give the customer a final opportunity to pay and to prevent an unfavorable credit record.
4. Restate the consequences of failure to pay the amount owed or at least to respond to your letter.

If you choose to send a notice stating what action you have been forced to take, explain precisely what you have decided to do. The actions open to you may include turning the account over to a collection agency or terminating the customer's credit. Your letter should express regret at the necessity for this action, but emphasize that the reader's lack of response has given you no choice.

Throughout the collection process, avoid scolding customers or judging them. You may try creative or off-beat approaches in the earlier letters to catch the customers' attention. If these approaches do not work, you can return to a more business-like tone.

Your letters should be courteous but firm at all times. If you must sever relations with a customer, express your regret at the loss.

Your goal should be to preserve your customer/client relationship and recover the amount due. Well-written collection letters that treat customers sensitively yet state your own position with firmness can help prevent the loss of both customers and revenue.

COLLECTION LETTERS

First Letter (Semiblock Format)

August 1, 19--

Mr. Michael Jensen
892 Draper Lane
Milwaukee, Wisconsin 53214

Dear Mr. Jensen:

Probably it's just an oversight on your part . . . but our records show that you have a balance of $14.50 due with us.

We realize this is a small amount and could easily have escaped your notice. We have included a copy of the invoice in case you have misplaced your bill.

Please remit the amount due in the enclosed return envelope at your convenience. We look forward to your continued business.

Sincerely,

GOLDEN-C JEWELERS

Len Stroder

LS:pm
Enclosure

Second, Tougher Letter (Semiblock Format)

September 15, 19--

Ms. Angela Wilson
8 South 99th Street
Des Moines, Iowa 50312

Dear Ms. Wilson:

We have appreciated your business in the past and would like to keep you as a customer. However, the current balance of your account, $85.60, is now 120 days overdue.

We have sent two reminders requesting payment or an explanation for the delay in clearing your account. So far, we have had no response from you regarding the overdue balance.

Ms. Wilson, please do not jeopardize your fine credit record over so small an amount. Send a check or money order for $85.60 in the enclosed return envelope or notify us when we may expect payment.

We value our customers and make every effort to accommodate their needs. Please take care of this matter so we may restore your credit account to its former excellent standing.

Sincerely yours,

IDEAL PHARMACY

Bruce Gregory
Customer Service

BJ/hs

Final Notice (Full Block Format)

May 1, 19--

Mr. and Mrs. J. A. Appleton
324 Main Street
Santa Vista, California 93063

Dear Mr. and Mrs. Appleton:

We have attempted to contact you repeatedly over the past four months regarding your overdue balance of $567.42. You have not responded to our letters or phone calls.

Your account is now eight months overdue. At this point, we have no choice but to cancel your credit privileges immediately and pursue legal action to collect the $567.42 balance due.

We are reluctant to take this step, since it means a black mark on your credit record.

However, you can still preserve your credit standing by discussing repayment of your account with us. Please contact us immediately.

If we do not hear from you within three (3) days, we will be forced to turn your account over to a collection agency.

Sincerely,

Norman Cross
Credit Manager

/ab

Credit Letters

Credit represents a trust extended by a seller to a buyer. It is based on the seller's confidence that the buyer can and will pay what is owed within a reasonable time, usually fixed by agreement. Credit can encourage spending and foster a strong buyer-seller relationship among firms and customers.

Credit letters are written to grant or refuse credit to individuals and businesses. As a result, it is essential that your letters convey consideration, fairness, and tact. You will need accurate information about your customer's financial circumstances to make your decision. Requesting additional information must be done tactfully, without appearing to pry into personal affairs. Refusing a customer credit also demands the utmost tact and diplomacy to retain the person's goodwill.

Granting credit privileges is a fairly straightforward matter of letting the customer know the good news. You can also take the opportunity to restate conditions of credit terms and include a list of benefits, such as bonus buys, coupons, discounts, and special privileges credit customers earn.

Refusing credit is more difficult. Here are a few guidelines to help you write successful refusal letters.

1. In the opening paragraph show that you care about the reader's situation. Put yourself in the reader's shoes.
2. Explain the credit policy and the reasons for the refusal, then state your decision.
3. Offer an alternative solution, if possible, or a time when the customer can apply for credit privileges again.
4. End on a positive note. Suggest that the customer buy C.O.D. or on a cash basis until another application for credit can be considered. Offer to discuss the matter further in person or over the phone. Always be able to back up your refusal with objective reasons and facts.

Refusal of credit is a sensitive issue and may even lead to legal action on the customer's part if he or she feels that any type of discrimination influenced the decision. Make sure you state your case clearly and keep the door open for future applications.

CREDIT LETTERS

Acceptance of Credit Application (Block Format)

December 10, 19--

Ms. Mary Locke
125 South First Avenue
Detroit, Michigan 48237

Dear Ms. Locke:

Congratulations! Your application for an Alben's Department Store charge card has been approved. You are the proud owner of a credit card you can use for all your household and clothing needs.

As a special welcome to new cardholders, we invite you to accept our money-saving offer:

> If you purchase more than $50 in merchandise from any of our stores within 30 days, you can deduct $15 from your February statement!

To make it easy for you to take advantage of this offer, we've enclosed a list of our many fine stores.

Remember—you can order any of our catalog items by phone and simply charge the order to your Alben's card. Catalog purchases are included in the special offer above.

We are pleased that you selected Alben's as your store and look forward to serving you. Welcome to Alben's credit card family!

Sincerely yours,

Carol Whitte
Customer Service

CW:pm
Enclosure

Refusal of Credit Application (Semiblock Format)

May 15, 19--

Mr. Carl Johnson
14 West Dearborn
Columbus, Ohio 43228

Dear Mr. Johnson:

Thank you for applying for our CARCON Oil Company credit card. Your application has been carefully reviewed by our Credit Department.

Based on the financial information you have provided, your expenses/income ratio is slightly below the level we have established for our credit accounts. As a result, we cannot at this time approve your application.

However, if you have additional information that would improve this ratio—other assets, savings accounts, extra earnings—we would be happy to review your application again. An "Additional Financial Information" form has been included for your convenience. Please complete the form and return it to my attention.

Thank you again for your interest in our CARCON credit card. We hope we can approve your application, and we look forward to serving you.

Sincerely,

CARCON OIL COMPANY, INC.

Cecil Bennett
Credit Advisor

CB/ts
Enclosure

Goodwill or Public Relations Letters

Goodwill or public relations letters are often an important part of a company's and an individual's correspondence. While these letters are not used to transact business or communicate strictly business matters, they do help build the personal and community relations that make good business possible.

You may have many occasions in your business career to write goodwill or public relations letters. They can be written to show appreciation, acknowledge achievement, provide information, propose solutions to community problems, offer support or assistance, and establish committees or philanthropic organizations.

Such communications are part of a firm's outreach and strengthen the company's reputation as a firm that cares about people and the community in which it does business. Today, more companies are realizing the importance of building good public relations with the many "publics" they serve.

A simple, effective plan for writing goodwill letters follows these three steps:

1. State the purpose of the letter clearly and briefly in the opening paragraph. Perhaps you want to congratulate the local Little League team on winning the state championship.
2. Provide specific details in the body of the letter and stress their significance and benefits to the reader. For example, if you are welcoming a new employee into the firm, you might list the advantages of working for your company.
3. Close by stressing your confidence, appreciation, or concern on behalf of the reader. You may be congratulating a colleague on a promotion and stating your confidence in his or her ability to perform the new job.

Focus on the "you" approach; make the reader the central consideration of the letter. Your goodwill letters will be most effective if you appeal to the reader's loyalty, honesty, persistence, excellence, or other positive characteristics when phrasing your message. Study the sample letter to see how the writer accomplished the letter's purpose.

GOODWILL LETTER

(Block Format)

March 23, 19--

Ms. Marsha Tanner
Vice President
Metropolitan Public Relations
100 First City Plaza
New York, New York 10017

Dear Ms. Tanner:

We are delighted that you have selected L-D Long Distance Service from among the many long-distance services available.

To establish a strong working relationship with you from the start, we have assigned Mr. Dennis Trebel as your personal account representative. Dennis has developed communications systems for some of the largest Fortune 500 companies and knows the complex needs of a large public relations firm.

Dennis will arrange a meeting with you and your staff to discuss details of our service from installation to billing. He will also ensure that any future questions or problems are handled to your complete satisfaction.

We are confident that L-D Long Distance Service can provide you with features unmatched by any other communications service.

- L-D Long Distance Service is the only service that allows you to make long-distance information calls, <u>free</u>!

- L-D Long Distance Service is the only service that gives you <u>instant</u> credit for wrong numbers.

- L-D Long Distance Service is the only service that gives you an additional <u>20% discount on</u> each call longer than 20 minutes.

March 23, 19--
Page Two

- L-D Long Distance Service is the only service that provides a 45-day payment period.

And there's more! Your personal account representative will be happy to discuss all our special features and services with you.

The staff at L-D Long Distance Service guarantees that your company will always receive efficient, friendly service. Again, we are pleased you have selected our firm to meet your communication needs, and we look forward to working with you.

Sincerely,

Jill Scott
President

JS/gt

Letters to Government Officials, Agencies, and the Press

As a business person, you may find it necessary to write to a government official, an agency, or the editor of a newspaper or journal to express an opinion or ask for help. You may be doing research on a particular issue, preparing a proposal, responding to an editorial, or asking for more details regarding a story or report you have seen.

In addition, companies may wish to make their positions on issues known and will ask representative members of their management staff to write a statement. The relationship of business, government, and the media to one another is traditionally dynamic—with the players alternately confronting and cooperating with one another.

Government officials are often sensitive to the opinions and positions of their constituents, particularly when important policies or legislation are being developed. Likewise, newspaper and magazine editors and radio and television managers need to know their readers' or viewers' reactions to articles or programs. If those views are expressed in a clear, courteous, and persuasive manner, they are likely to impress editors and managers.

Whether your message is a request, protest, or word of support, it must be clearly stated. Your opinions or requests will be more effective if you plan your message to make your points carefully and convincingly. If you are writing on behalf of your company, you will want to make doubly certain that you have represented your firm's point of view accurately.

Keep the following guidelines in mind as you write your next letter to a member of Congress, government official, editor, or station manager.

1. State the subject of your message and your reason for writing in the first paragraph.

   "I am extremely concerned about the proposed corporate surtax bill H.R. 6544 now before the House . . ."

2. Explain your interest in the matter and support your position with facts, statements from well-known spokespersons, or other pertinent information to show why you are concerned.

   "William Morris, former chief economist to President Ford, has pointed out the potential harm such a surtax could do in a time of sluggish economic recovery."

3. Suggest ways to improve the situation or solve the problem. You may offer a plan of your own or support the plan of someone else. The important consideration is to be helpful. You are not simply raising an issue but offering some action step that can be taken. You can shoulder your share of the responsibility while holding government officials or the media accountable to the public.

   "We at Allied Technomics join with other major corporations in urging you to consider Senator Wayne's proposed tax on imports instead of supporting H.R. 6544. We feel that any additional revenue should come from foreign imports rather than from the earnings of American companies."

4. Urge immediate action on your proposals or the proposals of others, and indicate your willingness to help in whatever way you can.

   "We ask you not to support H.R. 6544 and to examine Senator Wayne's proposed tax bill when Congress resumes session next week. If you would like supporting data, we can supply you with the latest industry figures on earnings and profit."

By organizing your letter according to this plan, you will give readers the information they need to consider your message seriously. The attention your letter receives depends largely on how effectively you present your argument or appeal.

LETTER TO GOVERNMENT AGENCY

(Simplified Format)

April 10, 19--

Ms. Margaret Renner
Internal Revenue Service
20 West Street
Phoenix, Arizona 85025

Document: #33-45-6778

QUARTERLY TAX RECORDS AND REPORT: TORBES MARKETING, INC.

Enclosed are copies of cancelled checks for our quarterly tax payments made in 1984. In addition, we have included a report of our auditors' meeting with you and several other IRS agents.

We ask that you review the enclosed report, verify that each of the tax payments has been properly credited to Torbes Marketing, Inc., and advise us of our tax status to date.

Should you require any further documentation or have any questions regarding the attached information, please call me. We would like to be sure that our tax records are in order as we enter the 19-- tax year.

MICHAEL CRAIN
TORBES MARKETING, INC.

Enclosures (2)

LETTER TO THE EDITOR

(Full Block Format)

November 6, 19--

Editor
Miami Herald
445 Biscayne Drive
Miami, Florida 33132

To the Editor:

Your recent feature story on the role of business in easing youth unemployment ("Business Gives Youths a Break," October 16) failed to mention the fine work of Milton Brothers, Inc.

This company, a small dry-cleaning establishment, actually introduced the innovative youth jobs program now so proudly publicized by the city. Interestingly enough, the city has neglected to include one important part of the Milton Brothers' program—day care for the children of teenage mothers.

Without day care, teenage girls with children cannot participate in the jobs program. Yet statistics released by the mayor's office in September 19-- showed that 72% of unemployed youth are young girls with preschool children.

The day-care model proposed by Milton Brothers is simple. Retired people with nursery, elementary teaching, or related experience are hired at minimum wage to care for the children, often in a rented space or at one of the worker's homes.

The Miami metropolitan area has one of the highest percentages of retired persons in the country. Milton Brothers discovered that finding paid or volunteer workers was no problem. When they advertised for three day-care workers, they received over 250 calls in one day from people eager to apply for the jobs.

Editor
Page 2
November 6, 19--

The city could easily put this model to work, setting aside low-rental space or providing a small subsidy to help pay day-care workers. Other businesses could be encouraged to adopt the Milton Brothers' model. This would put hundreds more teenage mothers to work and take them off the city dole.

Now <u>that</u> would be a feature story worth syndicating!

Bernard Sterling
President
EXECUTIVES URBAN YOUTH LEAGUE
Dade County, Florida

Inquiry Letter

Inquiry letters are written for many purposes. You may be conducting research and need help locating sources or finding experts whom you can interview. You may need to know if a product is appropriate for your company's needs or if a price list is up to date. Your inquiry may range from a simple request for a catalog to more complex matters such as the per capita consumption of sugar in the United States from 1970-1980.

The principal weakness of many inquiry letters is a lack of clarity. The writer fails to state the request clearly, fails to let the reader know precisely what information is desired, or fails to direct the request to the proper person. As a result, the writer may receive the wrong information in reply or a letter asking for more details about the request. Do not assume automatically that the recipient of your letter is at fault should this happen to you. You need to do your homework before writing an inquiry letter.

First, make sure you have identified the proper source—is the person you are writing actually the one who can fulfill your request? Second, include enough detail in your request to obtain the action or information you desire. Don't assume that the reader knows what you want. If you are writing in response to an advertisement or other promotional medium, mention the source or name in the letter. Companies change advertisements and promotions frequently and need to know which one caught your attention. Make sure your return address is on the letterhead or clearly typed in the signature block.

In some cases you will be writing on your own initiative to ask for help or request information that may require some time and effort on the reader's part. You will get the best response if your letter includes the following:

1. A clear statement of the type of information or help you are seeking. For example, if you need to know the per capita consumption of sugar in the United States from 1970 to 1980, you should include this exact information in your request. Otherwise, you may get yearly consumption rates, not per capita rates.
2. Pare down your questions to those that only the recipient can or must answer. List them in your letter to make them easier to read. Make sure your questions are phrased clearly and concisely.
3. Explain why you need the information and why your reader should respond. Is the reader an expert in the field? Will the person receive acknowledgement for the work or a copy of the finished material? In this section of the letter, do a little selling to gain the reader's cooperation.
4. Express your appreciation for their consideration of your request. Do not "thank them in advance" for their help. They may not be able to assist you or they may decline to do so. Rather, express your gratitude for the time they have taken to read and consider your request.
5. Include a self-addressed, stamped envelope where appropriate. The cost of a reply should be borne by the one who asks for information or help.
6. Indicate your willingness to pay any fees or cover the cost of any materials that the reader may send to fulfill your request.

Inquiry letters should accomplish two objectives: state clearly what you need and persuade the reader to help you.

INQUIRY LETTER

(Semiblock Format)

July 14, 19--

Mr. Colter Hughes
Consultant
Satellite Software Services
45 Orange Road Suite 1443
Orem, Utah 84057

Dear Mr. Hughes:

Recently, our firm, Anconda Manufacturing Industries, purchased Edition 3.0 of your software package WordPerfect. Our dealer has informed us that we are eligible for a free update of the program—Edition 4.0.

We use word-processing for our reports and surveys, and we will need several of the added features of the updated program. We would like to know the following:

1. When will you have the new version in stock? The dealer informed us you were backordered for at least the next three weeks.
2. Can we have the software shipped to us via Federal Express at our expense?
3. Will we be eligible for future updates at no cost?

Enclosed is a business reply envelope for your convenience. We would appreciate your immediate attention to this matter since we are planning to expand our word-processing capability by mid-August. Thank you.

Sincerely,

(Ms.) Norma Greenwood
Supervisor, Report
Production

NG:mc

Request Letters

Customers' letters of request should be answered in a manner that shows you care about their problems and needs. You have an opportunity to build goodwill by personalizing your replies. This in turn tends to make customers loyal to you as a supplier of goods and services. As a result, your reponses to request letters can serve as public relations and sales pieces at the same time.

Use the following structure when answering letters of request. Remember that every contact with customers is an opportunity to strengthen their confidence in your ability to meet their needs.

1. Set a friendly, positive tone in the opening paragraph that tells the customer they are valued and appreciated. For new customers you might begin by saying, "We are pleased that you came to us for help . . ." The long-time customer can be addressed with, "It's good to hear from you again . . ."
2. Let them know how their request is being handled. If you are responding to an order, tell them when and how the order will reach them. "We will be shipping the cartons UPS. You should receive them by July 15 . . ."

   If they requested information, give them all the data they need. "You will find a complete price list enclosed for all our paper products."

   Try to anticipate problems or questions the customer may raise and deal with them in your letter. Put yourself in the reader's position and ask what you would need to know from a company.
3. Show confidence in your product or service and invite further business contacts. Your closing should include a message that says, in effect, "We would like your continued business. How can we be of further service to you?" Your friendly tone is meant to foster goodwill so that the reader remembers not only your product or service but also your attitude toward customers.

Your response to a request letter can work as both a public relations and sales piece for you. Look over the sample letter. Notice how the writer has conveyed the message "the customer is our major concern."

REQUEST LETTER

(Block Format)

June 8, 19--

Ms. Jean Klein
Tri-Products, Inc.
2502 Central Avenue
Flint, Michigan 48553

Dear Ms. Klein:

Thank you for your telephone order of June 6. As you requested, we have ordered the following items:

- 10 packages of white, 3 x 5 pressure-sensitive labels imprinted with your company name and address.
- 5 dozen yellow, 4 x 6 memo pads imprinted with your company name only.

We will ship the memo pads to your attention via UPS by June 15.

However, we are presently backordered on pressure-sensitive labels. We anticipate receiving your imprinted labels by June 29 and will ship them by air express, at no additional cost. We apologize for the delay.

Thank you for your order—we appreciate your continued business.

Sincerely,

Martin A. Train
Order Department

MAT:rw

Refusal Letter

Knowing how to say "no" to a customer, applicant, or associate is an important skill. You must refuse someone yet preserve their goodwill, offer an alternative solution or course of action, and end on a positive note. The reader should know clearly that you cannot grant the request or accept their offer.

The basic principle of writing refusal letters is courtesy first and refusal second. This principle applies to any type of refusal letter, from turning down a customer's request for credit, to refusing an extension on a contract, to declining an offer to head the local charity drive.

The following guidelines should help you write tactful, friendly, yet firm, letters of refusal.

1. Respond immediately so the writer can seek help elsewhere. This action shows consideration of the reader's problem.
2. Open by assuring the writer you have given the request careful consideration. Do not mention in the first paragraph whether the request will be refused or granted.
3. Give your reasons for the refusal. List them in a clear, straightforward manner so the reader will be able to understand them quickly. You are setting the stage for your no and preparing the reader to accept it. Even if the reader does not like your decision, the person will probably respect your reasons for making it.
4. Where possible, suggest an alternative course of action or solution to fulfill the writer's request. For example, if you must turn down a request for reservations because your hotel is filled, you can suggest alternative accommodations at other hotels nearby. Your primary message is that you care about the writer's situation and will offer whatever assistance you can.
5. Close with a positive statement. Don't overly apologize for your refusal; state that you hope you will be able to grant other requests in the future. Your closing paragraph can wish the writer success or provide encouragement to try other companies or institutions that may be able to help.

A refusal should not be a rejection. Readers should understand clearly that you are unable to grant their request, yet at the same time feel that you have considered their needs, respected their feelings, and handled your no diplomatically.

REFUSAL LETTER

(Full Block Format)

February 2, 19--

Mr. Jerry Guerton
Central Heating & Air Conditioning
First and Grant Streets
Midland, Texas 79701

Dear Mr. Guerton:

Thank you for submitting specifications and a cost estimate for the heating and air conditioning work on the Panhandle Plaza project. Your references and list of previous clients are impressive.

We received over fifty bids for the plaza work. Each bid was carefully reviewed in light of our budget and the qualifications of each company.

Your firm was among five finalists we considered. After careful deliberation, however, we selected HI-VAC, Inc. for the plaza project. Their bid was closest to our budget and their experience most in line with the variety of office and business sites to be built in the plaza.

We appreciate your interest in our project and the time and effort you took in preparing your bid. We hope you will consider bidding on future projects we supervise. Your firm's qualifications are excellent.

Truly yours,

PLAZA DEVELOPMENT, INC.

Estelle Kitteridge
Project Supervisor

/dk

Sales Letters

The principles of effective sales letters are the same as those for effective personal sales. First, identify the readers' interests, needs, and motivations. Second, know your products and services thoroughly. Third, convince your readers that what you have to offer will satisfy their needs. The more creatively you can match products or services to the particular needs of your readers, the more successful your letters will be.

Two of the most effective formulas for organizing sales letters are AIDA and IDCA.

A	Attention	I	Interest
I	Interest	D	Desire
D	Desire	C	Conviction
A	Action	A	Action

Either of these formulas can be used when you begin writing your sales letters.

1. Start by capturing the readers' attention or interest. You may ask them a question about saving time, money, or work. You may start with an offer, free product or service, or discount. Your opening statement may be a startling fact about their business or industry, a testimonial from satisfied users, a promise, or guarantee.
2. In the following paragraph, create a desire for your product or service. You can describe the product or service in terms of the reader's motivations for profit, comfort, convenience, leisure, savings, pleasure, or any one of a number you have identified for your readers. The details should be carefully chosen to appeal directly to the needs of the reader, not simply be an exhaustive list of qualities and characteristics about your product or service. Every sentence should reinforce the reader's need for what you have to sell.
3. Support the desirability of your product or service by offering evidence to convince readers of your credibility. You might mention results from independent testing services, statistics from market tests, comments from satisfied customers, and a guarantee, refund, or replacement for any defective parts. You want readers to believe your message.
4. Motivate the reader to act. If your letter has done its job well, the reader is already eager to take the next step—order the product or service, give you a call, invite a sales representative to

> call, or whatever action you indicate. Avoid giving two or three alternatives; the reader may end up deciding to do nothing. Your action step should be easy—mark an enclosed business reply card, fill out and return an order form, telephone for further information.

In writing your sales letter, focus on both your product and the reader. Consider carefully the product or service's appeal and benefits for potential customers. Below is a quick checklist to help you write effective sales messages:

1. ***Attention (or Interest):***

   Have you identified the reader's needs and interests?

   What benefits does your product or service offer the reader?

   Can you state the benefit in a question or arresting statement?

2. ***Interest (or Desire):***

   What motivations are you addressing—profit, savings, comfort, convenience, prestige?

   If the reader has a problem you have identified, does your product or service offer a solution?

   Did you point out what emotional satisfaction the reader would gain from your product or service?

3. ***Desire (or Conviction):***

   Have you supported your statements with interesting facts, statistics, tests, testimonials?

   Did you offer any warranty, money-back promise, or evidence of your support for your product or service?

4. ***Action:***

   What specific action do you want the reader to take?

   Did you avoid alternatives or ambiguous choices?

   Have you made it easy for the reader to act?

   Is your desired action the last sentence of your letter?

SALES LETTER

(Simplified Format)

April 7, 19--

Mr. John Crown
Mail Room Supervisor
Kurtiss Manufacturing Co.
1410 Bloom Street
San Francisco, California 94110

SEAL-IT . . . A SUPER-FAST, SUPER-STRONG TAPE!

SEAL-IT tape moves your mail system into the 21st century. Its one-step application lets you seal any size package or envelope quickly and securely.

SEAL-IT:

- Has a self-adhesive backing strong enough to withstand the roughest treatment.
- Meets all postal shipping requirements.
- Comes with a hand-held dispenser to seal boxes and envelopes quickly and securely.
- Guarantees no more shipping losses from broken seals.

Try the sample SEAL-IT enclosed. Test its convenience and strength for yourself. Once you've tried it, we think you'll want to order a supply for your mail room.

Simply fill in the enclosed order form or call our Order Department at our toll-free number: 1-800-243-5550.

MARK EBERHARDT
MARKETING DIRECTOR

P.S. As an added bonus, we will send you a free portable tape dispenser with your first order!

Social Business Letters

Not all business letters have to do directly with business. As in the case of goodwill letters, social business letters communicate on a more personal level.

You will use the social letter to write business associates, colleagues, and friends. You may want to congratulate them on a promotion, console them for a loss, or request a contribution for a charitable cause. These situations call for a letter that is genuine, spontaneous, and warm.

Oddly enough, it is those qualities that often cause people the most trouble in writing social business letters. It is one thing to compose a letter summarizing a meeting or explaining a new product. It is quite another to write a personal letter in which you express your private thoughts and feelings. This is particularly true for most people when they must write letters of sympathy to the friends and relatives of someone who has died. Yet such instances are as much a part of business life as congratulating someone on their achievements. It is important for you to be able to express yourself in many ways.

The following guidelines are an effective pattern for writing social business letters.

1. Strike a conversational tone. The key to writing social letters is to sound as if you were speaking to the reader in person or over the phone. Engage your emotions as well as your thoughts.
2. Begin your letter with a statement that mentions the occasion that prompted you to write. If you are soliciting funds for charity, describe the reason the funds are needed. If the letter is in response to a personal matter involving the reader, add your reactions to the occasion and your personal wishes. For example, if your reader has recently been promoted, you may want to express your confidence in the person's ability to take on added responsibilities.
3. Close the letter with a statement that reinforces what you have expressed or states what action you would like the reader to take.

By following this pattern, you will be able to write well-organized and sincere messages, even for difficult situations, such as a death in the reader's family. Look over the sample letters. With practice, you can learn how to write appropriate and sensitive social letters.

SOCIAL BUSINESS LETTER

(Semiblock Format)

October 5, 19--

Ms. Irene Orlando
Director, Sales
Richmond & Forrest, Inc.
8760 West Union Boulevard
Oklahoma City, Oklahoma 73159

Dear Ms. Orlando:

It was with deep sorrow that we learned of the sudden passing of Mr. Sam Schroeder. We thought highly of Sam both as a sales person and an individual of considerable integrity and charm.

I remember how many times Sam helped speed through rush orders for us or worked until an order was filled to our satisfaction. He was a great favorite with the staff, and we looked forward to his visits.

Please accept our deepest sympathies for the loss of a fine man. He will be greatly missed.

Sincerely,

Louis Stewart
President

LS/wr

SOCIAL BUSINESS LETTER

(Full Block Format)

April 23, 19--

Ms. Elizabeth Graham
Director, Financial Services
St. Mary Hospital
1110 East River Road
Santa Fe, New Mexico 87501

Dear Ms. Graham:

As president of the Animal Shelter League of Santa Fe, I would like to invite you to chair our annual fund-raising dinner to be held February 5, 19-- at the Palace Hotel.

Because of Santa Fe's rapid population growth, hundreds of pets are abandoned or lost in the city each year. Every day we receive an average of twelve homeless pets who need medical attention and foster homes.

Our work is supported in part by private donations and some city funds. But we look to our fund-raising dinner to keep our doors open to the city's abandoned and lost pets.

We know of your interest and concern for animals, and we would be honored if you would accept our invitation to chair our annual dinner. May I call you Friday to discuss the matter further? Thank you for considering our invitation.

Best regards,

Larry Barnes
President
ANIMAL SHELTER LEAGUE

Transmittal or Cover Letters

Transmittal letters, also known as cover letters, perform a vital function in business communication. They accompany an item or document sent to a customer and identify what is being sent, the person receiving it, and the reason the item or document is being delivered to the recipient.

The letters act as valuable references for sender and receiver, since they document what items were sent and the mailing date. If there is any question about either of these matters at a later time, the transmittal letter can be consulted as an accurate record of the transaction. Such documentation is particularly important when legal claims are involved.

Transmittal letters that accompany items such as a check, catalog, brochure, or other material requested by a customer cover the following:

1. Describe the material being sent and number of copies or, in the case of money, the amount.
2. Specify any action the recipient might need to take.
3. Identify the purpose of the material enclosed. If you are sending money, your letter would state the purpose for which the money is to be used.

Transmittal letters are also used to accompany reports and proposals sent to a client. They often summarize the main points of the document or, in the case of a report, condense the findings and conclusions contained in the full document. When writing a transmittal letter of this type, keep the following guidelines in mind:

1. Make sure your remarks are brief and focused. Do not rephrase the entire proposal or report.
2. Highlight some of the major points that you believe are of particular interest to the reader.
3. Express appreciation for any help the client's staff may have given you during the proposal or report process.
4. Use the letter to help sell your ideas or recommendations.

TRANSMITTAL LETTER

Accompanying an Enclosure (Block Format)

September 25, 19--

Mr. Richard Perry
6778 Dempster Street
Evanston, Illinois 60202

Dear Mr. Perry:

Thank you for your interest in our custom-made suits and fine evening jackets. The enclosed catalog describes our tailored clothing line and current prices.

Our customers include some of the most well-known names in the entertainment and business worlds. We are proud to serve such a discriminating and exacting clientele.

We feel sure your elegant evening wear needs will be met to your complete satisfaction. When ordering any of our custom-made items, be sure to include all your measurements on the order form.

We look forward to serving you.

Sincerely yours,

Dina Vandenberg
Customer Service
Consultant

DV/js

Enclosure

LETTER OF TRANSMITTAL

Accompanying Report (Semiblock Format)

March 4, 19--

Ms. Georgia Patterson
Vice President
Holton National Bank and Trust
334 East Sheridan Road
Des Moines, Iowa 50312

Dear Ms. Patterson:

Enclosed is the report on customer demographics in the greater Des Moines area completed for your Marketing Department. We concentrated on the 24 to 45 age bracket as requested in your January 6 letter.

Our study revealed a growing affluent customer base in the 24 to 45 age group. This group should respond particularly well to your investment and savings instruments, mortgage financing, and consumer loan programs. According to our findings, your institution is moving into the consumer financial market at the right time.

If you have any questions regarding our findings, please call me at the office or my home. It has been a pleasure to assist your institution in its continued growth.

Yours truly,

MACOMB MARKETING
CONSULTANTS, INC.

(Mrs.) Lucille Tuskey
Senior Marketing
Consultant

LT/eb
Enclosure

Section 3
Dictation, Memos, Form Messages

Chapter 8 Mastering Dictation

Dictation is a valuable skill to have in today's business world. Technological improvements in recorders and tape machines now make it possible for busy managers and executives to dictate letters, reports, memos, and other data practically anywhere outside the office. The tapes or cassettes can then be sent in for transcription. Whether you work for yourself, a small company, or a large multinational firm, mastering the art of dictation can increase your productivity and save you time.

The three steps for effective business writing can be adapted to help you dictate your messages. Your first step is to plan your message beforehand and gather any data you may need. The second step involves the actual dictation itself, whether you dictate in person to a secretary or assistant, or record your message. Finally, you will need to revise, edit, and proofread the finished copy of your material.

This chapter assumes that you will be using dictating machines, but the guidelines also hold true for personal dictation.

Step One: Preparation

1. ***Make sure you know how your equipment works.*** Although this step may seem obvious, too many people overlook it. Learn the features and conveniences of your dictating machinery.

2. ***Arrange a comfortable and quiet work area.*** If you are dictating while you travel, try to find a room or area in which background noise is reduced to a minimum. You want your voice to be heard clearly and distinctly. If you dictate at home, do so away from distractions such as television, record or cassette players, video games, and the like. The transcriber must be able to hear every word.

3. ***Collect reference materials you may need to use or mention as you dictate your message.*** References could include notes from meetings, previous correspondence, price lists, sales figures, and so on. Arrange them in the order you will need them. You don't want to spend valuable time searching for information once you have started to dictate your message.

4. ***Develop an outline before you start.*** The outline, as in the case of written work, gives you a structure from which to develop your letter, report, or memo. It will help you keep your purpose, audience, and subject in focus.

5. ***Practice dictating before you begin to dictate the messages to be transcribed.*** Beginners often collect their material, write their outline, turn on the machine, and freeze. "Mike fright" is common when people first use dictating machines. Practice by reading material into the mike. Write out a short message and dictate it, then either have someone transcribe the message or transcribe it yourself. Don't worry about doing the job perfectly. You will soon be able to relax and focus on *what* you are saying rather than *how* you are saying it.

Step Two: Dictating Techniques

The art of dictating is the ability to state verbally what you want to appear as final typewritten copy. You will need to verbalize paragraph breaks, punctuation, underlining, capital letters, spacing, reference lines, and the spelling of all proper names, products, and any unfamiliar terms.

Your instructions to the transcriber at the beginning of the dictation should begin with the person's name, if you know it, or with the title "operator" or "typist." By using the person's name or title, you are warning them that your instructions are not to be typed.

Other guidelines for effective dictation include:

1. Identify yourself by stating your name, department, and any other information to let the typist know who is dictating the message. Leave a phone number where you can be reached should the transcriber have any questions.

2. Describe the material you are dictating, whether it is a letter, memo, or report. Estimate its approximate length and whether it is to be a rough draft or final copy. Include any special instructions such as the format, number of copies, distribution, mailing instructions, stationery, and priority of each message.

3. Speak distinctly and slowly. Enunciate each word and the final endings of words. Keep the volume of your voice even, maintaining a uniform distance from the mike. It is frustrating for the transcriber to hear your voice rise and fall, obscuring the message.

4. Learn to be aware of and to control any distracting personal mannerisms. If you drum your fingers on the desk as you dictate, jingle keys or loose change in your pockets, or tap objects with a pencil or pen, these sounds will be picked up by the microphone and may distort or cover your words.

5. Give adequate instructions as you dictate the message.

- Indicate any special formatting such as use of bullets, underlining, spacing, indentations, and the like.
- Spell words that are likely to be problem terms—foreign words and names, cities, technical terms, words that sound alike (cite, sight, site), and all proper names. Sound-alike letters should be distinguished by such phrases as "B as in boy" or "F as in Frank," and so on.
- Indicate capital letters before you say the word you want capitalized (Example, ". . . send the invoice to the Capital S Sales Capital D Department . . .").
- State how you want numbers typed (". . . the sales totaled dollar sign one zero, zero, zero . . ." or ". . . we have about one thousand orders for January. Operator, spell out figure. . . .").
- Signal paragraph breaks by saying "Paragraph" before dictating the text.
- Dictate *all* punctuation. Indicate opening and closing dashes, brackets, quotation marks, and parentheses.
- Indicate how you want measures, weights, and other technical or scientific notations typed (". . . two five centimeters . . ." or ". . . two five cc . . .").

6. Indicate which complimentary close you will use, unless your company has a standard closing the typist uses for each letter.

7. Dictate any enclosures, copies, and other material that may follow the signature.

8. Indicate when you have finished a message and when you have dictated the last message of the tape. A typical conclusion would be "End of letter, end of tape."

9. Stop when you have said what you have to say. While this step might seem self-evident, one of the hazards of dictation is that you always have one more thing to add. Before you realize it, you have wandered far from your outline. Warning signs of this tendency are repeating points you have already made, including less important points, or using clichés and empty phrases that pad your message. With practice, you will be able to tell when you have finished the message and should close off the letter.

Step Three: Revising

When your dictated message has been transcribed, you will be able to correct any errors or make any changes you need to improve the letter. You may find that three sentences in a row start with the word *However*, that information in the first paragraph should be placed in the second, or that paragraph breaks should be revised.

Often people who are beginners at dictation are surprised to discover how carelessly they speak. Our conversational English cannot be transcribed directly into written English—spoken words usually contain too many sentence fragments, half-finished thoughts, and grammatical errors. In fact, dictation frequently has the effect of forcing people to pay more attention to the quality of their verbal communication with others.

As you become more skilled in dictation, you will begin to correct your errors as you speak. Study the sample dictation and typed version below. Notice that the speaker indicates how the typist should transcribe every item in the letter.

> "Operator, type this letter in Semiblock on letterhead stationery. The letter is one page long and should be sent by certified mail to the recipient. The date should be January 6, 19--. The inside address is as follows. First line. Mr. Francis (F as in Frank r-a-n-c-i-s) Inglewood (that's I-n-g-l-e-w-o-o-d). Next line. Four six seven Crain (C-r-a-i-n) Street. Next line. Chicago comma Illinois six oh six one one. Salutation. Dear Mr. Inglewood. Colon. Paragraph. I am enclosing a copy of the survey maps you requested in your October three-oh letter. Period. You will find that the maps numbered one through twenty-two cover Brown (B-r-o-w-n) and Quinn (Q-u-i-n-n) counties. Period. (Operator, type the numbers one and twenty-two as figures.) Paragraph. I am also including a copy of the government pamphlet quote marks initial capitals Choosing the Best Site for Your Small Business end quote marks. Period. I believe comma as you will see in the pamphlet comma that this publication offers valuable tips on selecting a prime location for your firm. Period. Paragraph. I hope you will find this information helpful. Period. Call me if you need further assistance. Period. Sincerely yours comma Frank Ritter. Type the word Enclosures after the signature. End of letter."

Do not assume that the typist will automatically understand how you want an item spelled or typed. Take the time to give clear, explicit instructions. Again, this process will become more automatic as you acquire skill in dctation.

Here is the transcribed version of the dictated letter.

January 6, 19--

Mr. Francis Inglewood
467 Crain Street
Chicago, Illinois 60611

Dear Mr. Inglewood:

I am enclosing a copy of the survey maps you requested in your October 30 letter. You will find that the maps numbered 1 through 22 cover Brown and Quinn counties.

I am also including a copy of the government pamphlet "Choosing the Best Site for Your Small Business." I believe, as you will see in the pamphlet, that this publication offers valuable tips in selecting a prime location for your firm.

I hope you will find this information helpful. Call me if you need further assistance.

Sincerely yours,

Frank Ritter

Enclosures

After you have edited your message, proofread the final typed copy for errors that may have slipped through.

Chapter 9 Memos and Form Messages

Memos and routine form messages, unlike letters, are generally meant for communication *within* a company or among various branches or divisions of the same company. They are used to route information, acknowledge receipt of goods or data, inform recipients about various matters, and initiate some action. In other words, these messages get things moving. Occasionally, they are also sent to clients.

Memos

Memos are used to provide a summary of important information and suggest actions that should be taken. They are designed to catch the reader's undivided attention.

Memos can move in all directions in a company—up and down the management ladder or horizontally across departmental and division lines. They can be sent to one person or hundreds. Occasionally, they may even go outside the company to suppliers, customers, government agencies or officials, or the press. Although memos can be ten pages or more, one- to two-page memos are more common. Also, they are more likely to be read and to accomplish the writer's purpose. All memos are typed single space with double spaces between paragraphs.

Keys to writing effective memos include:

- Organization
- Getting quickly to the point
- Accurate information
- Specific actions indicated

Whether your memos are long or short, you can use the three steps of business writing to prepare, write, and revise them. Most firms have printed forms for writing memos, although the format may vary slightly from company to company.

Memo Format

Each memo has five headings at the top of the first page:

1. Company name, usually contained in the letterhead.
2. The word "To" followed by a colon indicating the recipient of

the memo. Use the reader's full name with any professional title such as Dr. but without the complimentary titles of Mr., Ms., Mrs., Miss. If you are sending the memo to several people, list them after the word "To:". However, if the list is long, put only the primary recipient's name and list the other names at the end of the memo.

3. The word "From" followed by a colon indicating the sender. Your name and professional title go after this heading.
4. The word "Date" and a colon. All memos must be dated. As in business letters, dating a communication gives the company a record of its correspondence.
5. The word "Subject" followed by a colon introducing the topic of the memo. State the subject in a few words but make sure it communicates the point of the memo. For example, a subject heading that says merely "Employee Benefits Program" does not tell the reader what aspect of the benefits program you are going to discuss. A more specific heading would be "Changes in Employee Medical Benefits."

Optional Headings. Optional headings may also be used when necessary or required by your company. These headings include references to other documents such as memos, letters, reports, invoices, and the like. If readers will need to review reference documents, make sure you supply the information necessary to retrieve the material: authors, names of issuing companies, dates, file or document numbers, subjects, and so on. In the text of your memo, refer to these documents by their assigned numbers.

Attachments. In some cases, you may need to attach photographs, charts, calculations, correspondence, or other types of documents to your memos. You may list attachments as you do references, either at the top of the memo or at the end, as the enclosure line in letters.

Address of Writer. In most cases, the address of the writer is contained in the company letterhead. But in firms with 500 or more employees or with branch offices in several cities, it may be necessary to include the address, division or department, and plant name in the memo to identify the writer. You may also wish to include your personal phone number within the company if you would like a quick response.

The order of these headings may vary from company to company, depending on in-house style. They may be placed flush with the left margin:

Company Letterhead

TO: All Division Heads
From: R. I. Richards, Vice President Sales
Date: December 5, 19--
Subject: EMPLOYEES' CHRISTMAS BONUS

Or headings may be placed on either side of the page, particularly if some of the optional headings are included:

Company Letterhead

To:	Edwin Green Yolanda Benning Martin Garcia	Date:	June 4, 19--
		References:	Contact #45 Ace Products 445 Kind Drive Jayne, OH 45642
From:	Marcia Davenport		

Subject: DELIVERY OF FURNITURE TO ACE PRODUCTS

Step One: Prewriting

As in a letter or report, you must first identify your purpose, determine your audience, and establish the scope of your subject. Your approach to memo writing will change slightly, depending on the situation and intended readership. You would use a different tone and include different information in a memo to the president of the company as opposed to a line manager.

Gather all references and data you will need before you start writing. Use your laundry list of topics as a guide to the background research you may need to do. Ask yourself what the reader *must* know from all the information you have gathered. What do you want the memo to accomplish?

Step Two: Writing

As you write your memo, keep the purpose and the readers' needs in mind. If you are informing employees about a company relocation, try to see the action from their point of view and anticipate their reactions or questions. What effect might the news have on company morale and efficiency?

Organizing

You can organize the memo in several ways. You may want to use a chronological approach, outlining the history of a project or situation. In other cases, a question-and-answer style might be more appropriate. For some readers, the general-to-the-specific approach or cause-and-effect method might be best. Each approach has its advantages.

1. Chronological. With this method you tell the history of the situation, beginning with the past and moving up to the present or starting with the current situation and bringing in past events to fill in the early history.

2. Functional. In this approach you discuss the functions of products or people such as marketing researchers, product developers, and the like. You focus on the product or person without bringing in historical or past information.

3. Cause and effect. You can start either with the causes of a situation or with the effects, depending on which one you wish to emphasize. An oil spill, for example, is the effect of an accident or natural catastrophe. You may want to discuss the implications of the effect—ecological or economic damage—or discuss the causes—an off-shore accident, a shipping collision, an earthquake or storm. This method focuses on the immediate situation and recommends immediate actions.

4. Question and answer. In this approach, you anticipate the reader's questions and answer them or ask those questions that reflect the reader's point of view. You then proceed to answer them in the memo both to inform the readers and to persuade them to take the action you outline. For example, this approach can be used to persuade employees to work an extra shift or accept a change in benefits.

5. Geographical. This method can be used for memos that report on routine activities such as monthly sales figures or production levels. You do not need to persuade or convince readers or bring a crisis or other type of situation to their attention. You are simply reporting information routinely.

These memos can also be organized from highest sales figures to lowest, largest to smallest divisions, and the like. The important point is to arrange the date to meet readers' needs.

6. The problem, analysis, solution approach. In this type of organization, you are using the memo to give a capsule account of a situation, your analysis of it, and your solution. The purpose is to draw attention to an issue that needs quick action. You are giving the reader important information on which to base a decision or call a meeting. By providing the reader with a preliminary analysis and solution, you have saved time and effort on the reader's part.

Organizing Long Memos

Memos longer than two typed pages generally have a more formal structure than shorter ones. However, the main point is still to apprise the reader of the topic quickly. The reader should not have to work through two pages to find the point of the memo or the essential information. A long memo should have the following sections:

1. A Summary. The summary, placed at the beginning of the memo, should condense the subject to five or ten lines. It should not contain jargon or highly technical language but be a clear, simple account of the subject. The summary can help readers decide quickly if they should read the entire memo or only certain sections. Summaries usually contain findings, conclusions, or recommendations.

If you expect a hostile reaction to your memo, you may want to begin your summary with a statement of the problem, a brief analysis, and conclusions or recommendations. By doing so, you may neutralize your opposition or at least get a fair hearing.

2. Introduction. The introduction orients the reader by stating the memo's purpose and scope. You may add a paragraph or two of background material if the reader needs more information.

The introduction may also be used to ask or answer key questions, make a thank-you statement, or give good news such as the approval of a proposal. If you must refuse a request or reject an offer, use the introduction to establish your reasons before saying no. If you are pointing out a mistake, avoid using statements that blame or judge.

3. Discussion. The main discussion may be limited to a few paragraphs or run to several pages of detailed analysis. The subjects may range from policy changes to reorganization of a department to a proposal for diversifying company holdings. Long memos usually discuss topics that will require considerable outlays of resources, time, and personnel. The arguments need to be reasoned and supported carefully, and the facts of a situation accurately identified and presented.

Your ability to outline and organize material will be crucial to this section of the memo. You can use various headings to separate your information into sections: Statement of the Problem, Approach to the Problem, Analysis, Evaluation, Conclusions, and Recommendations.

4. Closing or Concluding Remarks. The conclusion discusses what action is required of the readers. This section reviews and underscores the main points and problems your readers should keep in mind. The closing is also the place to acknowledge assistance, ask critical questions of the readers, or request a particular action or decision.

5. Optional Elements. Unlike business letters, the complimentary closing and signature are not included in memos. In some companies, however, it is customary to sign the memo.

You may want to include a distribution list, like the copies lines in a letter, at the end of the memo. Even though memos may be sent to hundreds or even thousands of employees, most go to fewer than a dozen people at any one time. To determine who should receive a copy, ask yourself if the person was involved in the project or issue and should be kept informed of the situation. If the answer to either question is *yes*, then include the person on your distribution list.

Copies of memos serve several purposes. They keep lines of communication open among all concerned individuals, they can protect you in sensitive or highly political situations within a company, and they can prevent your ideas from being pirated by someone else.

Names in the distribution list are usually typed in alphabetical order. However, if one of the individuals clearly outranks the others, place that name first. If the list is shorter than a dozen names, it follows the heading "To:" at the beginning of the memo. If the list is longer, place it at the end of the memo, referencing it after the "To:" line. For example:

TO: See distribution list on page 6

Attachments provide supporting material for the subject of the memo. You may wish to include quotes or tables from attachments in the text. How much material to include will depend on the situation, but it is usually good to limit the amount taken from attachments. Your text should stand on its own with attachments providing support.

Writing the First Draft

Regardless of the organizing approach you use, there are three guidelines for writing the text of the memo. Keep them in mind as you develop your first draft.

1. Tell readers only what they need to know. Memos by nature are concise packets of information. Elaborate details will obscure your point and frustrate the reader.

2. Tell them what the information means. You are not simply supplying information but interpreting it for the reader. If sales have declined by 20 percent over the past six months, give the reader a brief analysis of what that drop might mean. Is a product line failing? Has a division become a critical drain on operations? Interpreting the information leads to the next step.

3. Tell readers what action is needed and when it should be taken. Should the failing division be closed down or sold? When? Discuss ways of achieving the desired action, but keep it brief! Remember, a memo is like a telegram alerting the readers to a situation that demands attention.

The style of a memo emphasizes active verbs, descriptive words and phrases, and a brisk, conversational tone.

Descriptive words and phrases. Ask yourself questions about the subject. What makes it important? What does the reader need to know about it? There is a problem, but what kind of problem? A product is for sale, but what is the height, weight, performance, and feel of that product? Use your words to create a vivid picture of what you are describing and why it is important. Include photographs, charts, and other illustrations if necessary. For example, if you are trying to persuade the office manager to buy new carpeting for the department, explain the virtues of the carpeting you have in mind. Instead of "The carpeting will last long" say "The carpet's stain-resistant, nylon-wool blend will give us years of wear."

Active Verbs. Memos are used to urge the reader to take some action. Active verbs can underscore the impression that your message is important and needs an immediate response. "A decision must be reached by Tuesday" does not carry the same imperative as "We must decide this matter by Tuesday." The active voice involves the reader directly.

Conversational, positive tone. The style of most memos should approach that of natural conversation. Write as if the recipient were with you. Avoid stilted or artificial language like the following:

> It has come to my attention that the pronounced lack of worker attention to safety matters is jeopardizing all personnel in the docking and loading area. Effective June 4, instructions on safety gear and procedures will commence. All shifts are required to attend.

The writer meant to say:

> Our accident rate this year is 50 percent higher than it was for the same period last year. It is clear workers are not wearing safety gear nor following safety procedures in the loading and docking areas. Beginning June 4 we will conduct seminars in safety procedures and equipment for all shifts. Supervisors from each shift will see that all employees attend the seminars.

A positive tone in your memo can set the stage for cooperation and establish goodwill between yourself and your readers. If you must disagree with the reader's opinions or policies or criticize the reader's products or services, try to preface your remarks with a favorable comment. For example:

Poor: The new adhesive you recommended doesn't work. You must not have researched our products at all.

Better: Although the new adhesive works well in most fabrication plants, we have found that it does not hold up under the tests we give our products.

Avoid "firing off" a memo in anger; it is likely to provoke an angry reply in return. Read over your criticism carefully to make sure you are not letting a sarcastic, complaining, or demanding tone slip into your words. A negative tone would be:

> I realize that productivity matters more than the morale of the workers, so I am complying with the recent order to raise production output by 10 percent.

A more objective and pointed tone might be:

> The recent order to increase productivity by 10 percent does not address one of the major causes of reduced output. Worker morale is unusually low over employment cuts in the company. I propose that we delay implementing the new level until we have talked with the workers about their job future.

In the second memo, the writer points out a problem and proposes an action step to address it while tactfully criticizing the new production levels.

A positive rather than a negative tone is more helpful to both reader and writer. It suggests the writer has something more to offer the reader than simply a demand or a judgment.

Technical Language. In memos, you will be able to use technical language more than in general business correspondence. Memos are often written from one professional to another. Instead of saying to a fellow computer analyst, "The new model has an expandable memory that should meet our needs," you would be more likely to say "The new model's 256K memory can be expanded to 640K, more than enough for our short Lotus program." Since memos between professionals are not intended for a general or lay reader, using technical language can save time and prevent misunderstandings or delays while specific details are clarified.

Accuracy. Memos often urge immediate action or decision; as a result the facts on which those actions are based must be accurate. Double-check facts, figures, events, cause-and-effect relationships, dates, time lines, and other information essential to the decision. Distinguish fact from opinion, particularly when you are interpreting or offering recommendations on the subject of the memo. Check your grammar, punctuation, spelling, and format. Avoid sending out a memo that has strikeovers, obvious corrections, or erasures that may obscure or distort data. An attractive, clean copy can help ensure that your memo gets a quick reading.

When you have determined what you want to say, begin writing your first draft. Review your memo to make sure that the tone is appropriate, the ideas clear and concise, the style natural and flowing, and the information accurate. Take into consideration the reader's personality and surroundings. How is the reader likely to react when reading the memo? Consider the total context in which the message will be received, particularly if you are criticizing the reader's policies, products, or opinions.

Step Three: Revising and Proofreading

Look over your first draft and revise it for brevity, active language, and clarity. Make sure that you have explained technical or unusual terms adequately and that you have included only the most pertinent, essential information. Ask yourself what you would need to know if you were the reader.

Finally, proofread the memo carefully, paying particular attention to facts, dates, names, figures, and any other quantitative data. This step is your last chance to make any changes or corrections before the memo leaves your office. Double-check the distribution list, if you have one, to make sure you have not left out anyone who needs to see a copy.

Read over the following examples of memos. Notice the positioning of headings and closing material. How well does each memo accomplish its purpose?

To: All Support Staff Supervisors

From: Ruth Bennett, Controller

Date: December 5, 19--

Subject: YEAR-END BONUS FOR SUPPORT STAFF

I am pleased to announce that we will be distributing a year-end bonus to all support staff and middle management this year. Sales have increased by 25 percent in the past eight months and are up 36 percent from the same period last year.

Bonuses will be calculated according to employees' salary and length of service as follows:

Service	*Amount*
10 years or more	3/4 of monthly salary
5 to 9 years	2/3 of monthly salary
Less than 5 years	1/2 of monthly salary

All employees have contributed to the rise in sales revenue this year. The bonus is one way of expressing our appreciation for everyone's outstanding effort. Bonus checks will be issued to each employee on December 23 along with the regular paycheck.

TO: Theodore Gaynor, President
Gail Barton, Secretary
Richard Yin, Treasurer
Nissan Pushba, Corporate Counsel

From: James McKenna, Field Investigator

Date: October 27, 19--

Subject: SAFETY AND SECURITY OF OFFSHORE OIL-DRILLING PLATFORM #45

I have completed my investigation of the superstructure of offshore oil-drilling platform #45 as you requested. Several platforms sustained heavy damage in the October 25 hurricane. Platform #45 is still operational, but some serious structural problems must be corrected before another storm hits the area.

The pylons anchoring the platform were subjected to severe torque in the hurricane and no longer meet current safety standards. In addition, the drilling shaft has been cracked and could shear the cable if subjected to undue pressure.

I recommend that the platform be shut down until repairs can be made. To delay them could jeopardize the lives of the 45 permanent crew members and 10 part-time workers on the rig. A major accident could also spill crude oil into the bay and destroy nearby fishing beds and beachfront.

A decision on this matter should be made as soon as possible. I realize the economic consequences of shutting down the platform and disrupting the flow of oil, but the safety considerations should be paramount. The firm cannot afford a major oil spill.

I will remain on site until I hear from you. Please let me know your decision as soon as possible.

Other Form Messages

Memos are only one kind of interoffice messages used in companies. Many firms also employ routing slips, telephone and visitor message forms, and mailgrams and other telegraphic services. With computerized office communications, messages can even be sent via electronic mail, bypassing the post office, telegraphic office, and private mail carriers.

Routing Slips

Routing slips are used when material is sent to several people within a firm. The slips can be small (3″ × 5″) and are attached to the first sheet of the material to be sent—a book, magazine, report, memo, and the like. The slip lists the sender and those who will receive the material. Each person crosses his or her name off the list and forwards the material to the next person. This method of communication ensures that everyone who needs to read the information does so.

TITLE ______________________________

CODE # ____________________ DATE ____________

ATTACHED PLEASE FIND:

____________ GALLEYS ____________ REPROS

____________ PAGE PROOFS ____________ BLUELINES

____________ CAMERA COPY ____________ (OTHER)

PLEASE CHECK & INITIAL:		INITIAL	DATE
EDITORIAL	Tim Rogus	______	____
	Barbara Donner	______	____
	Michael Ross	______	____
	Judith Clayton	______	____
ART	Michael Tapia	______	____
EDITOR IN CHIEF	Leonard Fiddle	______	____
ADVERTISING	Bill Klein	______	____
SALES:	Charlie Liebowitz	______	____
BUSINESS	Mark Pattis	______	____

PLEASE RETURN TO PRODUCTION NO LATER THAN ____________

____

Warren Flint / Pat Martin

NTC National Textbook Company

Routing slips can also be used to send contracts or other documents that need the approval and signature of several people. The routing slip provides a record of all signatures and dates.

Often routing slips have the sender's name printed on them and a standard instruction at the bottom: "Return to company librarian" or simply "Return to __________." The slips can also be typed individually for each document circulated.

Routing slips save companies time and money by eliminating the need to duplicate and send material to all concerned. After being circulated, the original material can then be placed on permanent file.

Mailgrams and Other Telegraphic Services

Several services for sending messages are available from telephone and telegraph companies. The most well-known is the *telegram*. Telegrams are also the most costly, which is why they are seldom used in business.

Telegrams are sent by calling Western Union, giving the name and address of the recipient, and an exact message. Western Union sends the message to the branch office nearest the recipient and delivers the telegram to the door. Western Union delivers anywhere in the world where they have a branch office. The cost of a telegram is determined by the number of words and the location of the recipient.

In many offices, *teleprinter equipment* is used to send messages directly to branch offices or divisions. A company with offices in Chicago, Dallas, Los Angeles, Boston, and New York can install teleprinters in each office to speed up communications among the locations. Western Union offers two such services: TWX (teletypewriter exchange service) and Telex. Telex service is used so often it has given business language a new expression: *to telex* a message.

One of the more recent services to appear on the electronic message scene is *Mailgram*, offered jointly by Western Union and the U.S. Postal Service. Instead of wiring the message to a branch office, Western Union sends it to the post office closest to the recipient. The post office gives priority to Mailgrams and delivers them the day after they are sent. Mailgrams are effective attention-getters and can be used in advertising campaigns and other volume mailings when the sender wishes to call readers' attention to the message. Mailgram format is similar to a telegram and has the same eye-catching envelope.

Overnight or Same-Day Services

Overnight or same-day services have multiplied in the last few years. The post office offers Express Mail with a guaranteed overnight delivery time. Federal

Express, UPS, and other carriers promise overnight and same-day service to companies, in some cases assuring customers that their messages will reach the chosen destination within two to three hours, regardless of the distance.

The competition in overnight and same-day mail service has increased in the past few years. The computer revolution has accelerated the speed of business communications and cut into the territory of traditional quick-service messenger companies. As a result, these companies are attempting to broaden their services to keep customers happy and attract new business.

What does all this mean to you as a business person? You are in a position to "shop" for the least expensive way to send your letters and packages and to demand extra services tailored to the needs of your company. Competition has increased the choices you have for overnight and same-day carriers.

Electronic Mail

When it comes to speed, however, *electronic mail* has no competitors. Messages sent via electronic mail are relayed at the speed of light from one computer terminal to another or to several terminals via a telecommunications link.

At that speed, communications are virtually instantaneous. Terminals can be separated by a few blocks, a few miles, or an entire ocean and still receive messages as soon as they are sent.

Once a company has the hardware in place and is on-line in the network, electronic mail can be a rapid, relatively inexpensive way to send instant communications. The only obstacle preventing many companies from joining in the system is the cost of the hardware needed to make telecommunications links.

With advances in technology, however, such hardware should be within reach of even small companies within the next five to ten years. By the end of this century—even perhaps by the end of this decade—such communications networks should be commonplace in nearly all businesses.

Section 4
Special Writing and Research Projects

Chapter 10 Business Report Writing

Business reports are written for a variety of reasons. They may be requested by upper management to explore an area of concern to the company. They may be routinely prepared, as in annual reports, monthly sales reports, or quarterly production reports. Government requires many written reports from businesses each year to ensure their compliance with federal regulations, IRS requirements, equal employment practices, and other governmental orders.

In many cases, reports follow the acceptance of a written proposal. (Proposals are discussed in Chapter 11.) However, a report may also *precede* a proposal and serve as part of the background information on which the proposal is based. For example, your firm may publish a study on the energy problems of small businesses. You would then write a proposal to small firms detailing how an energy survey by your company could help them save money. If a firm accepts your proposal and hires you to do the work, the results of your survey would be the subject of a final report delivered to the client.

Some written reports may be only a page or two, much like a detailed memo, long letter, or government report. The content and form of these documents are usually set beforehand, as in the case of monthly sales reports, inventory reviews, and the like.

In this chapter, however, we will focus on reports written on an assigned topic at the request of management. The topics might include evaluating the communications skills of employees or determining the best marketing strategy for 19--. For these reports, you will need to determine the content and format for yourself.

When you are asked to do a report on an assigned topic, you can assume in most cases that other employees have written reports before you. Ask to see copies of these reports so that you can familiarize yourself with the company format and style.

To begin the report-writing process, we return to the three basic steps for effective writing.

Step One: Prewriting

As in the case of letters, memos, and other business communications, you begin by establishing the purpose of your writing. Assume that you have been asked to prepare a report on employee involvement in management decision making. Your first task is to determine the exact objective of the report. Is it to evaluate the possibility of using employee involvement at your own firm? Are you to study the results of the technique at other firms? If you are not sure about the purpose of your assigned topics, ask questions until you can state the objective in a sentence or two.

Who is your intended audience? Will the report be written for top management? the government? for other firms in the same industry? Will it be available to middle and line management or to workers at the support staff and production levels? Once you have determined your audience, ask yourself what they need to know. Will they need background information on employee involvement? Interview those who are requesting the report to find out what they would like included and use those answers to guide your research. Put yourself as much as possible in the readers' place as you work.

Finally, you will need to narrow down the subject to a list of topics that the report will cover. For this chapter, assume that the report will be read by top management. Also, assume they would like to know if instituting employee involvement in your company would improve decision making, productivity, and morale.

You now know you will need to research how employee involvement has worked in companies similar to yours. You may want to include information on employee involvement in other countries. Further, you will need to learn how workers view the program and how management feels about the results. The data you gather will need to be analyzed in terms of productivity, decision-making methods, efficiency, revenues, accident rates, turnover, morale, and labor-management relations. You will also be formulating conclusions and recommendations about whether employee involvement is appropriate for your firm.

Your initial plan for the report might be a list of the following topics:

1. Define employee involvement
2. Determine success or failure of such methods in similar firms over the past five to ten years
3. Compare U.S. experience with that of Japan and Europe
4. Determine worker and management attitudes and experiences with employee involvement
5. Evaluate program in light of our company
6. Formulate recommendations

Background Research

Your main research sources are libraries, industry and government data; other people; and your own knowledge and experience. For your report on employee involvement—or many other assigned topics—you would probably institute a literature search of books, articles, and reports written on the subject. Your company librarian or the reference librarian in the business section of a public or private library can help you. Computer-assisted research can provide printouts listing all the work published on your topic, giving you author, title, publication, year, and a synopsis of the work. Ask the librarian about computer-assisted research; it can save you considerable time and effort in gathering data. (See Chapter 12: Finding Business Information for a discussion of resources.)

To gain information from other people—in this case, primarily workers and managers—you will need to conduct interviews and use questionnaires. Questionnaires give you access to a large number of people in a short time, but the information gathered is limited by the number and type of questions you can ask. Most people are not willing to fill out a lengthy or detailed questionnaire. They may also wonder if the results will be reflected in their personnel records, particularly if they are criticizing the company. In addition, devising unbiased, probing questionnaires requires professional skill.

Personal interviews generally yield more information but will also limit the number of people you can include in your survey. Interviewing is time consuming. You must win the confidence and trust of each person you interview and learn how to probe without offending people. Skilled interviewers are rare, and you may need to hire someone to interview for you.

You can also investigate industry and government sources for information on your topic. The government offers an astonishing array of free data. Industry associations also do surveys, reports, studies, and seminars on various topics or may publish the proceedings from a conference or convention. Again, the reference librarian can help you locate the specific material you need.

Don't overlook your own knowledge and experience. Think back over your own career and see if you have resources you may have forgotten or simply put aside. For example, you may have participated in employee-involvement programs without realizing it. Examine your own background for helpful material.

The important point is to generate *quality* information on which to base your conclusions and recommendations. You want to gather the most reliable and up-to-date information possible. Talk with others to help you determine which information to use, which to discard, and which to include with qualifications.

You may need to go back to an information source more than once, particularly if your interviews, for example, yield widely different data. Part of the information-gathering process involves analyzing and evaluating the data.

Keep careful records of all sources used. Document author, title, publication, publisher, date, and number of pages or pages used in your search. Put each reference on a separate index card and keep your cards in a special file. You can save yourself considerable frustration when you are ready to type the bibliography if all your sources are documented. It can take hours, even days, to track down a missing reference. Make sure any quotes, opinions, figures, or facts cited are accurately referenced. You should know where all background information originated.

To summarize the prewriting phase:

1. Establish the purpose of your report.
2. Identify the audience and its needs.
3. Determine the scope of your topic.
4. Plan and conduct background research and data gathering.
5. Document all reference material collected.

Step Two: Writing

Now that you have gathered the information you need, your next step is to organize it into logical sequence before you begin writing your rough draft. You can make this a two-step process: Develop a rough plan and then write a final outline of the report. Splitting the process into two stages can be especially helpful when you have gathered a large amount of data.

Organizing the Plan

The written plan is less formal or detailed than the outline and can be adjusted and amended more easily. You would include the following items in your plan:

1. The subject of the report. State the subject in one or two sentences. In the case of our example, you might state the subject as "Evaluation of employee involvement in medium-sized corporations, and its impact on productivity, profits, labor-management relations, and decision making."

2. Purpose of the report. State the purpose in a single sentence. It might be, "To determine if employee involvement techniques would be suitable for our company." Keep refining the purpose until you can state it clearly and briefly.

3. Special terms. Define any special terms. "Employee involvement" may be a new concept to some of your readers. If you use other terms like "quality circles" or "quality of work life," define them as well. Establishing your definitions will give your readers a common basis for understanding.

4. Data. Specify the kinds of information you will be using in the report—interviews; questionnaires; literature from public, industry, and government sources; personal experience; and the like. This will give your readers some idea of your methods in researching the subject.

5. Sources. Keep a working bibliography so that you will be able to compile your sources at the end of the report.

6. Rough outline of content and organizational approach. You might want to start with the chronological method and give a history of employee involvement in U.S. companies. Or you may want to begin with the functional approach, describing employee involvement and how the technique is applied. Make a rough outline of the report, choosing one of the organizational approaches discussed in Chapter 10: Memos and Form Messages.

7. ***Conclusions and recommendations.*** Formulate possible outcomes of the report based on your information. Would you recommend instituting employee involvement in your company? Under what conditions? What training and education would labor and management require?

8. ***Estimated budget for producing the report and a time line for completion.*** How much will printing and binding cost? When can you deliver the finished report? Setting budgets and schedules will help you move from one step to the next without getting caught at any one stage.

The rough plan paves the way for the second step in the organization process, preparing the detailed outline.

Outlining the Report

The detailed outline will serve as the basis for writing the report. You have had a chance to go through your data and organize it, to evaluate what you will include and discard, what the information means, and what conclusions and recommendations you can make.

The outline should be detailed enough to help you develop each section of the report, yet flexible enough so that you can change it if necessary. The outline is your way of thinking through the structure and content of the report in detail. Final adjustments and corrections can be made when you write the first draft.

An outline for your report on employee involvement might look like the following:

I. Summary or synopsis (summarizes major points of the report and conclusions)
   A. Employee involvement can be used in medium-sized companies to improve labor-management relations, develop human resources within a firm, improve productivity and efficiency, develop better decision-making processes, and increase overall company performance.
   B. Employee involvement needs to be introduced carefully or it will not be successful. Top management and labor leaders must be committed to the process and seek to involve workers and middle and line managers. Adequate training in employee involvement procedures must be given. The success of the method depends on commitment and education.

II. Introduction (explains the reason for writing the report)
   A. Purpose of the report: to determine if employee involvement is suitable for our company.
   B. Scope of the topic: definition of employee involvement and its application. Description of what will be covered in the report.
   C. Methodology: how data was gathered and analyzed.
   D. Structure of the report: the organizational approach chosen.

III. Historical review of employee involvement in the United States
   A. Introduction of employee involvement in U.S. firms.
   B. Overall success and failure rate of the method.
   C. Comparison of U.S. and foreign programs, focusing on Japan and Europe.

IV. Evaluation of employee involvement in medium-sized firms
   A. Description of firms chosen and explanation of their programs.
   B. Interviews, questionnaires, and data from published literature revealing characteristics of successful and unsuccessful programs.
   C. Summary of findings.

V. Evaluation of our firm and employee involvement
   A. Current structure and organization of firm.
   B. Ways in which employee involvement would impact firm—pros and cons.

VI. Conclusions and recommendations
   A. When instituted and administered properly, employee involvement improves a company's productivity, decision-making process, profits, morale, labor-management relations, and development of human resources.
   B. Recommend that employee involvement be instituted in our company.
   C. List of conditions for instituting and administering program successfully: commitment from management and labor leadership, selection of training and education programs, means of administering and phasing in new system, follow-up and monitoring.
   D. Estimate of time and cost to institute program and get it running effectively.

VII. Bibliography

VIII. Appendixes
  A. Charts of four companies showing increase in productivity, morale, revenue; decrease in absenteeism, turnover, labor-management conflicts.
  B. Questionnaires used and transcripts of selected interviews with workers and management in four companies.
  C. Summary of historical data from government reports.

After developing and refining the outline, you are ready to write.

Writing the First Draft

Although the format of the report will vary from company to company, most reports have eleven elements. Not every report will contain all eleven parts. You may want to omit some parts, depending on the length and kind of report and your readers' needs. Nonetheless, you should be aware of the purpose and function of each part.

The eleven elements can be divided into preliminary materials, body of the report, and supplemental materials.

Preliminary Materials. Five of the eleven elements fall into this category: title page, letter of authorization, letter of transmittal, table of contents, and summary or synopsis.

1. Title page. The title page contains all the identifying information—title of the report, company, recipients, date, and writer's name. Each company usually has its own format for the title page. Some may set all information flush with the right or left margin, others may center everything at the top third and bottom third of the page. Check copies of previous reports to see which format your company uses.

Right Flush:

EMPLOYEE INVOLVEMENT IN
MEDIUM-SIZED COMPANIES

Prepared for

TECTRONICS INCORPORATED

August 31, 19--

Presented by

RUTH WHITMAN-JONES

Centered Top Third

EMPLOYEE INVOLVEMENT IN MEDIUM-SIZED COMPANIES

Prepared for

TECTRONICS INCORPORATED

Bottom third

August 31, 19--

Presented by

RUTH WHITMAN-JONES

The title page is followed by a blank sheet of paper.

2. ***Letter of authorization.*** The letter follows the blank sheet of paper after the title page. It is typed according to the company's format for business letters. The letter should come from the person or persons who authorized the report, and it should outline the purpose or importance of the material. It might come from the president of the company—as in the case of an annual report—or from a division manager, head of a department, or vice president.

3. ***Letter of transmittal.*** This letter indicates who is the audience for the report. It may be written in the form of a regular business letter or memo. It may contain a checklist of all persons who will receive a copy of the report. Make sure that everyone who needs to see the report is included in the list. (Chapter 7 contains a sample letter of transmittal accompanying a report.)

4. ***Table of contents.*** The table of contents lists all the topics and materials in the report. All preliminary pages—letter of authorization, letter of transmittal, table of contents, and synopsis—should be numbered with lower-case Roman numerals. The body of the report should be numbered with Arabic numerals. Each company may have a slightly different format for typing the table of contents. Check previous reports to see how the table has been done in your firm.

A table of contents for the report on employee involvement might look like the following:

TABLE OF CONTENTS

The table of contents may be typed in upper/lower case or in all capitals. You may want to list the titles of appendixes by letter (A. Charts of Four Medium-sized Companies). Appendix titles are indented under the heading Appendixes.

5. Synopsis or summary. The summary gives the reader a quick, concise overview of the report. It is usually one-half to one page long and does not include data or figures. A good summary (1) provides enough information to specify the aims and results of your project, (2) is brief without omitting essential information, (3) is written in a fluid, easy style, (4) is consistent in tone and emphasis with the body of the report, and (5) makes use of accepted abbreviations to save space but does not include any tables or illustrations.

Body of the Report. The body of the report contains the introduction, body, conclusions and recommendations. You may not always have both conclusions and recommendations, but generally you will have one or the other.

6. Introduction. The introduction describes the reason the report was written. It contains the purpose, methods of gathering data, sources, definitions, and a brief discussion of the report's organization. A good introduction arouses readers' interest and gives them some background information on the subject, preparing readers for the material contained in the body of the report.

7. ***Body.*** All the pertinent data you have gathered and analyzed is included in this section. This is the heart of the report in which you state your case and substantiate your points, presenting the results of your research and analysis. You may also include illustrations—charts, graphs, pictures—to support or enhance your discussion.

This portion of the report is usually organized under various headings. Major headings indicate main points of the report. Subheadings and sub-subheadings indicate subordinate and supporting ideas. The organization might look like the following:

Major head centered:

EMPLOYEE INVOLVEMENT IN JAPANESE FIRMS

The public first began hearing about employee involvement or quality circles from foreign business observers in Japan. The circles were composed of workers and management from all levels in the company. The objective was to elicit suggestions from employees and to solve work-related problems.

Subheading centered:

Toyota Quality Circles

The Toyota auto firm was among the first to institute quality circles. Within six months, workers had produced over 500 suggestions that resulted in savings to the company of over $35 million in one year.

Sub-subheading flush left:

Methods of Eliciting Worker Ideas

One of the biggest complaints of workers in U.S. companies is that information flows only one way—from management on down. Workers have little chance to impact the decision-making process. At Toyota, managers in quality circle meetings are not allowed to run the show. They can only listen or ask questions while workers discuss problems and propose solutions.

Make sure the wording of your headings is parallel. For example, if you use a noun phrase for your first major heading (Employee Involvement in Japanese Firms), use noun phrases for all your major heads. Do not use participial phrases one time (Examining Employee Involvement in the United States) and a noun phrase another time (Quality Circles in U.S. Firms). Subheads and sub-subheads should also be parallel.

Additional headings can be used if necessary, but generally three headings are enough. Again, each company has its own individual format for reports.

8. Conclusions. Readers may skim through the body of the report to get to the conclusions. They want to know what the data and supportive materials mean. What patterns, trends, or observations did you find in your research? Your conclusions should be stated briefly and clearly, perhaps in a series of numbered statements. Be sure that your conclusions are logical outcomes of your data and are supported by the information and research you have completed. For example, you may conclude that employee involvement can be successful only if management and workers understand how to implement and administer the technique.

9. Recommendations. You may be asked to develop recommendations for further study or action in your report. You will be taking your conclusions to the next step and answering such questions as What should be done? How do we achieve the desired outcome? How can we persuade people to agree with our plan of action? Your recommendations will be action steps or suggestions for action that give the readers a starting point for the next phase in the process. In some cases, when the situation is urgent, you may want to place your recommendations at the beginning of the report in the introduction. For the most part, though, they will come at the end of the report after you have presented your findings and conclusions.

Supplemental Materials. This section lists the sources of your information and any supporting data that did not appear in the body of the report but that you wish to include.

10. Bibliography. The bibliography lists all sources used in writing your report. You should also list the names of people with whom you corresponded or interviewed. You will need to give complete information on all books, reports, articles, documents, and other references so that readers can retrieve these materials if they wish.

Entries in the bibliography should be alphabetized by the author's last name, or, if no author is indicated, by the document's title. Articles *an, a,* and *the* are not used as the first word. Each entry is single-spaced with a double space between entries. The first line is flush with the left margin, and run-over lines are indented five spaces. Your company may have its own style for typing bibliographic entries. If not, a common style used in many business reports is given below. Notice the spacing and punctuation.

Books with one author:

Adler, Afred. Six Great Ideas. New York: William Morris, 1978. 245 pp.

Books with two authors:

Morgan, John H., and Rachel C. Haynes. Corporate Culture in the '80s. Chicago: Contemporary Books, 1981. 342 pp.

Magazines and newspapers:

"Getting Management and Labor to the Round Table," Business Week, January 6, 1982, pp. 15-17.

"Motorola Invests $3 Million in Quality Circles," Chicago Tribune, March 19, 1980, pp. 1, 15-16.

Quincy, Teresa. "How the Japanese Did It." Forbes, March 24, 1981, pp. 23-26.

Smith, Hedrick. "Giving Labor Authority in the Workplace." New York Times, April 10, 1983, pp. 1, 17.

Unpublished materials:

Roberts, Norman. "Effects of Employee Involvement on Management's Perception of Power and Authority in the Workplace." Doctoral thesis, University of Michigan, East Lansing, Michigan. 1982. 156 pp.

Government documents:

U.S. Department of Labor. "Worker Productivity in Five Major Industries, 1978-1983." Washington, D.C.: U.S. Government Printing Office, 1984. 76 pp.

Institutional/company materials:

Bell Laboratories. Annual Report, 1983. Niles, Illinois: Bell Laboratories, Inc., September 30, 1983. 53 pp.

All bibliographical entries must include the author or authors, title of the material either underscored or in quotation marks, the publisher's city and state and the publisher's name, the date and year, and the total number of pages contained in the reference or the pages covered by the reference if it is found in a larger work.

11. Appendixes. This section contains information that supports the data in the body but is too lengthy or detailed to include in the text. Appendixes can include charts, questionnaires, short reports or documents, photographs, explanations of statistical methods or computer programs used to gather data, transcripts of interviews, or any other data you feel the reader would find valuable.

Illustrations.

Illustrations can add impact to your report by *showing* readers, not simply *telling* them, about a situation. You can use many forms of illustrations—graphs, tables, drawings, charts, and the like. Since many offices have computer graphics capabilities, creating illustrations is relatively easy. Make sure you have a clear need for an illustration. Readers will find it difficult to follow your line of reasoning if it is lost in a forest of charts and tables.

Make sure illustrations stand on their own, enhancing what has been stated in the text instead of merely repeating it. For example, if you have listed production rates in your report, don't repeat the same information in a table. You have duplicated your data for no good purpose and wasted the reader's time.

Instead, list the production rates in the table and use your text to explain the data—for instance, why the rates go up or down. You have used the *illustration* to highlight your data, putting it in a form the reader can easily grasp. You have used your *text* to tell the reader what the data mean.

Keep these points in mind when you create any type of illustration. Ask yourself, does the reader really need to see the data in the form of an illustration? If so, what form would present the data most clearly: a table, chart, or graph? What conclusions do you want the reader to draw when viewing the illustration?

Several kinds of illustrations can be used, each having advantages and disadvantages, as described below. Look them over carefully. Examine other reports with illustrations to determine how the authors used each type of chart, table, or graph. Experiment with each type, putting your data into several forms and noting the different effects each form has on the information presented.

1. Graphs. Graphs are visually more interesting than tables but often less accurate since data must be drawn along a continuum. The main advantage of graphs is that the reader can spot trends, cycles, or other movements more easily. Graphs can condense a large amount of data into a small space. Reports commonly use several kinds of graphs.

a. *Line graphs* indicate the relationship of a series of data along a continuum. The movement of sales and number of products sold, for instance, can be charted as two lines moving from one time period to another.
b. *Bar graphs* are horizontal bars crossing the page from left to right. They indicate varying quantities of an item over time or from one location to another.
c. *Column bar graphs* show a row of columns rising from the base of a chart.
d. *Pie graphs* are circles cut into sections like a pie. Each section represents a percent of the total.

Line Graph

Figure 4.1—BROWN, INC. NEW AND USED AUTOMOBILE SALES IN 19--

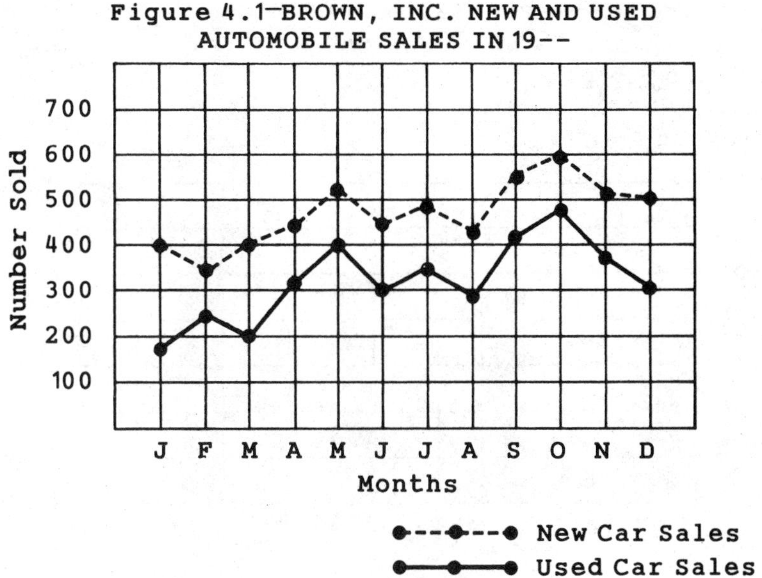

Bar Graph

Figure 4.2—NUMBER OF EMPLOYEES INCREASES AS CHEMICAL COMPANY EXPANDS

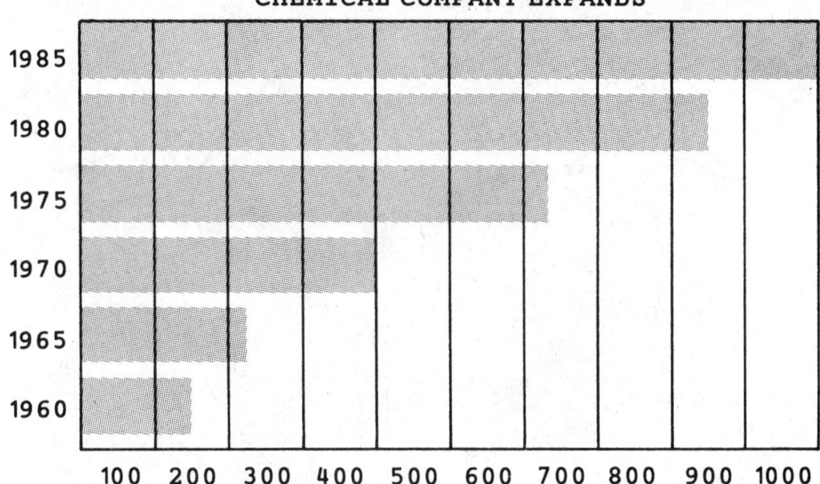

Bar graph illustrates an increase in the number of employees in the A & D Chemical Company.

Column Bar Graph

Figure 4.3—EMPLOYEE DISTRIBUTION AT SOUTHLAND ELECTRIC COMPANY, INC.

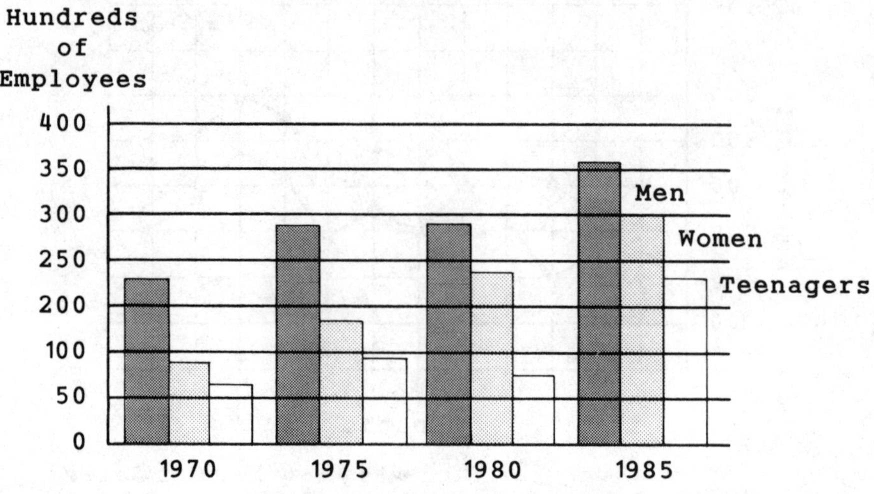

Pie Graph

Figure 4.4—BARLEY EXPORTS TO FOREIGN NATIONS 19--

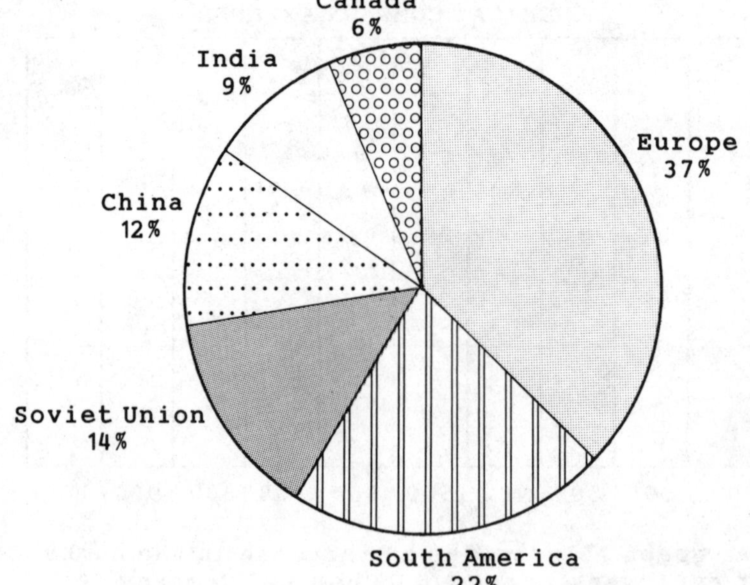

2. ***Tables.*** Tables present data in columns and are used to summarize changes over time or to compare information such as total sales among company divisions. Tables can include more detailed and complex information than either charts or graphs. They may even contain some narrative material explaining the various parts or data in the columns. However, trends or other movements over time are more difficult to spot in tables.

3. ***Photographs.*** Reports that deal with organizational behavior, as in our sample report, can be enhanced by photographs. Pictures can also be used effectively in reports discussing site locations or new plant facilities. Keep in mind, however, that photographs are generally expensive to reproduce.

Number illustrations consecutively within a chapter or throughout the report if you do not have chapters. Number tables by including the word "Table" followed by the chapter and table number and title. For example:

> Table 3.1 Company Performance by Yearly Income
> (The designation 3.1 means Chapter 3, first table.)

Figures are numbered in the same way, with the word *Figure* preceding the chapter and figure number and title.

> Figure 1.1 Production Trends from 1970-1980

If you have no chapters in your report, number tables and figures consecutively.

> Figure 1 Production Trends from 1970-1980
> Figure 2 Absenteeism Rate from 1970-1980

Illustrations in the Appendix would be numbered according to the letter of each appendix. For example, illustrations in Appendix A would have the following notation:

> Figure A.1 Historical Revenues for Automotive Firms

Each company usually has a particular style for labeling illustrations. Whichever style you use, follow it consistently throughout the report.

Step Three: Revising

If possible, let your first draft "cool off" for a few days. When you are ready to revise, read it through several times, keeping in mind the following questions.

1. Did I achieve the purpose defined in my working plan and outline?
2. Does the introduction establish the scope and methods of the report?
3. Is the presentation of data in the body of the report logical? (In the process of writing your first draft you may discover that you need to rearrange paragraphs or sentences.)
4. Is the information presented complete? Does the reader have all the data necessary to understand the situation? Are my facts well documented and supported?
5. Have I presented the information concisely? (Read through your material carefully and see where you can cut unnecessary words and phrases, condense information, or eliminate repetition. Such editing can make your report more effective. Keep the *reader* in mind as you work.)
6. Have I separated opinions from facts? (You may report that in one plant management resisted employee involvement programs. You speculate that management did not want the program to succeed because of its reluctance to surrender decision-making power (an opinion). The real reason may be that it felt unprepared and needed more training in shared management techniques (a fact). Where you need to express an opinion, label it clearly with such phrases as "In my judgment . . ." "These facts suggest that . . ." "The situation seems to be . . .")
7. Have I chosen the precise word to convey my meaning? (When you say, "The workers found the change difficult," does the sentence give the reader a clear idea of what happened? Can you be more precise and say, "The workers did not like having to make so many decisions"? Check for vague claims or results. Specify exact amounts or degrees of what was achieved or changed. Ask yourself, "How much?" "What kind?" "In what way?" "How long?" "Who was involved?")
8. Have I checked my facts? (Accuracy is essential in any report. The company may make major decisions on the basis of your information. Double-check statements, figures, charts, and sources for accuracy.)

9. Do my titles accurately reflect the material discussed? (Edit your headings to make sure they indicate precisely the subjects that follow. Avoid headings that are general and abstract. For example, "Quality Circles" covers too wide a subject area. "Quality Circles in Japanese Plants, 1960-1980" is specific. Study the titles of articles and newspaper stories. How do the titles convey the information that follows?)
10. Have I checked for errors in spelling and grammar? (Read through your report once for grammar and spelling errors. Such mistakes will detract from your credibility. In one report, for example, the writer did not notice that he had misspelled "values." His report title read, "Reviewing Company Valves"!)
11. Have I asked someone else to read through the report? (If possible, have another person read your manuscript. Carefully consider their questions or suggestions. False pride as an author will not help you produce the best report possible. Good writing is often a joint project.)

Finally, proofread your report carefully for typos, misspelled words, or any mistakes that may have been overlooked in previous readings. Neatness and accuracy in grammar and spelling will enhance your report's credibility and influence readers in your favor.

Chapter 11 Proposals and Press Releases

Proposals and press releases represent two other forms of business communication often used by companies in their daily operations. Proposals function as sales pieces while press releases are meant to inform the public about an event, discovery, or change associated with your firm. You will broaden your writing skills by learning to create these types of business communication.

Proposals

Proposals are usually based on studies conducted by an individual or group within a company and are often used to solicit business for the firm. Architectural companies, management consultants, independent contractors, and special service companies frequently submit proposals to potential clients.

Proposals can also be used *within* a company. In our sample report, personnel might be called upon to prepare a proposal for implementing employee involvement programs. Often an oral presentation follows the submission of a proposal.

Although proposals contain some elements of a formal report, their structure conforms more to the AIDA formula of a sales piece. Your primary goal is *persuasion*—either to convince management to accept your recommendations or to sell a client on your firm.

Since a written proposal must sell an idea, you need to support your argument in a compelling and convincing manner. You must show readers what you have to offer, how they will benefit, and why, therefore, your proposal should be accepted.

Step One: Prewriting

As in letter and report writing, the prewriting stage for proposals involves posing key questions that your finished work must answer. Asking these questions can help you plan your writing.

1. What is the purpose of your proposal—beyond selling your ideas? Why are you writing it? What does the client need to know? For example, if the client asked for a proposal on implementing an affirmative action program, you would tailor your purpose toward that end. In a sentence or two, state the purpose of the report.

2. Who is the audience and what are their needs and motivations? Effective persuasion depends on your ability to identify and appeal to the recipients' needs and motivations. Who are the readers—upper management, the board of directors, your immediate supervisor? Research your audience so that you know how to appeal to their self-interest. The client or other readers should understand clearly how they will benefit from your efforts.

3. How do you catch the readers' attention? Once you have identified their needs, capture the readers' attention by addressing their primary concern first. Do readers want to save time and money? Increase profits? Change procedures? Are they motivated by prestige or convenience?

4. What results or outcomes would the reader like to have? A proposal asks for some change, perhaps a new policy or procedure, or the solution to a problem. Your job is to identify what outcomes the reader would like and then consider other outcomes the reader may have overlooked.

For example, if an affirmative action program is implemented, how might it affect the company's clients and competitors? How would the company's advertising change? Where would they recruit new employees? Anticipating other outcomes and providing suggestions or possible solutions can help you gain the client's confidence.

You should also anticipate objections to your proposal and be prepared to counter them.

5. What information or background research will you need in writing the proposal? Once you have determined the purpose, audience, and scope, you are ready to gather data.

Background Research. For a client proposal, you will need to research the client's needs and problems thoroughly. Your information will come from the company's management and personnel, its publications, information about the industry in which it operates, its markets and suppliers, and other historical documents that will give you an accurate picture of the company's current situation. If you are writing a proposal on implementing affirmative action programs, you would gather data on such programs in similar companies. What success or failure rates are available? How have these companies handled the impact on personnel, management, clients, competitors, market image, and daily operations? What methods of implementation have worked best for companies similar to the client's?

Estimate the time and cost of the project. Can costs be measured against specific gains or benefits? For example, in the affirmative action proposal, what advantages would the company gain once the program was operating smoothly? Explain time and cost estimates in terms of benefits to the client.

These same preparation steps hold true if the proposal is for an individual or a group within your own company. Any change will cost a company time and money. Your proposal should persuade readers that the time and money will be well spent.

Step Two: Writing

Many companies have a standard format for proposals. If so, it can simplify the job of organizing and outlining your document. A standard proposal format might look like the following:

I. Background of the situation

II. Description of the current problem

III. Our approach to the problem

IV. Methodology and research
   - A. Methods of gathering data
   - B. How research would be conducted

V. Expected results
   - A. Proposed outcomes
   - B. Specific action steps

VI. Time and cost requirements
   - A. Budget for proposed work
   - B. Estimated time for completion

Writing the First Draft. A standard format can provide headings and subheadings for your proposal. Keep in mind that you are not simply presenting facts or information but that you are seeking to persuade the reader to accept your ideas and approach. As a result, all information should support your position. You will want to put your ideas in their best light, tailored to the specific needs and purposes of the readers. Do not offer detailed explanations or technical facts unless the client asks for them.

Every paragraph and sentence should convey the impression that your ideas and approach are well-reasoned and appropriate. Where graphs, charts, or other illustrations will present the material more persuasively use them. Otherwise, keep them to a minimum to avoid distracting your readers.

Remember, your goal is *to sell your ideas*. Look over the material in Chapter 8: Sales Letters for additional guidelines on writing persuasive messages.

Step Three: Revising the Proposal

Review, edit, and revise every part of the proposal. In many instances, thousands even millions of dollars may hinge on a proposal being accepted or rejected. Check and recheck all your facts about the client's situation. Pay particular attention to the choice of words and tone of the proposal. Is your tone positive without being too optimistic? The readers must believe you have appraised their problems realistically. Have you stated the situation clearly and tactfully—suggesting how the problem can be approached rather than focusing on how the client created the situation? Are your suggestions for the proposed work tailored to the client's specific needs?

If your proposal convinces your readers that you have done your research carefully and clearly understood their problems, you will probably sell your ideas. Ultimately, the acceptance of a persuasive message depends on the sender's credibility and the receiver's perception of direct benefits.

After the proposal has been typed in final copy, proofread it carefully. Check for errors in grammar and spelling, for careless mistakes that previously escaped your eye, and for any inconsistencies in format.

Study the sample proposal letter below.

SAMPLE PROPOSAL LETTER

February 25, 19--

Mr. Bernard R. Wright
Wright Heating Systems, Inc.
1886 North Diversy
Crystal Woods, Illinois 60014

Dear Mr. Wright:

Last week, you spoke with Mr. Stephen Chutus, our senior consultant, about some of the organizational problems your firm is experiencing. At that time, you asked our firm

Mr. Bernard Wright
Page 2
February 25, 19--

to submit a proposal outlining our approach to those problems and including an estimate of time and expenses. This letter is in response to your request.

OUR UNDERSTANDING OF THE CURRENT SITUATION

Wright Heating Systems, Inc. was founded by Charles Wright in 1935. The company grew modestly through the 1930s and 1940s and confined its business to the sale of heating equipment to small companies and private homes.

In 1958, Bernard Wright assumed leadership of the company and began diversifying into office appliances, service contracts, and some international sales. By 1965, company sales had reached $25 million. The number of employees had grown from 32 to over 120, and two branch offices had been opened in New York and San Francisco. Over the next 20 years, the company continued to enjoy steady growth, with only two periods of decline during the 1970s oil embargo and severe recession of the early 1980s.

However, the company has been experiencing organizational problems along with its growth. Communications among management levels and with support staff are often poor. Goals and objectives are not communicated clearly throughout the organization. Sales and service areas overlap in some cases, and there is considerable confusion about who services which customers. Quality control is spotty at best, and faulty equipment and appliances have been turning up in customers' orders at an alarming rate. Worker morale is poor, and the company has been approached by union organizers within the past month to recruit union members from among employes in the firm.

In short, the company is experiencing "growing pains" in making the transition from a small,

Mr. Bernard Wright
Page 3
February 25, 19--

family-owned concern to a medium-sized firm with multinational connections.

OUR APPROACH TO THE PROBLEM

Wright Heating Systems is on the verge of entering a new phase in its development. We have assisted many firms in making the change from a small company to a larger concern. We can offer consulting services on reorganizing your management structure without losing key individuals or disrupting the flow of business. These services include setting up new office systems, accounting procedures, and distribution networks to help you manage your business more effectively. We will also provide training for support staff to involve them in the changes that need to be made.

We can help you devise forcasting and planning strategies that will define your goals and develop plans to achieve them. You will be able to see where you are headed and what the greatest growth areas are likely to be. These strategies, together with your new management structure, will ensure that company goals are communicated clearly to all management and support staff levels.

ESTIMATED TIME AND EXPENSES

On the basis of our past experiences with companies similar to yours, we estimate that the transition period will take about six months to complete. At the end of that time, you and your management staff will have an organizational structure with clearly defined functional areas and responsibilities and well-designed channels of communication.

We will assign Mr. Stephen Chutus as senior consultant in charge of this project and form a team of consultants from our corporate staff. Mr. Chutus has worked with many of the Fortune 500 companies. His most recent project was overseeing the complete reorganization of

Mr. Bernard Wright
Page 4
February 25, 19--

Hyatt Industries, a multi-million dollar corporation. The resumes of other proposed team members are included with this proposal.

We estimate the cost for the project will range from $135,000 to $150,000. This would include implementation of recommended changes and follow-up visits three months and six months after completion of the project.

Wright Heating Systems, Inc. has an excellent record in the industry. We would be pleased to assist your firm in its continued growth, and we appreciate the opportunity to work with you.

Sincerely yours,

Barbara Tholin
FARBER & THOLIN ASSOCIATES

Enclosures: (5)

Press Releases

Press releases are the most journalistic of all business communications. They are written to inform the public of events sponsored by, or occurring within, a company or industry. As such, they are part public relations message, promotional piece, and fact-finder all in one. Press releases announce promotions within a company, changes in product line, creation of new departments or divisions, expansion into diversified products, mergers, and divestitures. They publicize grand openings, research findings, unusual events, humanitarian projects, and any other "newsworthy" items.

Nearly every major corporation and many smaller firms produce press releases for the public. They are published in newspapers and periodicals and may even be picked up by wire service, radio and television if the news is sufficiently interesting. For example, a company may achieve a breakthrough in an artificial sweetener or new diet medication. Since public interest in weight control is high, press releases announcing the new products would receive wide distribution and may even appear on the nightly television news.

Occasionally, reporters from newspapers or magazines are assigned regular industry beats and will write the press releases. More often, someone within the company will be assigned the release. If that someone is you, your job will be to keep the public informed through the media about company events and activities. Press releases may be among the most creative and enjoyable writing assignments you do. They stress not only basic information but also human interest.

Since press releases may receive widespread attention, you must be sure that every statement is accurate and clear. A misquote, an ambiguous statement, a wrong fact could damage your company's reputation and your own. In addition, if an outside reporter is writing the story and asks to interview you, make sure you have clearance from your superiors for the interview and that you discuss with them the subject of the release. A careless or off-hand remark can be distorted or misunderstood. Whether you are the writer or the one interviewed, watch your language!

Step One: Prewriting

The first step in preparing your press release is to identify the newsworthy "story" in each topic assigned to you and research the story thoroughly. For example, suppose your company has discovered a way to double the life of AA batteries. In itself, this advance would be news. But suppose the person who discovered the process is a 17-year-old high school intern hired by the company as part of a field education project with the local school? The story now has a strong human interest element and might attract the national media. The company enhances its reputation on two counts—as an innovator in youth job training and a technical leader in its field.

Once you have identified your story follow these steps:

1. Establish the facts. Remember the five Ws of journalism—*who, what, where, when,* and *why*. If you cannot answer all of them, go back for additional information.

2. Verify the facts. Remember the three rules of journalism—*accuracy, accuracy,* and *accuracy*. Check your facts by consulting at least two sources until you are confident your information is correct.

3. Secure releases or permissions. You must secure permission from a responsible source in the company to make the information in your press release public. Never assume that the data you have are free for the taking. If you have secured permission from a superior, or if your superior has requested the release, give the person a preview of what you intend to write. Make sure you have approval for the use of specific information.

4. Choose the media you will use. Generally, the press release will be meant for general distribution and can be sent to all media and appropriate associations and individuals. In some cases, however, you may want to select a specific publication or media outlet for specialized press releases. If the material is urgent and needs immediate release, radio and television outlets are best. If the release has considerable detail, such as a list of names or scheduled events, the print media are better. Choose the media before you begin writing, since your choice will influence the presentation.

Step Two: Writing

Most companies have a standard format for press releases. The general rules for such a format are as follows:

1. If the company does not have a standard press release form, type "News Release" centered at the top of the first page.
2. At the top right-hand side of the first page, type "FOR:" followed by a date that tells the media when the release should be printed. In most cases you would type:

   FOR: Immediate Release
3. Two spaces down from "FOR:" type "CONTACT:" followed by your name or that of the person the media should call for further information. The contact's address and/or phone number is typed below the name.

   FOR: Immediate Release

   CONTACT: Ruth White
445-7866
4. Double-space the release and leave one and one-half inch margins on all sides.
5. If the story runs more than one page, type "More" at the bottom of all pages but the last one.
6. Type (End) or X X X at the bottom of the last page to indicate the end of the release.

Press releases generally should be written in the "inverted pyramid" style, that is, the most important facts appear first. Answer the five Ws in the first paragraph. Succeeding paragraphs provide supporting details and further explanations. Avoid stylistic tricks such as surprise endings or posing questions that are not answered until the final paragraph. Your readers should be able to scan your story quickly for the main points. Remember, other stories and events are competing with yours.

Writing the First Draft. As you write the press release, ask yourself the following questions:

1. What is special or different about this person or product?
2. Who is my audience?
3. Which media should receive the release?
4. What does this product or this person's story mean for the readers?
5. What costs or savings are involved?
6. Are the facts verified?

Keep your paragraphs short. Short paragraphs move the story along and cover the main points quickly while holding the reader's interest. Keep the press release to one or two pages, unless the story is particularly newsworthy—such as a new heart transplant technique or the latest innovation in computer memory. A concise release is more likely to be read and distributed.

Aim for a conversational, journalistic style. Make your language lively and fresh. Avoid superlatives like "brilliant company executive" or "outstanding corporate achievement." Most editors will simply delete them. Use quotes where you can. They add interest to a press release. Compare these two published releases.

FT. LAUDERDALE, FL., April 8, 19-- Company officials at Intertel Corp. announced today they have succeeded in producing a commercially viable flat panel TV screen. The breakthrough, said one company official, means that ordinary television sets can be built only three inches thick. Printed circuitry replaces the electron gun and phosphorous cathode ray tube in the current TV sets. The achievement will revolutionize the television manufacturing industry.

FT. LAUDERDALE, FL., April 8, 19-- Company officials at Intertel Corp. announced today they have succeeded in building the first commercial flat panel TV screen.

"Flat panels will revolutionize the television industry," one company official said. "In three years you'll see wide-screen TV sets only two to three inches thick."

Printed circuitry replaces the cathode ray tube and electron gun now in TV sets. The new technology will allow manufacturers to produce thin, pocket-sized TVs with all the resolution and quality of current black-and-white and color sets.

In the second release, the writer not only used quotes to add interest but also showed readers how the discovery would affect their own lives. Well-chosen quotes and details bring your press release to life and add to its immediacy and impact. Always verify your quotes to make sure the words accurately state what was said.

You may want to include a title with your press release, but avoid clever or catchy headlines. Editors and newscasters usually rewrite or discard them. In addition, let the editors decide on matters of style. Avoid underlining statements for emphasis. Use quotation marks only for actual dialogue or when a passage is quoted from another source. Do not use quotation marks for titles of books, songs, documents, films, and the like. The names of departments, products, inventions, and the like should not be capitalized even if the company style tends to do so. The editor receiving your press release will adapt it to the style of the publication.

At times it is appropriate to include pictures or other illustrative material with your press release. Camera-ready photos reproduce well in print media. Contact the editor to find out what photos or visual aids are preferred. Mail photographs and other illustrations in well-protected envelopes. To avoid damage, do not staple or paper-clip photos to your release.

Step Three: Revising

In revising the press release ask yourself:

1. Have I answered the five Ws of journalism?
2. Is the language lively and concrete?
3. Have I put the most important facts first and supporting facts and explanations after?
4. Are paragraphs concise?
5. Have I checked all my facts and obtained permission to use quotes, sensitive information, and proprietary data?
6. Do readers understand the story's implications for their own lives?
7. Have I checked for errors in grammar and spelling?

Proofread your final copy carefully and make sure you have addressed the press release to the proper media contacts. A well-written and carefully prepared release will help keep your company's name in the public eye. Study the sample press releases on pages 163-164.

Sample Press Releases

Quality Co. Press Release

TO: All news media FOR: Immediate Release

CONTACT: Wendell Sims
Corporate Communications
Quality Co.
22 South State
Chicago, IL 60603
(312) 861-4423

QUALITY CO. APPOINTS FIRST WOMAN PRESIDENT

Quality Co. announced today its appointment of Virginia Weston as the company's first woman president and chief executive officer.

Ms. Weston, 42, first joined the firm in 1974 as the company's chief financial officer. She was responsible for saving several company stores from bankruptcy and urging corporate expansion into consumer electronics.

Over the past ten years, Ms. Weston has been known for her outspoken views about the direction Quality Co. should take.

"No retail chain can afford to remain lost in the past," she stated in a speech before the Chamber of Commerce Thursday. "By shifting our product emphasis from clothing and hardware to electronics and career-oriented products, we can still offer customers the best service and maintain our market share. The Quality Co. catalog should be a look at the future, not a reminder of the past."

Ms. Weston will assume her office September 30 at the annual stockholders' meeting. Shareholders appear pleased with her choice as president. They sent her a congratulatory telegram when the company announced her appointment last week in the company newsletter.

X X X

Triton Electronics Press Release

TO: All news media

FOR: Immediate Release

CONTACT: Cynthia Fostle
Public Relations
Triton Electronics
41 Juniper Road
Menlo Park, CA 94110
(415) 228-6424

Triton president Barry Dietz was on hand today for ground-breaking ceremonies for the new cultural arts building to be erected at the corner of Lake and Central in Menlo Park. The building will house art collections from three nations and feature a special Native American wing.

Mr. Dietz first proposed the idea of a cultural arts building ten years ago. Since then he has worked to raise funds and foster public support for the building. This year, donations from Triton Electronics and matching grants from the National Historical Society and California Arts Program have made Barry Dietz's dream a reality.

"I believe that art belongs to the people," Dietz said. "For too long we have viewed culture as something only the elite can enjoy. Beauty shows us we are capable of more in this life than simply surviving."

The cultural arts building has been designed by Robert VanDeroue, whose architectural innovations have won him an international reputation. The building will feature three fountains in the central courtyard and an open-air café for visitors.

The building, which will take a year to complete, will cost an estimated $3.5 million. There will be a small admission charge for adult visitors but all children under 12 will be admitted free.

X X X

Chapter 12 Finding Business Information

At some point in your career you may have to prepare a report, write an article, or make a speech. Or you may work for someone who will need your help in finding information quickly. The ability to locate the right reference and gather information that can be used readily is an invaluable skill in business writing. This section lists some of the basic research and information resources available to business people. Also, books such as *A Business Information Guidebook* by Figueroa and Winkler, published by the American Management Association, can be a useful tool in finding what you need to know.

Libraries

Public and special libraries are among the greatest sources of information. A good reference librarian can act as a guide through these treasure houses. Most good libraries contain the following:

1. *Excellent general encyclopedias* such as the *Encyclopaedia Britannica, Encyclopedia Americana*. These works are especially strong in business, science, and government.

2. *Special encyclopedias* such as *The Encyclopedia of Banking and Finance*. These volumes explain and define terms in banking, financial, and allied vocations. The work is a complete digest of the financial world without being too technical.

3. *Fortune Directory*, which lists major United States industrial firms by sales, assets, and net profits. Issued by the publishers of *Fortune* magazine. Similar works include *Standard & Poor's Corporate Records*, published by Standard & Poor's Corporation, and *Moody's Industrial Manual*, published by Moody's Investor's Service. These two volumes give up-to-date information on large corporations' sales, acquisitions, mergers, major product areas, stock and bond ratings, names and titles of officers and directors, history of the firms, financial statements for the previous five to seven years, and many other facts.

4. *Indexes* to periodicals and books on business topics. These works index articles and books by subject and author. They are useful for locating information quickly, especially facts within the past one to two years. Examples of these works include the *Industrial Arts Index, Business Publications Index, Engineering Index,* and *Applied Science and Technology Index.* In addition, the Public Affairs Information Service indexes over 900 periodicals and many books, pamphlets, government documents and special publications.

5. *Government publications.* Most libraries carry standard U.S. government references such as the *Statistical Abstract of the United States,* a digest of the most important statistical data gathered in the United States. It covers population, education, finance, utilities, commerce, transportation, manufacturing, and the like. *United States Government Publications: Monthly Catalog* is a comprehensive listing of all publications issued by the various departments and agencies of the U.S. Government. These catalogs also list bureaus and agencies issuing publications.

6. *Other reference sources* such as out-of-state telephone directories, trade directories listing the names and addresses of trade associations, directories listing the names and addresses of foreign companies doing business in the United States.

The public library can also help you find specialty libraries and government libraries.

1. *Directory of Special Libraries and Information Centers,* published by the Gale Research Co., Book Tower, Detroit, MI 48226, lists approximately 14,000 special libraries and information centers in the United States and Canada and includes an extensive subject index.

2. *Federal Government Document Depository Libraries.* These libraries were established to give the public access to publications of the federal government. The depository library program currently distributes 3,800 classes of U.S. publications to more than 1,200 depositories located in colleges and universities and special and public libraries.

Computer-Assisted Research

Many major cities throughout the United States have established computer-assisted research facilities in their public and specialized libraries. Through these facilities, businesses and individuals can arrange to search through and retrieve information from over 250 databases covering a wide range of subjects including business, education, science and technology.

Most databases are computerized versions of abstracting and indexing publications that list articles, documents, theses, books, journals, and other publications. Computer searches provide a display and printout of references on any topic you choose. Each reference includes the author, title, publication, date, and in many cases a synopsis of the contents.

Major database services include Dialogue Information Services (DIS), System Development Corporation (SDC), Bibliographic Retrieval Services (BRS), Dow Jones & Company, The New York Times Information Service, Info Globe, Legi-Slate, Inc., and Mead Data Central. These databases also offer commercial contracts, a type of subscription service, to individual companies or business people. Fees may run from $50 to $100 a month. If the services are used only a few times a year, such a subscription is not cost effective. As a result, most companies work through reference centers like those in public libraries.

Setting up a Computer-Assisted Search

Computer-assisted research can save you considerable time and money when you need to do background research. For example, if you were searching for references on the recovery of Chrysler Corporation, you would set up a computer search using the company name and a key word or phrase like *Chrysler Corporation, recovery of*. The computer would then search all relevant databases for material published on that topic. A reference librarian can help you focus your topic and select the proper key words or phrases to initiate the search. Computers can even combine two or more subjects in a single search, organize the printout alphabetically by author or publication, include abstracts or synopses of the references, and perform other specialized functions.

The printout may run from a few to several hundred pages, depending on how extensive a search you requested. You can then select the best references for your work, locate the publications in the reference section of the library, and photocopy the articles from each publication.

Business Databases

Computer searching can help you gather information for market research, grant proposals, and current developments in your field; locate experts in various specialties; obtain information on companies; and keep abreast of government actions and proposed legislation affecting your industry.

The items listed and the years covered vary with each database. Most databases index material published after 1970. The reference librarian can help you find the right information source or additional sources not available through the computer.

Major databases for business include the following:

1. ABI/INFORM indexed from 1971
Covers over 500 international periodicals for general business, management, personnel, and administration.

2. AMI indexed from 1979
Provides information related to advertising, marketing, and communications. Includes new products, promotional programs, consumer trends and marketing research.

3. DISCLOSURE indexed from 1982
Contains extracts from financial and administrative reports from more than 9,000 public companies filing with the SEC.

4. EIS covers only current articles and publications
Two files provide information on individual manufacturing and nonmanufacturing plants in the United States. The database includes sales, location, employment, industry, and size.

5. ELECTRONIC YELLOW PAGES current only
Provides enhanced Yellow Pages information for the United States. Classified by SIC. Areas covered include financial, professional, wholesale, manufacturing, retail, and construction.

6. MANAGEMENT CONTENTS indexed from 1974
Indexes cover-to-cover 200 U.S. and foreign periodicals in general business, management, personnel, and administration. Includes some course materials.

7. PREDICASTS indexed from 1972
A series of files providing information on domestic and foreign companies, products, industries, markets, statistics, and forecasts.

The reference librarian can provide a complete list of all databases that may be useful in your business writing. Fees for computer searches vary from database to database and may range from $0.05 per reference to $1.50. The convenience and time saved in gathering information through computer-assisted research can be well worth the investment.

Industry Sources of Business Information

Each industry has its own sources of information. The problem—where to look for it? Many public libraries do not carry company publications or trade journals and magazines. The following list provides a few references for selected industries. For further references, see handbooks like *A Business Information Guidebook.*

1. *National Directory of Newsletters and Reporting Services,* published by Gale Research Co., Book Tower, Detroit, MI 48226, lists and provides information on newsletters and other related publications issued by businesses, associations, societies, clubs, government agencies, and other groups. There is a reference guide to national and international services, financial services, association bulletins, and training and educational services.

2. *Membership Directory: Association of Data Processing Service Organizations, Inc.,* published by Association of Data Processing Service Organizations, Inc., 210 Summit Avenue, Montvale, NJ 07645. Lists companies providing data processing services to all types of companies.

3. *Energy Directory Update,* Environment Information Center, Inc., 292 Madison Avenue, New York, NY 10017, provides energy information for state and federal governments; trade, professional, and research organizations; oil, gas, coal, electric, and nuclear power companies; large energy consumers; and information centers, systems, libraries, and publications.

4. *The Directory of Market Research Reports, Studies, and Surveys,* published by FIND/SVP, 500 Fifth Avenue, New York, NY 10036, lists and describes writings on market research regarding consumer and industrial studies and surveys, syndicated and multiclient studies, audits, and subscription research services. Industries are arranged under various industry categories.

Resources for Practical Business Problems

At times you will need to know the best way to ship goods, where to look for travel information, and how to find the latest postal rates for business mail. The references listed below should answer these and many similar questions.

Mail and Transportation

1. *United States Postal Manual,* published by the U.S. Government Printing Office, Washington, D.C. 20402. Issued in two parts. Part I gives a variety of information on domestic postal services such as mail classification and rates, postage, collections, and delivery, special mail and nonmail services. Part II describes international postal services.

2. *Air Cargo Guide,* published by Reuben H. Donnelley Corp., 2000 Clearwater Drive, Oak Brook, IL 60521, provides information on air cargo services to points throughout the world. Contains such information as domestic and international flight schedules, rates, pick-up and delivery programs, small package service, and international documentary requirements.

3. *Bullinger's Postal and Shippers Guide for the U.S. and Canada,* published by Bullinger's Guide, Inc., 63 Woodlawn Avenue, Westwood, NJ 07675, provides information on post offices, railroad stations, and steamboat landings. Contains information on rates, schedules, and freight shipping lines and receiving stations.

4. *Leonard's Guide; Parcel Post—Express; Motor—Freight; Rates and Routing,* published by G. R. Leonard Co., 79 Madison Avenue, New York, NY 10016, contains shipping information on various air mail and parcel post shippers and rates, postal, and express regulations, United Parcel, warehouse locations; and traffic terms and abbreviations.

Traveling—Domestic and Foreign

1. *Hotel Red Book,* American Hotel Association Directory Corporation, 221 West 57th Street, New York, NY 10019, provides a current geographical classification of principal hotels in each state and Canada, with a further breakdown by cities.

2. *Leahy's Hotel-Motel Guide and Travel Atlas,* published by American Hotel Register Company, contains hotel, motel, and travel information with maps for The United States, Mexico, and Canada.

3. *Owen's Commerce & Travel and International Register,* Owen's Commerce and Travel, Ltd., 886 High Road, Finchley, London, N12 9SB, England, provides detailed information concerning travel and trade in approximately 50 countries—primarily in Africa, the Near and Middle East, Southeast Asia, and Far East. Entries include travel agents, airline offices, hotels and automobile hires. A classified list of firms providing services in each of the countries, covering importers, exporters, and manufacturers, is included as well.

Section 5
Business Writing and the Job Search

Chapter 13 Résumés, Applications, Employment Letters

Your first job search usually follows the completion of your formal education. By that time you have identified some of your interests, skills, and abilities, and you are looking for a position to match those qualities. In most cases the search involves visiting employers' offices, completing an application form, and interviewing for the position. This process is the simplest and is most commonly used for finding your first or even your second job.

As you gain experience in the working world, the nature of your job search is likely to change. Perhaps you have decided to switch career fields or to look for a position that offers greater opportunities for growth and advancement. You may want a job that has less security and more risk. Your company may move to another location, and you decide to remain where you are. There are many reasons you may find yourself job hunting several times during your working life.

As a result, you should know how to write employment-related letters; put together a résumé summarizing your work history, experience, and skills; and complete a variety of job applications. As a job seeker, you must prepare all the written material that will help you sell yourself and obtain the job you seek.

Identifying Your Abilities, Interests, and Skills

The job search process has its preparation and background research stages as does business writing. To start your search for a specific job, you will need a sound understanding of your qualifications. You can then list specific skills and knowledge that would benefit an employer and decide which jobs match the qualities you possess.

How do you identify your skills and abilities? Some will be obvious, such as skills in electronics, computers, mathematics, writing, and professional skills gained through education in medical, legal, business, and other fields. You will acquire other skills as you work. But some abilities are not so easily recognized. For example, a woman who has spent most of her working years raising a family may feel she has no marketable skills. Yet through the years of child-rearing she has had to be organizer, manager, budget-keeper, and volunteer worker. With some additional training, these skills translate well to the modern office.

On the other hand, you may need to reach back into your childhood to recall what gave you the most pleasure. Perhaps you liked sports, crafts, exploration, solving problems or puzzles, building with your hands, working with machines, raising animals. All these activities contain clues to skills you have developed and may not recognize. In one instance, a man who had organized neighborhood clubs as a child found a satisfying career directing fund-raising efforts for national charities.

Various vocational assessment and skill tests are available to help you identify your skills and abilities. Local colleges and universities or state employment offices can help you find where such tests are given and how much they cost. The investment could net you a new career and more satisfying work life. In addition, many books on the market describe how to organize your skills and abilities and to discover those still unknown to you. Take the time to know yourself better—it can be one of the most valuable steps you take in your career.

Background Research—Job Sources

Once you have assessed your qualifications and determined which jobs you would like to have, you need to locate the right position. Several employment sources can help you find job openings that match your qualifications. Some will be more appropriate than others at different times in your life, but you should know the variety of sources available.

1. ***School placement offices.*** If you are still in school or have recently graduated, the school placement office is a good place to start your search. If your school has a good reputation for providing occupational training and support for graduates, you may have a wide range of job opportunities to choose from. Your teachers may also be able to supply additional leads or have direct contacts with companies looking for qualified graduates.

2. ***Classified ads.*** Newspapers and professional journals also provide job leads. Employers advertise openings in newspapers and journals to attract qualified candidates. These ads may request either a letter of application or a phone call to set up an interview.

If you are experienced in your field, you may want to confine your search to professional journals such as the *Journal of the Modern Language Association*, the *Los Angeles Daily Journal*, *The Wall Street Journal*, *Publisher's Weekly*, and others.

3. ***Employment agencies.*** State and private employment agencies also help match up job applicants with job openings. State agencies provide their services free of charge to both employer and employee.

Private employment agencies charge either the applicant or employer a fee for matching a candidate and a job opening successfully. Some companies prefer to work through employment agencies since candidates are prescreened before being referred to the employer. This process saves the employer considerable time and ensures that only qualified candidates will be applying for the job. From the applicants' point of view, the process guarantees that only jobs matching their background and interests will be recommended.

4. Professional groups and associations. While the above three sources work in many cases, they are part of the "numbers game" in which candidates simply comb through job listings and eliminate the unsuitable ones. You will probably go through this process for your first and second jobs.

But as you build experience and get to know others in your field, you build a network of contacts you can use to locate new positions. Professional groups and associations are excellent sources of job leads since you share in the same profession and know the field, the employers, and job opportunities well. Joining professional groups at the outset of your career can help you move up in your profession.

5. Personal referrals and recommendations. Of all the ways that people find new jobs, personal referral or recommendation is by far the most common and effective. One employment expert estimated that 80 percent of the jobs people hold are obtained through someone else's personal recommendation. When you let people know you are job hunting, you activate your network. Others will pass on information about job openings.

6. Civil service and institutional offices. Job openings in civil service at the federal, state, county, and city levels are also excellent employment opportunities. Various levels of government regularly publish notices of positions available. If you are interested in such a career, contact your local government employment office for information on applications and civil service exams.

In addition, hospitals, colleges, universities, and other institutions have business offices that employ clerks, typists, secretaries, managers, administrators, and data analysts. If you would like to work outside the traditional business field, you might consider one of these institutions.

7. Individual companies. Many companies do not actively recruit candidates through the usual channels of classified ads or employment agencies. Applicants can apply directly to the personnel office of the company and inquire about job openings. Even if there is no immediate job opportunity, your résumé can be placed on file for future reference.

In larger companies, the turnover rate is sometimes high, and the personnel office is constantly recruiting and hiring new employees. If you contact these firms directly, you may find your call coinciding with an opening in the company. At the least, you have contacted the firm and made your qualifications and interest known.

Preparing Your Résumé

Now that you have completed your preparation and background research steps, you are ready to write your résumé. You have identified your qualifications and the jobs best suited to them. A résumé—with your cover letter and your interview—can help sell employers on your skills and abilities.

A résumé is a written summary of your qualifications, experience, and education. It usually includes your career objective, employment record, references, a summary of your formal education, and other information such as professional memberships, awards, publications, or any other items that will highlight your abilities.

Your résumé is a sales piece and must be prepared as carefully as any sales letter. It must represent you in the best possible light to an employer. Like a sales letter, a résumé can be tailored to the needs of various employers. For example, you may have two or three résumés on hand, each one emphasizing a different aspect of your abilities. You may have one that highlights your writing skills, another that summarizes your management abilities and experience, and still another that emphasizes your work as an information analyst. Research the companies you are interested in and tailor your résumé to their job openings. The more exactly you fit the requirements of the job, the more likely you are to secure it.

The physical appearance of your résumé is important. As a sales piece it should attract the eye of a busy employer. The résumé should be typed or, if you have the time and money, typeset by a professional printer. As a rule, keep all information to one page. As you gather experience and further your education, you may wish to use two pages—one for the basic information summarizing your qualifications and work history, and the other to list publications, achievements, awards, and the like.

The résumé should be printed or photocopied on good bond paper. If you are applying for a job in a bank, insurance office, or other conservative institution, use a white or off-white bond and a conservative format. But if you are interested in a more creative organization such as an advertising agency or graphic arts company, you may want to be more innovative and use tinted paper and a more experimental format.

Layout of the Résumé

There are no fixed rules for résumé format and layout in presenting all the information you will need to include. The sample résumé on page 178 uses a basic format that displays the information in a clear, concise, and readable manner. It contains major headings to highlight various aspects of your work history: position sought, experience, education, honors, activities, and references. Your name, address, and telephone number appear at the top of the page and may be centered or flush left. You are not required to list your age, marital status, state of health, birthdate, or height and weight.

1. Position sought or career objective. The employer can see at a glance the position you would like and the job opportunities you are looking for in a company. If possible, use the specific title of the job for which you are applying.

2. Experience. This section is more than simply a list of places you have worked. It can serve as a summary of your responsibilities and indicate to a prospective employer the skills and experience you have gained through your work life.

For each job you have held, list your title, the name and address of the company, dates of employment, and a brief summary of your work responsibilities and skills. List your last job first and work back to the first job.

Be sure you account for any obvious gaps in your work history longer than one year. For example, you may have returned to school for your M.B.A. degree, had to care for small children, traveled overseas, or undergone medical treatment.

Also, you do not have to list every position held, particularly if the job lasted only a few weeks or months. Everyone makes mistakes and occasionally takes the wrong job. Or perhaps the company went out of business or laid off new workers soon after you were hired. You want your résumé to reflect your accumulated experience. Include only those jobs that add to the employer's knowledge of your qualifications.

3. Education. For recent graduates from high school or college who have limited, or no, job experience, the education section of the résumé will be the most important. Here you can give specific details about your education and training that qualify you for the job.

Also list special interests and skills. Make sure you include awards, honors, scholarships, and other recognition you received. Memberships or offices held in campus groups, team sports, and outside activities can demonstrate leadership, imagination, and management potential. Even though your outside activities may not relate directly to the position, employers are interested. Show the range and depth of your abilities.

4. References. In some cases you will list the names of people your prospective employer can contact for more detailed information about you. Make sure you obtain permission from references before listing them on your résumé. In general, you need only three or four names, but you should have backup references who can attest to your experience, work record, education, and character.

If possible, tailor your references to the job for which you are applying. If you are interested in an assistant editor's job, a reference from a writing or journalism instructor would be more appropriate than one from your minister. Also, tell your references the position you are seeking so they will know which of your capabilities to emphasize when an employer calls. When you ask someone to write a letter of recommendation for you, include a stamped envelope addressed to the employer.

The reference list should include the following information:

1. The full name and appropriate title of each person.
2. The name and address of their company or institution.
3. A work or home telephone number.

You may wish to consult a professional career counselor for assistance in creating your résumé. The counselor may suggest different types of résumés for you to use. For example, in a functional résumé, you focus on the skills you have acquired in your work life rather than on a chronological list of the jobs and responsibilities you have held. This type of résumé is particularly helpful when you wish to change career fields. You can show what skills and qualifications you have learned in one field that can be transferred to another.

Whatever form or style you select, keep in mind that the résumé is a sales piece representing you to a prospective employer. A sample résumé is shown on the next page.

Completing Employment Applications

Nearly all business firms have application forms that candidates fill out when they apply for work. Generally, you will be asked to fill out an application before you are interviewed and hired, although in some instances you will fill out the application after you have been hired. Applications are part of a company's personnel record for each employee.

The information you supply on the application form helps the interviewer know what questions to ask about your education, training, and experience. But interviewers can also tell a great deal about you from the way you complete the form. For example, how accurately and completely did you answer each question? Can you follow directions? Is your handwriting legible? This point may be important if your job involves taking handwritten orders or messages over the phone. How neatly did you complete the form? Although this concern might seem trivial, neatness, or the lack of it, says something about your ability to organize your surroundings and thoughts. If the job calls for precision and orderliness, the appearance of your application can provide important clues regarding your work habits.

Sample Résumé

Lillian Sample
1435 North Shore Drive
Chicago, Illinois 60611
(312) 328-7743

<table>
<tr><td>Position Sought:</td><td colspan="2">Buyer for major retail clothing store.</td></tr>
<tr><td>Experience:</td><td>Assistant Buyer
1978-1984</td><td>Carroll's Red Hanger Shop
566 North State, Chicago, IL 60606</td></tr>
<tr><td></td><td colspan="2">Responsible for ordering all men's ready-to-wear clothing and accessories. Handled budgets up to $250,000. Increased sales 20 percent in two years. Supervised three assistants and one secretary.</td></tr>
<tr><td></td><td>Sales Clerk
1976-1978</td><td>Geske's Clothes
34 Virginia Street, Urbana, IL 61801</td></tr>
<tr><td></td><td colspan="2">Handled all sales transactions in men's and boys' wear. Responsible for special orders and customer relations.</td></tr>
<tr><td>Education:</td><td colspan="2">B.A. in business and marketing, June 1976,
University of Illinois, Champaign-Urbana, IL</td></tr>
<tr><td>Honors:</td><td colspan="2">Edwin Ebert Marketing Award, 1975-1976
Delta Tau honorary business society, 1974
AID Scholarship, 1973</td></tr>
<tr><td>Activities:</td><td colspan="2">Vice President, Delta Tau, 1975-1976
Big Ten Marketing Exhibit, organizer, 1975</td></tr>
<tr><td>References:</td><td>Mr. Harold Walker
General Manager
Carroll's Red Hanger Shop
566 North State
Chicago, IL 60606
(312) 445-7384</td><td>Mrs. Leslie Geske
Owner
Geske's Clothes
34 Virginia Street
Urbana, IL 61801
(217) 459-6533</td></tr>
<tr><td></td><td colspan="2">Other references furnished upon request.</td></tr>
</table>

When you fill out an application form, keep the following suggestions in mind:

1. ***Make sure you have a reliable pen.*** A small detail, but, again, it shows you think ahead. You don't want to interrupt your session to ask for a pen or mar the appearance of your application by using a pen that smudges the page.

2. ***Bring two or more copies of your résumé.*** You can leave one with the interviewer or others in the company who may interview you. Keep a copy on hand as a reference in filling out the application form.

3. ***Take your driver's license, social security number, and any other special identification or information that you will need to complete the form.*** You may want to memorize your social security number for your job search.

4. ***Take the time to write legibly.*** Make sure figures are clearly written, particularly for addresses and phone numbers. Illegible handwriting can bias the interviewer against you. Interviewers who have difficulty reading your handwriting may decide not to make the effort and pass you over for another candidate—especially if they must sort through several hundred applications. Whether it is fair or not, most people equate legible handwriting with intelligence and aptitude for learning.

5. ***Double-check all information you have supplied.*** Have you given the proper year for your birth if the question is asked? Many people, under the stress of the moment, put the current year. Make sure you have provided the correct address and telephone number for yourself, previous employers, and references.

6. ***Don't leave blanks in the application.*** If the questions do not apply to you, draw a line through the section or write "Does not apply" or "Not applicable" in the space provided.

7. ***Read the directions for each section carefully and follow them exactly.*** Companies have reasons for requesting the information. If you ask questions that are answered by the directions, you are showing that you have difficulty following simple, written instructions. Read through the directions until you understand what they are asking you to do. If you still have doubts, then ask for assistance.

Be sure to follow directions carefully. If the instructions ask you to print, do not handwrite your answers. Check to see if the application calls for your last name first, your last place of employment first, and the like. If you show that you can follow written instructions accurately, the interviewer will have greater faith in your ability to follow more complex written and spoken instructions on the job.

A sample application form is provided on the next page.

APPLICATION FOR EMPLOYMENT

(PRE-EMPLOYMENT QUESTIONNAIRE) (AN EQUAL OPPORTUNITY EMPLOYER)

Date ____________

Name [Last Name First] ____________ Soc. Sec. No. ____________

Address ____________ Telephone ____________

What kind of work are you applying for? ____________

What special qualifications do you have? ____________

What office machines can you operate? ____________

Are you 18 years or older? Yes ______ No ____________

SPECIAL PURPOSE QUESTIONS

DO NOT ANSWER **ANY** OF THE QUESTIONS IN THIS FRAMED AREA UNLESS THE EMPLOYER HAS **CHECKED A BOX PRECEDING** A QUESTION, THEREBY INDICATING THAT THE INFORMATION IS REQUIRED FOR A BONA FIDE OCCUPATIONAL QUALIFICATION, OR DICTATED BY NATIONAL SECURITY LAWS, OR IS NEEDED FOR OTHER LEGALLY PERMISSIBLE REASONS.

☐ Height ___Feet ___Inches ☐ Weight ____Lbs. ☐ Are you prevented from lawfully becoming employed in the U.S.? Yes____ No____

☐ Have you been convicted of a felony or misdemeanor within the last 5 years?* Yes____ No____ Describe ____________

*You will not be denied employment solely because of a conviction record, unless the offense is related to the job for which you have applied.

MILITARY SERVICE RECORD

Armed Forces Service ______Yes ______No

Branch of Service ____________ Duties ____________

Rank or rating at time of enlistment ____________ Rating at time of discharge ____________

Do you have any physical limitations that prohibit you from performing any work for which you are being considered? Yes____ No____

If yes, what can be done to accommodate your limitation? Describe ____________

EDUCATION

SCHOOL	*NO. OF YEARS ATTENDED	NAME OF SCHOOL	CITY	COURSE	*DID YOU GRADUATE?
GRAMMAR					
HIGH					
COLLEGE					
OTHER					

*The Age Discrimination in Employment Act of 1967 prohibits discrimination on the basis of age with respect to individuals who are at least 40 but less than 70 years of age.

EXPERIENCE

NAME AND ADDRESS OF COMPANY	DATE		LIST YOUR DUTIES	STARTING SALARY	FINAL SALARY	REASON FOR LEAVING
	FROM	TO				

BUSINESS REFERENCES

NAME	ADDRESS	OCCUPATION

This form has been designed to strictly comply with State and Federal fair employment practice laws prohibiting employment discrimination. This Application for Employment Form is sold for general use throughout the United States. TOPS assumes no responsibility for the inclusion in said form of any questions which, when asked by the Employer of the Job Applicant, may violate State and/or Federal Law.

TOPS Form 3286 (84-3) Litho in U.S.A.

Employment Letters

Employment letters are used to apply for a job, request a reference or letter of recommendation, accept or refuse a position, acknowledge the help of others in your job search, and resign from a position you currently hold. Throughout your career you will need to write one or more of these letters. Knowing how to compose effective employment letters can help you compete successfully in the job search.

Employment letters include the following:

1. ***Letters of application.*** You have seen a position advertised, had a friend pass on a recommendation, or located a possible job opportunity yourself. A letter of application introduces you to the prospective employer and is usually accompanied by a résumé.

2. ***Letters requesting references or recommendations.*** You are asking people who know you well and have knowledge of your skills and experience to act as a reference or write a letter of recommendation to a prospective employer.

3. ***Letters of acknowledgement.*** These letters are used to follow up an interview, thanking the interviewer for the time given you. You can emphasize your qualifications for the job in this letter.

4. ***Letters accepting or refusing a job offer.***

5. ***Thank-you letters.*** You are acknowledging the help each person gave you in your efforts to secure the job.

6. ***A letter of resignation.*** You want to leave your current position under the best circumstances possible.

Application Letters

The application letter is not meant to secure a job. Its main purpose is to catch the interest of a prospective employer and help you secure an interview. Employers cull through application letters to weed out candidates who are obviously unsuitable and to select the few they will pursue further. You will need to make your letter of application, along with your résumé, stand out from all the others.

Since your letter of application is the employer's first introduction to you, think carefully how you would like to present yourself. What do you want the letter to say about your qualifications, work experience, and abilities? The appearance of the letter is important and can do much to help create a favorable impression in a prospective employer.

The following guidelines can help you prepare an application letter that will represent you in the best light.

1. Use a good grade of 8½ × 11 inch paper (white or off-white bond). Do not use erasable bond paper. Even though it makes correcting mistakes easier, it also smudges easily and picks up ink from the platen roll of your typewriter. Make sure your paper is free from fingerprints and other marks.
2. Balance your letters on the page, allowing at least one and one-half inch margins all around.
3. Make sure corrections are invisible. Use a self-correcting typewriter or liquid correcting material that hides your errors. Use a black ribbon that is new or relatively new. Discard any ribbon that is worn. Avoid strikeovers, erasures, or squeezing words into too small a space. Clean your typewriter keys so that letters appear sharp and clear.

   Though the steps may seem elementary, many applicants overlook them and prejudice their case at the outset.
4. If you are using a word processor to prepare your letters, make sure you have a letter-quality printer or its equivalent. Dotmatrix printers look too rough for high-quality letters. You want a polished, professional appearance for your application letter, not something that looks like a first draft.
5. Address the letter to a specific person. If you are answering a classified ad and have the name of the company, call to find out who will be receiving the letter. If you do not have the company name but only a box number to write, address the letter "Dear Sir or Madam:" In general, it is better to address a particular individual. It tells the reader you took the time and initiative to research the job opening.

Writing the Letter. The application letter must capture the reader's attention and focus on your qualifications that meet the needs of your prospective employer. You can use a creative approach to the opening, perhaps a question and answer technique such as the following:

> Are you looking for someone who combines word-processing skills with good telephone technique? Can you use a person who is a self-starter and can organize routine office work? If your answer is yes, I think I can help you.

> Is there a place in your company for someone who enjoys a high-pressure working environment and can keep on top of client work? Someone who can manage office staff and supervise the workload?
>
> Can you use a salesperson who has a knack not only for first-time sales but also for capturing repeat business? Someone who has been in sales since high school?

You may want to start your letter with a summary of your qualifications. This approach gives the reader an immediate appraisal of your abilities and training. If you have caught the reader's interest, the person will read further.

> My four years as an editor with Rand McNally have given me well-rounded skills in editing, production, writing, and permissions. These skills should qualify me for the editor's position in your company.

> A ten-year record in sales as one of the top sellers in chemical products has given me the seasoning and skills to meet the challenge of Sales Director, the position open in your firm.

> My two years as a lab technician in Midland Mercy Hospital have provided me with the experience in medical and clinical pathology that your lab assistant position requires.

If you learned of a vacancy through a friend, relative, employee of the organization, or other individual, it may be to your advantage to mention the person's name (after obtaining their permission) in your letter.

> Mr. Ralph Cardine, a former employee with your firm, told me that you needed a secretary with excellent dictation and word-processing skills. I have been executive secretary for three years with Landrum, Kall, and Watson, an advertising firm. I believe I have the qualifications you need.

> Ms. Carla Norris, the career counselor at school, told me that you are looking for a trainee to start in your shipping department. I have worked in a small manufacturing plant for three years, and I am familiar with ordering and invoicing procedures.

Once you have established the employer's needs and how your qualifications match those needs, you can support your case in the following paragraphs. Again, keep your letter brief and focused. Highlight aspects of your educational background and business experience that relate directly to the job you are seeking. If you have researched the company, you may want to mention why you are interested in that particular firm. Showing knowledge of the company's business and activities will generally impress the reader.

If you are applying for the secretarial position mentioned above, for example, the second paragraph of your letter might look like this:

> I am experienced in several word-processing systems and software programs, including WordStar, Microsoft, and WordPerfect. I have worked on IBM, TRS-80, and Apple systems.

If you were writing your letter in response to an advertisement for a telemarketing position, your second paragraph might state:

> My résumé, which I have enclosed, presents my training and experience in telemarketing over the past six years. I have developed programs for firms whose budgets ranged from $50,000 to $3 million. I believe this experience has given me a solid background in telemarketing techniques and will enable me to get results for your firm.

As in any sales letter, the concluding paragraph should tell the reader what action you want taken. In the application letter, you want the reader to give you a personal interview. Make your request easy to grant.

> I will be in Chicago June 9-12. May I talk with you about the job opening on one of those days? Please let me know a date and time convenient for you. My phone number is (312) 459-9244.

> I believe I can explain in just a few minutes why I am a likely candidate for your position. Can we arrange for an interview? I can be reached at 866-4311 after 6:00 P.M.

Remember that the purpose of the application letter is not to tell the whole story of your working career but to convince the employer to grant you an interview. The interview is the time to discuss your career skills and experience in more detail. Look over the sample letter of application on the next page.

August 23, 19--

Mr. Bernard Houston
Senior Editor
BioMed Publications, Inc.
723 Oriole Trail
Milwaukee, WI 53215

Dear Mr. Houston:

I am writing in regard to the medical writer's position that your company advertised in the August 21 issue of the *Milwaukee Chronicle.* As a medical writer with ten years' experience in the field of biomedical engineering, I am particularly interested in your company's publications and audience.

You indicated in your job description that you are looking for someone with experience in medical journalism and reporting. I have worked for several major medical and science journals, among them *Science News, Biomedical Products, Medicine & Science,* and *Journal of the American Medical Association.* My responsibilities included covering assigned topics, meeting tight deadlines, and interviewing experts in various fields. I have also assisted in magazine and newsletter production. I believe my experience gives me the special skills you are seeking.

The details of my education, work history, and publications are outlined in the enclosed resume. I would appreciate talking with you about the position at your earliest convenience. If you would like copies of my articles or any additional information, please let me know. I can be reached at the number below from 9:00 AM to 5:00 PM.

Sincerely,

Linda Pastan
562 Trailways Road
Madison, WI 54306
(321) 378-9902

Reference Letters

During your career, you will probably write two types of reference letters: letters requesting references *from* others and letters of recommendation *for* someone else.

Letters Requesting References. Employers need to have information regarding the character, work habits, training, and experience of their candidates. You can ask others to act as references for you and supply their names, addresses, and telephone numbers to the prospective employer. Or you can ask your references to write a letter of recommendation directly to the employer. In either case, you must ask permission before listing anyone as a reference. A letter requesting such permission might look like the following:

Dear Professor Halley:

I am applying for the assistant astronomer's position at Axel Observatory in Phoenix, Arizona.

Since I received my basic training in radio astronomy in your class and assisted you in research, I would like very much to use your name as a reference.

I have enclosed a stamped, self-addressed envelope for your reply.

Sincerely yours,

Notice that the writer (1) stated the position being applied for, (2) gave reasons for wishing to use the professor as a reference, and (3) enclosed a stamped, self-addressed envelope for the professor's reply. By telling your references the position you are seeking and why you would like to use them as a reference, you help them know in advance what questions a prospective employer is likely to ask.

At times, you may need to have a letter of recommendation sent directly to the employer.

Dear Professor Halley:

I am applying for the assistant astronomer's position at Axel Observatory in Phoenix, Arizona.

Since I received my basic training in radio astronomy in your class and assisted you in research, I feel you are the best judge of my abilities and work experience.

Would you be willing to write a letter of recommendation on my behalf to Dr. Beatrice McConnel, Director, Axel Observatory? Enclosed is a stamped envelope addressed to the observatory for your convenience.

Sincerely yours,

Letters of Recommendation. At times you may be asked to write a letter of recommendation for a friend, former employee, or colleague. Your letter should include the following:

1. How long you have known the person.
2. The nature of your relationship or acquaintance (boss, friend, colleague, teacher).
3. Your assessment of the person's qualifications, character, and work.

As you write the letter, keep in mind that it may be read by the person who requested it. This fact may tone down your frankness but may also increase your sensitivity about the information you are revealing.

Your enthusiasm about the candidate is reflected in the amount of detail you provide. You would give a few, generalized statements about someone you know slightly or about the work record of a person you observed but did not directly supervise. On the other hand, explicit detail in several paragraphs indicates that you believe the candidate has superior abilities, work habits, and skills. Employers appreciate knowing as much about candidates as possible, even about some of their weaknesses. An employer can then take steps to play up the strengths of the candidate and compensate for weaknesses.

The following letter is a strong recommendation of a candidate.

Dear Mr. Martin:

Norm Roberts has worked directly under me for seven years in the Electrical Engineering department. His assignments included setting up a thin-film prefabrication laboratory and working as a consultant on various biomedical projects. He has an excellent grasp of the overall objectives of a project as well as a sound understanding of intricate and complex details.

Over the past seven years, Mr. Roberts has developed various miniaturized circuits for biomedical applications in artificial limbs. His innovative designs have increased the range and efficiency of these limbs and improved their functions. He also has experience in thin- and thick-film processes, hybrid circuits, computer graphics, and computer modeling.

Mr. Roberts has an excellent reputation for integrity and thoroughness. He works well with a broad range of personnel from salespeople to suppliers and shop workers. His approach to problem-solving is creative yet practical. If he can be said to have a fault, it is his penchant for perfection. I would suggest that his supervisor establish clear-cut objectives for any project to which he is assigned.

Other than this tendency for perfection, I would highly recommend Mr. Roberts for the position of Project Engineer with your firm. You would be getting an exceptional employee.

Sincerely,

Follow-up Letters

If all goes well, your application letter and recommendations have secured you an interview with a prospective employer. After the interview, you will probably write one or more of the following: letters of appreciation for granting the interview; if a job offer is made, letters of acceptance or refusal; and letters acknowledging the assistance of others in your job search.

Letters Following an Interview. If you have obtained an interview with an employer, you are one of a select group being considered for the job. The letter you write after the interview gives you the chance to:

1. Thank the interviewer for the time and courtesy shown you.
2. Let the interviewer know of your continued interest in the job.
3. Remind the interviewer of your qualifications for the position and how the company would benefit from your experience.
4. Provide any additional data requested by the interviewer that you may have needed time to collect.
5. Turn in an application form or other standard company forms you may have received to complete at home.

Dear Ms. Hartley:

Thank you for discussing with me the position of assistant buyer in your firm. You were very helpful in explaining the exact job requirements.

I am even more interested in the job since our talk. I believe that my three years as a buyer for Inland Clothing have given me the experience I need to step into the position with a minimum of training.

I am enclosing my job description, which you requested, and have asked my references to write letters of recommendation to you directly.

I hope that my qualifications meet your criteria for the assistant buyer's position. Please call me if there is any additional information you would like to have.

Sincerely,

Letters of Acceptance. When you decide to take a job that has been offered, write a letter of acceptance. The letter should include:

1. A statement accepting the position.
2. A brief paragraph restating why you believe your new employer made the right choice.
3. A date when you can report for work.

Your letter of acceptance might look like the following:

Dear Mrs. Rhodes:

It is with pleasure that I accept your offer of a sales representative position at Field Enterprises. You can be assured that I will bring all my experience and enthusiasm to bear on this job and justify your confidence in me.

I will be able to start Monday, April 14, as we discussed on the phone. I will report to the personnel office at 8:30 A.M. and to your office at 9:00 A.M.

Thank you for this opportunity. I look forward to working with you and others in the Sales Office.

Sincerely yours,

Letters of Refusal. You might refuse a job offer for several reasons. Perhaps you have received another offer that you like better. Perhaps you have realized you are not really suited for the particular company or position. Whatever the reason, you should respond to any offer with a tactful, friendly letter of refusal. You want to keep the lines of communication open, because at some time you may wish to reapply at the company.

Use the standard rejection format for your refusal letter. Express appreciation for the offer and give your reasons for refusing before you state your decision.

Dear Mr. Hass:

Thank you for your kind offer of a position as security officer at the Lake National Bank. I would have enjoyed working with the other security personnel at the bank.

Three days before receiving your letter, however, I was offered a position at the Hillcrest Savings and Loan. Because this job is closer to my home and would require significantly less travel time, I have decided to accept their offer.

I appreciate the time and effort you spent on my application. I know you have many fine candidates who can fill your job opening.

Sincerely yours,

Letters of Acknowledgement. When you accept a job offer, you may want to write letters thanking all the people whose support, encouragement, and suggestions helped you get there. A letter of acknowledgement is a brief note to your supporters mentioning their specific contribution and letting them know which position you accepted.

Dear Miss Leland:

I would like to thank you for all the support you have given me during the past six months while I was job hunting. You will be pleased to know that I accepted the position of accountant in the legal firm of Young, Letterby, and Dunn.

Your advice on how to write letters of application and to conduct myself during the interview proved invaluable. I want you to know how much I appreciate your help. If you need a good tax accountant, you will know whom to call!

With warm regards,

Letters of Resignation

During your career you may need to write a letter of resignation when you leave your current job. Your reasons for resigning may be as different as a decision to go back to school or a personality clash with your supervisor.

Regardless of the circumstances, your letter of resignation should be written in a courteous, positive tone. Barring any overt hostility between you and your supervisor, you may want your former employer to act as a reference or to write a letter of recommendation for you.

Letters of resignation generally follow the rejection/refusal format. The following example uses this letter plan.

Dear Mr. Archer:

I have enjoyed working with you and Mr. Conroy these past four years at Carbon Tool & Die Works. The job has taught me a great deal, and I have made several close friends here.

Recently, I have decided to return to technical school in the fall for a degree in electronics. I would appreciate it, therefore, if you would accept my resignation, effective September 10.

Thank you for the time you took to show me all the company's operations. I will always remember your patience and consideration.

Sincerely yours,

The guidelines in this chapter for completing résumés, employment letters, and application forms should help you to design an effective job-hunting strategy. Keep in mind that luck favors the prepared!

Section 6
Review of Business Grammar and Style

Chapter 14 Parts of Speech

The parts of speech—*nouns, pronouns, verbs, adverbs* and *adjectives*, and *prepositions*, *conjunctions*, and *interjections*—each have their own forms, characteristics, and uses. Knowing how to use these parts will enable you to write with greater clarity, accuracy, and style. Good writing, like any skill, involves mastering basic guidelines and learning how to apply them.

Nouns

Nouns are words that name persons, places, or things (objects, events, or concepts).

Persons	*Places*	*Things*	*(objects, events,*	*concepts)*
worker	office	desk	picnic	freedom
woman	city	window	meeting	equality

Common, Proper, and Collective Nouns

Common nouns refer to a general category or class of persons, places, or things. *Proper nouns*, on the other hand, name a particular person, place, or thing and are capitalized. *Collective nouns* name a group or unit and can be singular or plural.

Common nouns	*Proper nouns*	*Collective nouns*
typist	Jack Bartell	staff
town	New Orleans	management
meeting	Housewares Show	team

Note: Common nouns used with proper nouns are not capitalized. For example: Xerox copiers, Radio Shack computers, Smith-Corona typewriters.

Functions of Nouns

Nouns can serve as the subject, direct object, or indirect object of a verb. They can be used as the object of a preposition. In some cases they can serve as adverbs or adjectives. Nouns can also show possession.

Subject:	The employees arrived early. (Tells who or what does or is something.)
Direct object:	The employees celebrated the anniversary. (Tells what is celebrated.)
Indirect object:	She gave Jim the book. (Tells to whom the book was given.)
Object of prep.:	She typed the name under the signature. (Completes the preposition by telling what was under.)
Adverb:	We'll be arriving tomorrow. (Tells when.)
Adjective:	She is an exeutive secretary. (Tells which one, what kind.)
Possession:	The office's air conditioning system shuts off automatically at night, except in Howard's section. (Shows possession.)

Plural Nouns

Nouns can be made plural in various ways. Most nouns form the plural by adding *s* to the singular form. For other plural forms such as *es* and *y* changed to *ies*, see Chapter 18: Spelling.

Singular	*Plural*
hotel	hotels
chief	chiefs
association	associations
name	names

Collective nouns can be singular or plural depending on the context in which they are used. If collective nouns refer to a unit, they are singular. If they refer to the individuals in that unit, they are plural.

Singular	*Plural*
The staff is adequate.	The staff vote on every issue.
The board meets tonight.	The board are still divided on the merger.

Plurals of compound and hyphenated nouns can be troublesome. For a fuller treatment of these plural nouns, see Chapter 18: Spelling, page 259.

Possessive Nouns

A *possessive noun* shows ownership or possession. The possessive is formed by adding *'s* or ' to the end of the noun.

To form the singular possessive, add *'s* to all nouns.

Singular	*Singular Possessive*
The profits of the company	The company's profits
The rules of the manager	The manager's rules

To form the plural possessive of nouns that end in *s* or *es*, add an apostrophe to the end of the word.

Plural	*Plural possessive*
Papers of the lawyers	The lawyers' papers
The wages of the secretaries	The secretaries' wages

For nouns that form the plural in any other way, add *'s* to the end of the word, except when the final *s* is a *z* sound (houses). Then add only the apostrophe (houses').

Plural	*Plural Possessive*
men	the men's jobs
children	the children's department
notaries	the notaries' seals

When you are uncertain whether to place the apostrophe before or after the *s*, follow this simple rule. Rephrase the sentence by substituting an *of phrase* for the possessive noun to help you decide if the noun is meant to be singular or plural.

The (employee's, employees') decision was made on the spot.

Of phrase		*Possessive form*
the decision of the employee	(singular)	The employee's decision
the decision of the employees	(plural)	The employees' decision

---

To show joint ownership, make the final noun possessive. To show individual ownership, make both nouns possessive.

Joint Ownership: Greg and Carla's assignment is to survey the west end of the city. (Greg and Carla share the same assignment.)

Individual Ownership: Greg's and Carla's assignments are due on Friday or Monday. (Each person has a separate assignment.)

Note: Generally, in individual ownership, the noun following the possessives is plural. Look for this clue when deciding whether to use joint or individual possession (Brenda and Larry's car, Brenda's and Larry's cars).

Pronouns

Pronouns are used to take the place of one or more nouns. Like nouns, they can refer to persons, places, events, objects, or concepts.

Examples:

The managers approved the report. They felt it gave them a clear picture of the problem. (The pronouns they and them take the place of the noun managers. The pronoun it replaces the noun report.)

The director and supervisor argued about equal employment. They couldn't agree on a definition of it. (The pronoun they replaces the two nouns director and supervisor. The pronoun it takes the place of equal employment.)

Personal Pronouns

A *personal pronoun* can be used as the *subject* of a sentence, as the *object* of a verb or preposition, to show *possession*, for emphasis (called *intensive* pronoun), or to refer action back to the subject (called a *reflexive* pronoun).

Subject: I am not going to the conference next month.

Object: Ruth told him to come Wednesday. Give the letter to her.

Possessive: Their talk was enlightening. I hope your job improves.

Intensive: The manager herself approved the change. (Pronoun herself emphasizes the subject manager.)

Reflexive: I taught myself to type. They criticized themselves. (The pronouns refer the action back to the subjects.)

The following table shows the personal pronouns in all their forms for the first person (I, we), second person (you), and third person (he/she/it).

Table 1. Personal Pronoun Forms

Person		*Singular*	*Plural*
First:	subject	I	we
	object	me	us
	possessive	my/mine	our/ours
	intensive/reflexive	myself	ourselves
Second:	subject	you	you
	object	you	you
	possessive	your/yours	your/yours
	intensive/reflexive	yourself	yourselves
Third:	subject	he/she/it	they
	object	him/her/it	them
	possessive	his/her,hers/its	their/theirs
	intensive/reflexive	himself/herself/itself	themselves

Possessive Pronouns

Unlike possessive nouns, *possessive pronouns* never take an apostrophe. As you can see from Table 1, personal pronouns have a possessive form *(my, mine, our, ours, your, yours, his, her, hers, its, their, theirs).* The pronoun *who* also has a possessive form, *whose.*

Examples:

Is this desk mine? My application has been accepted.

Will you look at her report or his? This file is hers.

The department has prepared its final statement.
We looked over their specifications. I think the best bid is theirs.
Our office is closed on Saturdays. Are these letters ours?
Whose messages were left on my desk?

Some possessive pronouns sound exactly like other pronoun or noun forms *(its/it's, whose/who's, your/you're, their/they're/there)*. One easy way to keep the possessive forms straight is to remember that possessive pronouns *never* take an apostrophe. When pronouns have an apostrophe, they are contractions, a combined form of the pronoun plus a verb. For example, *it's* equals *it is; they're* equals *they are.*

its	The company reported its earnings.
it's:	It's (it is) easy to work with Jim.
whose	Whose car should we take?
who's:	Who's (who is) coming to the conference?
your	Is this your proposal?
you're:	Let me know if you're (you are) available.
their	They sold their last shipment yesterday.
they're	Mark said they're (they are) low on this item.
there:	Put the box over there by the cabinet.

Gerunds

Gerunds are verbs ending in *-ing* that are used as nouns. For example, in the sentence *Typing is a valuable skill,* typing is a gerund used as the subject. If a pronoun precedes the gerund, the pronoun is in the possessive form.

Examples:
Did you hear about his calling sixteen clients in one morning?
I would appreciate your providing me with more work forms.
Note: Nouns are also in the possessive form before a gerund. (We heard about Julia's winning the top employee award last month.)

Pronoun-Antecedent Agreement

The word to which a pronoun refers is called the *antecedent*. Make sure that a pronoun refers to a specific antecedent. Many writers misuse the pronouns *this, that, which, it,* and *they* to refer to entire phrases or sentences.

Vague: The department's finances were in chaos. The sales records were incomplete. It was a difficult situation. (The pronoun it refers to the preceding statements.)

Precise: The department's finances were in chaos. They would have to be straightened out before the budget hearing. (The pronoun they refers to the antecedent finances.)

Vague: Company sales increased five percent. The sales staff were all given bonuses. This boosted morale in the sales department.

Precise: The company had a five percent sales increase. This boosted morale in the sales department. (This refers to the sales increase.)

Pronouns must agree with their antecedents in person, form, and number. Review Table 1 for the appropriate pronoun forms.

Incorrect: When the operator exits the program, you must use the proper sequence.

Correct: When the operator exits the program, he or she must use the proper sequence. (Operator as the antecedent requires the third-person singular pronoun, not the second-person pronoun.)

Incorrect: Each December the company publishes their report.

Correct: Each December the company publishes its report. (Company is a third-person singular noun and requires a third-person singular pronoun, in this case the possessive form.)

Incorrect: The caller asked, "Is this Carol?" Carol replied, "Yes, this is her."

Correct: The caller asked, "Is this Carol?" Carol replied, "Yes, this is she." (The pronoun she refers to the subject. When in doubt about which pronoun form to use, reverse the pronoun and noun. "Her is (Carol)" makes no sense. "She is (Carol)" is the proper form.)

When two antecedents are joined by *and*, use a plural pronoun. If the antecedents are joined by *nor* or *or*, or form a unit (research and development), use a singular pronoun.

Examples:
Robert and Arlene gave their boss the questionnaire.
Either Robert or John will take his car tomorrow.
The secretary and treasurer takes her duties seriously.

Who or Whom?

Even experienced writers sometimes confuse *who* or *whom*. In modern usage, the tendency is to drop the more formal *whom* and use *who* in all cases. Yet the rules for using these two pronouns can be mastered easily. Once you have learned them, you should have no trouble choosing the correct pronoun.

Who is used as the *subject* of a sentence or of a phrase or clause within a sentence. Who is never used as an object.

Examples:
Who talked to the director? (Who is the subject of the sentence.)
I can tell who is coming. (Who is the subject of is coming.)
Give the package to whoever can pick it up. (Whoever is the subject of can pick and not the object of the preposition to.)

Whom is used as the object of a verb or preposition. It is never used as the subject of a sentence or of a phrase or clause within a sentence.

Examples:
To whom did you give your time sheets? (Whom is the object of the preposition to.)
Whom did you see yesterday? (Whom is the object of the verb see.)
Is that the manager whom you met last week? (You is the subject of the verb met. Whom is the object of that verb.)
Give the package to whomever you call to pick it up. (Whomever is the object of the verb call. Compare this sentence with the one using whoever.)

Verbs

Verbs are words that express action or states of being. Verbs provide the power or drive for your sentences.

Examples:
He changed the title of the report. (action)
The company merged with Kascade Industries. (action)
She appears calm in front of a group. (state of being)
The office looks more attractive. (state of being)

Active and Passive Voice

Verbs have *active* and *passive* voices. If the subject of the sentence performs the action, the verb is in the *active voice*. If the subject receives the action, the verb is in the *passive voice*.

Active voice	*Passive voice*
We delivered the package. (The subject we performs the action delivered. Package is the object of the verb.)	The package was delivered by us. (The subject package receives the action was delivered. It no longer serves as the object.)
He has checked the message.	The message has been checked.

In general, use the active voice in your writing. It adds interest and liveliness to your message. However, the passive voice can be used for variety and in cases where you want to minimize the source of the action or in cases when the source of action is unknown. For example, compare *Your credit rating has been reviewed* to *We have reviewed your credit rating*. The passive voice establishes a more neutral, objective tone and places the emphasis on the customer's credit rating, not on the persons who evaluated it.

Basic Verb Forms

All verb tenses and phrases are built from a few verb forms. These include the base form (verb), the infinitive (to + verb), the past tense, the past and present participles, and the gerund (verb + ing, used as a noun).

Base form:	I invest my money.
Infinitive:	It is wise to invest your money.
Past tense:	I invested $500 last month.
Past participle:	He has invested $500 as well.
Present participle:	I am investing another $500 this month.
Gerund (noun form):	Investing is a good way to ensure your future.

Note: Avoid splitting the infinitive in your sentences. *For example:* We need to pursue this client aggressively. *Not:* We need to aggressively pursue this client. Also, in a series, repeat the preposition *to* before each infinitive verb form: We can change the program to provide more flexibility, to store additional data, and to save on file space.

Auxiliary Verbs

Auxiliary verbs are used with main verbs to signal a change in tense (he used, he *had* used) or a change in voice (she gave, she *was* given). The most commonly used auxiliary verbs are listed below.

Auxiliary	*Auxiliary plus main verb*
has/have	He has sent the cable. I have received it.
is/are	She is going tonight. They are going tomorrow.
can/could	I can do it. They could help.
should/would	The company should pay more. He would like it.
will/shall	It will happen. Shall we decide later?
must/ought	We must remain here. They ought to call.

Verb Tenses

Verb tenses enable you to place an action or state of being in the past, present, or future. They give you a way of talking about time. The various tenses in English are formed using the basic elements of the verb: base form (promote), past tense (promoted), past and present participles (promoted, promoting), and auxiliary verbs (*was* promoted.)

English has both regular and irregular verbs. You will need to know the basic verb forms of these words in order to form the tenses and to avoid mixing tenses in your writing. This section gives examples of regular and irregular verbs, the basic tenses, and how each tense is used.

Regular Verbs

Regular verbs form the past tense and past participle by adding *d* or *ed* to their base form. The present participle is formed by adding *ing* to the base form. Most verbs fall into this category.

Base form	*Past tense*	*Past participle*	*Present participle*
call	called	called	calling
watch	watched	watched	watching
create	created	created	creating
delay	delayed	delayed	delaying

Irregular Verbs

There are no fixed rules for forming the past tense and past and present participles of *irregular verbs*. As a result, you will need to memorize most of the forms or consult a good dictionary, which will tell you the correct verb forms. Some of the most commonly used irregular verbs are listed below.

Principal Parts of Irregular Verbs

Base form	*Past tense*	*Past participle*	*Present participle*
be	was	been	being
begin	began	begun	beginning
bite	bit	bitten	biting
blow	blew	blown	blowing
break	broke	broken	breaking
bring	brought	brought	bringing
burst	burst	burst	bursting
buy	bought	bought	buying
catch	caught	caught	catching
come	came	come	coming
do	did	done	doing
draw	drew	drawn	drawing
drink	drank	drunk	drinking
drive	drove	driven	driving
eat	ate	eaten	eating
fall	fell	fallen	falling
fight	fought	fought	fighting
flee	fled	fled	fleeing
fly	flew	flown	flying

Principal Parts of Irregular Verbs

Base form	*Past tense*	*Past participle*	*Present participle*
forget	forgot	forgotten	forgetting
get	got	got/gotten	getting
give	gave	given	giving
go	went	gone	going
grow	grew	grown	growing
hang	hung	hung	hanging
hide	hid	hidden	hiding
know	knew	known	knowing
lay	laid	laid	laying
leave	left	left	leaving
lend	lent	lent	lending
lie	lay	lain	lying
lose	lost	lost	losing
pay	paid	paid	paying
ride	rode	ridden	riding
ring	rang	rung	ringing
rise	rose	risen	rising
run	ran	run	running
see	saw	seen	seeing
set	set	set	setting
shake	shook	shaken	shaking
shine	shone	shone	shining
shrink	shrank	shrunk	shrinking
sit	sat	sat	sitting
speak	spoke	spoken	speaking
steal	stole	stolen	stealing
strike	struck	struck	striking
take	took	taken	taking
tear	tore	torn	tearing
throw	threw	thrown	throwing
wear	wore	worn	wearing
write	wrote	written	writing

Common Errors in Using Verb Tenses

People frequently use the wrong verb forms for various tenses. While an occasional error may be overlooked in conversation, such mistakes are glaringly evident in written communication. They lower the tone of your message and may cause the reader to question the accuracy of other parts of your communication.

Incorrect: He has went to check on last week's records.

Correct: He has gone to check on last week's records. (Most tenses formed with auxiliary verbs use either the present or past participle of the main verb (see p. 203). Gone is the past participle of to go and is the correct form. Went is the past tense of the verb and is incorrect.)

Incorrect: We done it yesterday and turned in the report.

Correct: We did it yesterday and turned in the report. (The action takes place in the past and requires the past tense. Did is the correct past tense form of to do. Done, the past participle, is incorrect.)

Incorrect: We are studying the effects of inflation and use the Friedman model.

Correct: We are studying the effects of inflation and using the Friedman model. (The action is ongoing in the present—the present progressive. Are is the auxiliary verb for both main verbs. Both verbs must be in the present participle form for the present progressive tense. This is referred to as parallel structure.)

Incorrect: We have mailed the questionnaire, wrote the personnel directors of the companies, and gave each firm a code.

Correct: We have mailed the questionnaire, written the personnel directors of the companies, and given each firm a code number. (The action was taken and completed in the present—the present perfect, formed by the auxiliary verb + the past participle. Have is the auxiliary verb for each main verb in the series. Therefore, the past participles mailed, written, and given are correct. Wrote and gave are the past tense forms and are incorrect.)

Another common error in written communication is mixing verb tenses in the same sentence or paragraph. When the action or state of being takes place in the same time frame, the verb tenses must be consistent.

Incorrect: We looked up the information, reported to the manager, and turn in our findings.

Correct: We looked up the information, reported to the manager, and turned in our findings. (The actions all take place in the past. The present tense confuses the time frame.)

Incorrect: We received the customer's order on Friday. We give the order to the sales department, although I was sure that there is an error in the part number. I have been filling these orders for a long time, and the number looks strange to me.

Correct: We received the customer's order on Friday. We gave the order to the sales department, although I was sure that there was an error in the part number. I have been filling these orders for a long time, and the number looked strange to me. (The paragraph refers to a sequence of actions taken in the past. The verb tenses must be consistently in the past tense and must not confuse past and present.)

Incorrect: The report is ready for the committee to study. It showed that sales were increasing over the past six months.

Correct: The report is ready for the committee to study. It shows that sales have been increasing over the past six months. (References to the report are in the present tense. The present perfect tense refers to something occurring in the past and continuing into the present such as the increase in sales.)

Subject-Verb Agreement

In the previous section, you learned that pronouns must agree with their antecedents in person, form, and number. Verbs must also agree with their subjects in person and number.

The *first person subject* is the person or persons speaking in a sentence (I, we). The *second person subject* is the person or persons addressed (you, you). The *third person subject* refers to the person or thing spoken about and can be any noun or third-person pronoun (he/she/it). Verb forms change to agree with changes in person.

Agreement in Person

First:	I am	we are
Second:	you receive	(singular and plural)
Third:	The chair falls. She returns. They come.	

Verbs must agree with their subjects in number. A singular subject takes a singular verb; a plural subject takes a plural verb.

Agreement in Number

Singular	*Plural*
The calculator is inexpensive.	The calculators are inexpensive.
The assistant writes quickly.	The assistants write quickly.
I am not ready to leave.	We are not ready to leave.
Jay, you get two boxes of pens.	All of you get two boxes of pens.

Compound subjects joined by *and* generally take a plural verb, even if one of the subjects is singular. Compound subjects joined by *or* or *nor* are plural if the subject nearest the verb is plural or if both subjects are plural.

Examples:

The president and vice president are available for interviews.
Three city workers and one company employee were injured at work.
There are one premium and two certificates for each customer.
I don't know if memo pads or time sheets are reordered first.
Neither the director nor the managers were invited to the reception.

Compound subjects joined by *and* take a singular verb when (1) the subject is considered a unit (research and development) and (2) when both parts of the subject are modified by *each* or *every*.

Examples:

Shipping and receiving is less efficient under the new system.
Each supervisor and every worker fills out the hourly sheet.

Compound subjects joined by *or* or *nor* take a singular verb if (1) the subject next to the verb is considered singular or (2) if both parts of the subject are singular.

Examples:
The top files or the bottom drawer is the place to store records.
The shop steward or the employee representative has responsibility.
Neither the secretaries nor the shipping clerk knows where he is.

Plural nouns used as the titles of courses or subject areas take a singular verb. Nouns used as measurements or units of quantity (dollars, pounds, inches, miles, etc.) also take a singular verb.

Examples:
Physics is not a required course in most business schools.
Human relations is an important subject area for most managers.
I notice mathematics has been added to the list of requirements.
Forty-five dollars is a good price for the ribbon we need.
Is twelve pounds over the limit?
Does three feet six inches sound right to you?
Fourteen miles is too far to travel without a car.

Collective nouns can take either plural or singular verbs. If you wish to emphasize the group as a unit, use the singular verb. If you are emphasizing the individuals within the group, use the plural verb.

Examples:
Management is as concerned about job security as the unions are.
Top management are never sure of their long-term successes.
We appreciate the efforts the staff makes.
The staff are used to taking their coffee breaks early.

Prepositional phrases following the subject or material set off from the subject by commas does not influence the form of the verb. If you are in doubt about which form to use, simply block out the prepositional phrase or additional material and look only at the noun or pronoun and the verb.

Examples:
Each of the managers is due for a raise. (Each ~~of the managers~~ is)
All of the managers are due for a raise. (All ~~of the managers~~ are)
Our plant, along with other plants, has expanded production.
Many plants, particularly the one in Blue Ridge, have expanded production by thirty percent.

Adjectives

Adjectives modify nouns, pronouns, and other adjectives by describing some quality or characteristic about them. Adjectives can be used to give your writing more varied shades of meaning and to add pertinent information about the main topic. Adjectives answer the questions *Which one? What kind? How many?*

Examples:
We need four graphs tomorrow. (How many?)
The director wants a tiny, two-color one. (What kind?)
Let me have the blue file. (Which one?)

Limiting Adjectives

Many adjectives are used to identify or number the nouns they modify. Some of these limiting adjectives are listed below. In nearly all cases, the limiting adjective comes before the noun it modifies.

Limiting adjective	*Noun*
a/an	a dictaphone, an audit
the	the client, the clients
this/these	this account, these accounts
that/those	that carload, those carloads
few	few deliveries
many	many receivables
every	every worker
each	each rule
both	both workers
several	several orders
some	some letters
any	any paper
most	most employees
one	one day

Comparisons

Many adjectives show comparisons between or among persons, places, or things. The positive, comparative, and superlative forms represent different degrees of a quality or characteristic. The *positive* form is simply the base word (high). The *comparative* is formed by adding the suffix *-er* or the word *more* (higher, more careful). For the *superlative,* the suffix *-est* or the word *most* is added (highest, most careful).

Positive	*Comparative (er/more)*	*Superlative (est/most)*
hard	harder	hardest
sound	sounder	soundest
fortunate	more fortunate	most fortunate
critical	more critical	most critical

Note: There are several irregular comparison forms as well.

far	farther	farthest
good	better	best
bad	worse	worst

When you are comparing two items, use the comparative form. When you are comparing more than two items, use the superlative.

Examples:

Today's shipment is larger than yesterday's. (comparative)
Today's shipment is the largest one of all our orders. (superlative)
Greg's judgment is better than Jim's. (comparative)
Greg's judgment is the best in the company. (superlative)
This case is bad, that one is worse, but the one over here is the worst of all. (positive, comparative, superlative)
My opinion is more negative than yours. (comparative)
He has the most negative opinion of anyone. (superlative)

Compound Adjectives

Compound adjectives usually are hyphenated when they precede the noun they modify. When they follow the noun, they are two words.

Examples:

A fast-thinking executive	An executive who is fast thinking
The decision-making process	A process of decision making
A two-foot retaining wall	A retaining wall of two feet
A part-time job	A job which is part time
A past-due bill	A bill which is past due

Adverbs

Adverbs modify verbs, adjectives, and other adverbs. They answer such questions as *When? Where? How? How much?* Adverbs give additional information and describe an action or state of being in greater detail.

Examples:

She never leaves the office before I do. (when?)
I think they went upstairs. (where?)
Please type this quickly. (how?)
I agree somewhat with your decision. (how much?)

Types of Adverbs

Most adverbs end in *ly;* many do not. Those indicating direction, place, time, or degree look the same as nouns, prepositions, or adjectives. Listed below are examples of the different types of adverbs.

Adverbs of time/frequency (when)

now	once
before	never
forever	immediately
seldom	Monday
occasionally	frequently
eventually	often

Adverbs of place/direction (where)

in	over
upstairs	by
under	down
through	sideways
here	out
there	across

Adverbs of degree (how much)

somewhat	completely
most	much
more	less

Adverbs of manner (how)

carefully	nicely
earnestly	arrogantly
resentfully	orderly

Adverbs of degree (how much)		*Adverbs of manner (how)*	
totally	thoroughly	painstakingly	carelessly
entirely	excessively	quickly	tirelessly
nearly	however	contentedly	equally

Comparisons

Many adverbs—like adjectives—are used in comparisons. The comparative is formed by adding *er* or *more* and the superlative by adding *est* or the word *most*.

Examples:
They work fast. (positive)
They work faster than the night crew. (comparative)
They work the fastest of any group. (superlative)
She types as well as Frank. (equal comparison)
She types better than the younger workers. (comparison)
She types best when working alone. (superlative)
He speaks softly. (positive)
He speaks more softly than Lucille. (comparison)
He speaks the most softly of any trainer. (superlative)

Adverb Position and Meaning

The position of the adverb, particularly the word *only*, can affect the meaning of a sentence. Make sure that the adverb position reflects what you intend to say.

Unclear: He has only talked to the line supervisor and not to the workers. (Has he only talked and not done something else? Or has he talked only to the line supervisor? The meaning of the sentence is not clear.)

Clear: He has talked only to the line supervisor and not to the workers.

Unclear: I frequently order supplies for the department. (Does the subject *I* order the supplies more frequently than anyone else? Or does the subject *I* order supplies many times?)

Clear: I order supplies frequently for the department.

Prepositions

Prepositions always appear in a phrase. Nouns or pronouns serve as the objects of the preposition. A preposition and its objects form a *prepositional phrase.* Prepositional phrases can serve as either adjectives modifying nouns and pronouns or as adverbs modifying verbs, adjectives, or other adverbs.

Examples:

on the board (the noun board is the object of on)
to them (the pronoun them is the object of to)
through the office (the noun office is the object of through)

Below is a list of some of the most commonly used prepositions.

about	from
above	in
across	into
after	like
against	near
along	of
among	off
around	on
at	over
before	past
behind	through
below	throughout
beneath	to
beside	toward
besides	under
between	underneath
beyond	until
by	up
concerning	upon
down	with
during	within
except	without
for	

Phrasal Prepositions

Although most prepositions are one word, some consist of phrases and are called *phrasal prepositions*. They are familiar constructions in any type of communication.

in back of	because of	in spite of
in case of	by means of	on account of
in lieu of	instead of	in front of

We had to work weekends because of the tight schedule.
We shipped the order in spite of the transit strike.
In case of bad weather, we will cancel our seminar.

Common Errors to Avoid

Do not put unnecessary prepositions at the end of the sentence.

Incorrect: Where are the envelopes at?
Correct: Where are the envelopes?

Incorrect: Can we go with?
Correct: Can we go? *Or* Can we go with you?

Incorrect: Where did the Smith document get to?
Correct: Where is the Smith document?

In formal writing and in most of your business communications, avoid putting the preposition at the end of the sentence.

Avoid: I'm not sure which data they're referring to.
Better: I'm not sure to which data they're referring.

Avoid: Whom did they ask for?
Better: For whom did they ask?

Conjunctions

Conjunctions are words used to join words or groups of words. There are four basic types of these connectors: coordinating, correlative, and subordinating conjunctions, and linking adverbs.

Coordinating Conjunctions

Coordinating conjunctions *and, but, or, nor* join two or more elements of *equal rank*. These elements can be single words such as nouns, adjectives, adverbs, pronouns, or verbs; or they can be phrases or clauses. (Clauses are groups of words with a subject-verb combination. For more about clauses see p. 223.)

Examples:
The receptionist and switchboard operator are here. (nouns)
We have talked and argued for days. (verbs)
We have a tired but happy work crew. (adjectives)
This file doesn't go on the desk but in the drawer. (phrases)
Did you type this letter quickly or carefully? (adverbs)
Choose between him or her for the job. (pronouns)
The bank has never closed its doors, lost an account, nor refused a qualified borrower. (verb phrases)
The contract was not signed nor did the lawyer approve it. (clauses)

Note: The conjunctions *but, nor* are usually used with the adverbs *never* or *not*.

Correlative Conjunctions

Correlative conjunctions are coordinating conjunctions used in pairs. Their function is to emphasize the elements being joined. Some of the most frequently used correlative conjunctions are the following:

both . . . and
not only. . . but also
neither . . . nor
either . . . or

Correlative conjunctions also join words or groups of words of *equal rank*. Make sure that the elements following each part of the construction are truly equal.

Examples:

Either the janitor or the security guard is on duty. (nouns)

She is both intelligent and sensitive. (adjective)

Neither you nor we are taking a vacation this year. (pronouns)

You should not only tell the manager but also clear it with me. (verb phrase)

Linking Adverbs

Linking adverbs join two *independent clauses*. (Independent clauses are groups of words with a subject-verb combination that can stand alone [see page 223].) Linking adverbs indicate how two ideas expressed in clauses or sentences are related to one another. Generally, linking adverbs reflect results, contrast, or continuation.

Results	*Contrast*	*Continuation*
consequently	however	furthermore
therefore	nonetheless	further
thus	nevertheless	
as a result		
accordingly		

Linking adverbs can occupy two positions in a sentence. They can come at the *beginning* of the second clause or sentence they are joining. In such cases, they usually are preceded by a semicolon and followed by a comma. They can stand *within* the second clause or sentence and often are set off by commas.

Examples:

The ledger entries seem correct; however, check them again.

The programmer made a mistake; as a result, everyone's check was four days late.

He was appreciative of Angie's work; furthermore, he gave her a raise that following month.

She encouraged two-way communication; the employees, accordingly, felt free to discuss their concerns.

The production date was moved up; many changes, therefore, had to be made.

Subordinating Conjunctions

Subordinating conjunctions join *unequal elements* in a sentence, usually a subordinate clause (a group of words with a subject-verb combination that cannot stand alone) and an independent clause. Commonly used subordinating conjunctions are listed below. Notice that some of them also serve as prepositions and relative pronouns.

after	how	than	when
although	if	that	where
as	in order that	though	which
as much as	inasmuch as	unless	while
because	provided	until	who/whom
before	since	what	whoever/whomever

A subordinating conjunction can come at the beginning of a sentence as well as between the sentence parts it joins. When the subordinate clause comes at the beginning, it is followed by a comma.

Examples:

While I was in the bank, I filled out an application for a loan.

I filled out an application for a loan *while* I was in the bank.

As soon as the position opened up, three employees applied.

Three employees applied *as soon as* the position opened up.

Restrictive and Nonrestrictive Subordinate Clauses

When a clause, joined to a sentence by a subordinating conjunction, is essential to the meaning of that sentence, the clause is *restrictive*. When the clause is not essential to the meaning of the sentence, it is *nonrestrictive* and is usually set off by commas.

Restrictive: The secretary who reorganized the office has been asked to speak at Working Women conventions. (The clause who reorganized the office distinguishes this secretary from all others.)

Nonrestrictive:	Her secretary, who reorganized the office, has been asked to speak at Working Women conventions. (The clause is incidental information. It could be eliminated without changing the meaning of the sentence.)

Remember, restrictive clauses are essential to the meaning of the sentence. Nonrestrictive clauses are descriptive but not necessary.

Interjections

Interjections are words or phrases used to express emotion or to capture the reader's attention. Strong interjections (wow! call today! act now!) are punctuated with an exclamation mark. Milder interjections (indeed, yes, well,) are used with a comma.

Interjections are rarely used in formal business writing. They appear mainly in advertising and promotional materials.

Mild interjections:	Yes, we can complete your order today.
	Indeed, we appreciate our customers' concern.
Strong interjections:	Outstanding! That's the verdict from first-time users of Florentine Vinyl.
	Your suppliers may be saying, "Hey! What's happened to the old-fashioned cardboard box?"

Words Used as Interjections

Here are some words that are commonly used as interjections.

ah	hurry	no way
alas	hey	oh
congratulations	hooray	ouch
good grief	my goodness	outstanding
great	never	ugh
help	no	wow

Punctuating Interjections

Interjections may be followed by either an exclamation point or by a comma. The word following the exclamation point is capitalized because it is the first word in a new sentence. When a comma is used after an interjection, the next word is not capitalized because it does not begin a new sentence.

Examples:

Yes, we are very pleased with the new word processor.

You got an "A" on the test? Great!

Good grief, Fisby! A creature is emerging from the laboratory!

Chapter 15 Sentences and Sentence Patterns

In Chapter 14 you studied the individual elements of the sentence—nouns, pronouns, verbs, adjectives and adverbs, prepositions, conjunctions, and interjections. In this section, we look at the building blocks of sentences—phrases and clauses—and the various ways sentences are constructed. These different constructions can add variety to your writing and communicate your message more effectively.

Sentences, Fragments, and Run-Ons

A sentence is a group of words that expresses a complete thought. It begins with a capital letter and ends with a period, question mark, or exclamation point. Sentences can be declarative (a statement), interrogatory (a question), imperative (command or request), or exclamatory (for emphasis).

Declarative:	Two-way communication is essential in an office.
Interrogative:	Why is motivation so important to productivity?
Imperative:	Give him the key. Please return the file.
Exclamatory:	We get three weeks' vacation this year!

Fragments

Not every group of words is a sentence. *Fragments* are groups of words that appear to be sentences but do not express a complete thought.

Examples:
Received by the front office
Decisions made yesterday
When the client accepts

Fragments make no sense by themselves and leave important questions unanswered. What is received? What about the decisions made yesterday? When the client accepts, what happens? Fragments must be joined with other sentence parts to form a complete thought.

Run-Ons

Run-ons are two or more complete thoughts—often unrelated—that are strung together without punctuation.

Examples:
We cannot fill your order because shipment has been delayed and we tried to call you earlier this week. (The run-on connects two unrelated thoughts together. The meaning is not clear.)
The board voted on the measure and the stockholders approved the new management plan. (The run-on connects two related thoughts but without punctuation.)

Revised: We cannot fill your order because shipment has been delayed. We tried to call you earlier this week to discuss possible substitutes for the parts you wanted. (The reason for the attempted call is now clear.)
The board voted on the measure, and the stockholders approved the new management plan. (A comma before *and* separates the two complete thoughts and corrects the run-on sentence. The run-on can also be corrected by making the two thoughts into separate sentences. For example: The board voted on the measure. The stockholders approved the new management plan.)

Reread your communications carefully to make sure you have no fragments or run-on sentences. They can be confusing to the reader and can distort your message.

Sentence Structure

Besides the various parts of speech, sentences are constructed out of phrases and clauses.

Phrases

Phrases are related groups of words that do not contain a subject-verb combination. You have already encountered the prepositional, verb, participial, and infinitive phrase in Chapter 14.

Phrases

Prepositional	*Verb*	*Participial*	*Infinitive*
on the corner	has been told	writing the speech	to sell
among the files	was sent	connected to us	to return

Clauses

Clauses are related groups of words that do contain a subject–verb combination. *Independent clauses* can stand by themselves as complete thoughts or sentences. Dependent or *subordinate clauses* cannot stand by themselves but serve as part of a complete sentence.They are subordinate to an independent clause.

Clauses

Independent	*Subordinate*
she was hired today	when she was hired
each one of us called	when each one of us called
I'm five minutes late	because I'm five minutes late
the routine is changing	why the routine is changing

She was hired today <u>when the manager approved her application</u>.
I'm five minutes late <u>because the train was delayed.</u>
<u>When each one of us called</u>, we asked the same survey questions.
<u>Why the routine is changing</u> I haven't any idea.

Sentence Variety

There are four types of sentence constructions: simple, compound, complex, and compound-complex. Each of these constructions uses the same basic elements of the sentence—individual parts of speech, phrases, and clauses—as building blocks.

Simple Sentence

The *simple sentence* is an independent clause with no subordinate clauses. It is distinguished from an independent clause by a capital letter and an end mark—period, question mark, or exclamation point. Simple sentences can vary considerably in length.

Examples:
The Praedo file is on the back shelf.
We gave the Praedo file to the consulting team from Arizona.
We gave the Praedo file to the consulting team from a vocational school affiliated with the University of Arizona and connected with Shell Oil's field-study program.

Compound Sentence

The *compound sentence* contains two or more independent clauses but no subordinate clauses. The two independent clauses can be joined by a conjunction (but, and, either . . . or, not only . . . but also), by a semicolon followed by a linking adverb (; however, ; therefore,) or by a semicolon alone.

Examples:
We have two weeks to fill the order, or we lose the account.
The secretaries complained about the cold, but there was no way to regulate the heat.
I like the benefits at this company, especially the life insurance and the major medical; however, I think the pay raises are too small.

Complex Sentence

The *complex sentence* is made up of an independent clause and one or more subordinate clauses. The subordinate clause can act as an adverb, adjective, or noun in the sentence.

Examples:
After he read the letter, he gave it to his assistant.

Note: The subordinate clause is usually followed by a comma when it comes before the independent clause.
That we should reorganize the department was an excellent idea.
We read that the company would be offering stock option plans and that employees would be allowed to participate.

Compound-Complex Sentence

The *compound-complex sentence* is composed of *two* or more independent clauses and *one* or more subordinate clauses. In the examples, the subordinate clauses are underscored to help you see the sentence structure more clearly.

Examples:

We need more keypunch operators, but we cannot hire them until we have decided on our budget.

The mail clerk, who is usually efficient, lost the letter; I don't know what to tell my boss.

You should open the mail as soon as it arrives, but if you have a rush job put the mail off until noon.

I asked her about the figures; and she replied that she had looked them up, that they were accurate, and that I could use them.

Rearranging Sentence Order

The basic sentence pattern can be rearranged to place the predicate and part of the verb phrase before the subject.

Examples:

When the clock struck five, I looked up. (predicate, subject, verb)

Has the tax form arrived at the home office? (aux. verb, subject, verb, predicate)

Only when the payroll department complained did she turn in her weekly time sheets. (predicate, aux. verb, subject, verb, predicate)

When rearranging your sentence patterns, be sure the modifiers are clearly joined to the word or words they modify. Descriptive phrases or clauses that are joined to the wrong words are called "*dangling modifiers.*" They can create some odd images in your sentences.

Incorrect: Exhausted and bleary-eyed, the report was finished by morning. (An exhausted, bleary-eyed report?)

Correct: Exhausted and bleary-eyed, the staff finished the report by morning.

Incorrect: The secretary left the typewriter pleased with the work. (The typewriter is pleased?)

Correct: Pleased with the work, the secretary left the typewriter.

Incorrect: After standing up well under the stress tests, the company was convinced that the product was sufficiently strong. (The company stood up well?)

Correct: After standing up well under the stress tests, the product was judged to be sufficiently strong.

Incorrect: After considering the report, it was accepted by the committee. (The report considered the report?)

Correct: After considering the report, the committee accepted it.

A Practical Application

Read the following paragraphs to see how sentence variety can make your writing more interesting and informative. Study the differences in sentence structure between the two paragraphs.

1. The following is a report on employee productivity. It was prepared for the personnel office. Each worker was studied for three months. They were studied for efficiency, ability to work with others, and level of skills. A variety of conditions was considered. Some of the conditions were heat, light, ventilation, noise, equipment, and workload. Employees worked alone or in groups of six or more people. Solitary employees had slightly lower rates of productivity. Workers in groups tended to support one another. Their productivity rates were somewhat higher.

2. The following is a report on employee productivity prepared for the personnel office. Over a period of three months, each worker was rated for efficiency, ability to work with others, and level of skill. The study team considered a variety of conditions including heat, light, ventilation, noise, equipment, and workload. Some employees worked alone while others worked in groups of six or more people. That solitary employees had lower productivity rates should come as no surprise. Employees who work in groups tend to support one another; as a result, their productivity rates are somewhat higher.

Chapter 16 Punctuation and Punctuation Style

Punctuation serves two main purposes in written communication. First, punctuation helps you present your ideas clearly and accurately. It indicates where one thought ends and another begins, how ideas are related to one another, how to separate items in a series, and the like.

Second, punctuation is used in abbreviations and in figures expressing time, quantities, measures, and the like.

In this section, we look at the proper use of end marks, the comma, semicolon, quotation marks, apostrophe, hyphens, dashes, brackets, parentheses, and ellipses.

End Marks — Period, Question Mark, Exclamation Point

End marks usually come at the end of a sentence. However, they also have other uses within a sentence and in individual terms.

Period

The *period* marks a full stop at the end of a complete sentence. It is a visual marker that one idea has ended and another will follow. The period is followed by two full spaces before another sentence begins. The period is used at the end of a statement, command, or request.

Examples:
We will ship your order on the third of each month . (statement)
Order your copy today . (command)
Would you please return the enclosed card . (polite request)

Periods are used in many abbreviations. (For a fuller discussion of abbreviations, see pages 246-249.)

Ave. (Avenue)
Blvd. (Boulevard)
F.O.B. (free on board)
Dec. (December)
M.B.A. (master of business administration)
C.O.D. (cash on delivery)

Question Mark

Question marks are used at the end of a statement that asks a question but not at the end of a statement that contains an *indirect* question.

Direct question: Do you know who the new consultant is ?
Indirect question: She wants to know who the new consultant is .

Although polite requests in many business letters usually are followed by a period, a question mark is also acceptable.

Examples:
Will you please indicate your preference by June 30 .
Will you please indicate your preference by June 30 ?

Question marks are used after each question in a series of questions.

Examples:
What price did you quote for machine parts ? for replacement ? for maintenance and repair ? for field testing ?

Question marks are placed *inside* quotation marks when the quotation is a question. Otherwise they should be placed outside quotation marks.

Examples:
The supervisor asked, "How many parts can be welded in an hour ? " (The quoted material is a question.)
Did you say "return the package today" ? (The quoted material is not a question. The entire sentence is the question.)

Exclamation Point

Exclamation points add emphasis to complete sentences, phrases, or clauses. In business writing, exclamation points are used to call attention to a particular message or urge the reader to take some action. They are seldom used in formal writing.

Examples:
You can't allow the competition to get ahead!
This offer represents an unusual opportunity!
Order the NEC Printer today!

Comma

The *comma* is the most frequently used—and abused—punctuation mark. It is used basically to group words that belong together and to separate those that do not. Other uses have little to do with meaning and are simply traditional ways of punctuating various items.

Series Commas

Commas are used to separate items in a series. In most business writing, a comma comes before the final conjunction *(and, or, nor)* to avoid confusion.

Examples:
We learned how to use the keyboard, daisy wheel printer, and modem.
Do you want this on the table, on your desk, or near the door? (Series of prepositional phrases)
The sales department ordered men's and women's slacks, sports shirts, boots and shoes and laces. (Is the final category boots and shoes or shoes and laces? A comma would make the categories clear: boots and shoes, and laces.)

Joining Independent Clauses

Use a comma before *and, but, or, nor, for, yet* when they join two independent clauses, unless the clauses are very short.

Examples:

Please have Mr. Church reply by Thursday , and I will have his check ready for him.

The meeting was canceled , for no one could get to the office.

Have him go ahead and I'll follow soon.

Note: A comma is not used when *and, but, for, yet* join two verbs that share the same subject.

Marlene asked her co-workers for suggestions and received several good ideas from almost everyone.

Nonessential Material

Commas are used to set off nonrestrictive material or expressions that interrupt the sentence.

Examples:

Sheila Brown , who was appointed director last year , has been recommended for membership in the local Jaycees. (The material set off in commas is incidental to the meaning of the sentence.)

The arrangements depend , of course , on the number of people coming.

The Control Data order , the one we discussed , has been sent.

Expressions such as *I am sure, on the contrary, indeed, naturally, in my opinion, for example, that is, incidentally* are set off by commas whether they come at the beginning, middle, or end of the sentence.

Direct Address

Words in direct address are set off by commas no matter where they fall in a sentence.

Examples:

Jack , I think you need to trim your expense account.

Please call the field representative , Elaine , and tell him to come this afternoon.

Can you find this address , Dee?

Introductory Expressions, Phrases, Clauses

Use a comma after introductory elements such as *no, yes, well, why* when they begin a sentence. Use a comma after an introductory phrase or subordinate clause, unless the phrase or clause is very short.

Examples:
No , we can't change the schedule at this late date.
By the way , can you work this weekend?
When the final results were compiled , the interviewer was surprised.
Throughout the long meeting , he kept looking at his watch.
At five o'clock we left the office.
Note: Phrases or clauses at the end of a sentence are not usually set off by commas.
He kept looking at his watch throughout the long meeting.

Traditional Comma Uses

Commas are used in certain conventional situations including dates, addresses, the salutations and closings of a friendly letter, and certain forms of proper names or names followed by a title.

Examples:
We would like to set March 5 , 19-- , as our target date. (When only the day and month are used, no commas are necessary:
The stock offering on May 10 was for 5,000 shares.)
You can write Mr. Richards at 355 South LaSalle , Chicago , Illinois , for a copy of the brochure.

Dear Frank ,	Sincerely yours ,	Truly yours ,
Bill Waters , Jr.	Sarah Wellington , Ph.D.	Jill Hall , director

But: Bill Waters III

Comma Faults

Do not use commas to separate subject from verb.

Incorrect: The sales force from Dallas , arrived two hours late. (The subject sales force should not be separated from the verb arrived.)

Correct: The sales force from Dallas arrived two hours late.

Do not separate two subordinate clauses joined by a conjunction.

Incorrect: The supervisor recommended that we work longer hours , and that we divide the work among more typists.

Correct: The supervisor recommended that we work longer hours and that we divide the work among more typists.

Semicolon

Semicolons represent a stronger break between independent clauses or in a series than a comma but not as complete a break as a period or colon. A semicolon, like a comma, is followed by one space when used in typed or printed communications.

Independent Clauses

Use a semicolon to join two independent clauses similar in thought when they are not joined by *and, but, or, nor, for, yet*.

Examples:
We have repaired your TRS 8000 ; it should run perfectly now.
Check off the items you wish restocked ; leave blank those items you have in sufficient supply.

Use a semicolon between two independent clauses joined by linking adverbs such as *accordingly, however, for example, therefore, instead*. The linking adverb is usually followed by a comma or set off by commas.

Examples:
Our hiring practices need to be improved ; for example , we are not reaching the junior colleges.
I approved your recommendation ; however , I'm not sure Leonard will.
He received a copy of the complaint ; he has suggested , accordingly , that his assistant look into the matter.

Use a semicolon to separate two independent clauses if one or both of them contain internal punctuation.

Examples:
Carl said we needed a disk drive , a backup system , and a modem ; and he recommended we look at the IBM or Apple III.

Nancy , who talked to the people in the mail room , suggested we mail the letters today ; the mail delivery will be slow tomorrow.

Series

Use a semicolon to separate items in a series if the items contain commas within themselves.

Example:
The list of conferees includes Carol Hilliard , vice president ; Arthur Little , director of research ; Gayle Schmidt , director of finance ; and Alan Berman , office manager.

Colon

Colons represent a more complete stop than a semicolon but not as full a stop as a period. Insert two full spaces after a colon when using it in a sentence.

Before a Series or List

Use a colon to indicate "Note what follows." Colons are used correctly after complete thoughts, particularly after such expressions as *the following, as follows*. When a series immediately follows a verb or preposition, do not use a colon.

Correct: The manufacturer gave us five color choices : blue, orange, yellow, green, and red.
The application form covers the following : schooling, work experience, references, outside interests, and medical history.

Incorrect: The assistant expressed an interest in : telephone surveys, field research, and report writing.
Our best markets are : St. Louis, Chicago, and Des Moines. (The colons should be omitted in both sentences.)

Between Independent Clauses

Use a colon to introduce a question or related statement following an independent clause. In general, a question begins with a capital letter.

Examples:
Our biggest problem lies ahead: How do we repay the debt?
There is one reason for our success: we have an excellent staff.

Time

Colons are used in numerical expressions of time. When writing time in figures, do not use the words *o'clock*.

5:00 P.M.
12:00 noon
4:15 A.M.
10:00 in the morning

Business Letters

Use a colon after the salutation in a business letter or a memo.

Dear President Field:
Dear Customer:
Dear Ms. Johnson:
To the Staff:
To All Line Managers:
To All Secretaries and Clerk Typists:

Quotation Marks

Quotation marks are used to enclose a direct quotation, that is, someone's exact words.

Examples:
The shop supervisor said, "We must deliver the product today."
"We were told," he said, "to deliver this product today."
"I remember distinctly," he said. "We were told today."

Note: When quoted material is interrupted by *he said, she asked,* and the like, the second part of the quote begins with a small letter. If the second part is a new sentence, it begins with a capital.

Punctuation with Quotation Marks

Commas and periods are always placed *inside* the closing quotation mark. Semicolons and colons, on the other hand, are always placed *outside* the quotation marks.

Examples:
I know we are " off the mark, " but I'm not sure what that means.
She didn't say she was " disappointed in the group's performance. "
" The group has failed, " she said.
Look at the manual under " double-sided copying " ; then proceed.
His assistant considered the following as " unnecessary frills " : glass mugs and gold-stamped pens.
The manager said, " Please type these letters today. "
" Send this order right away," the supervisor spoke hurriedly.

Question marks and exclamation points, if they are part of the quoted material, are placed inside the quotation marks. Otherwise, they are placed outside the quotation marks. Only one end mark or comma is used at the end of the quotation.

Examples:
Did the article say " all employees share in the plan " ? (The question mark refers to the entire sentence.)
" Why hasn't this letter been typed? " she asked.
" We set a new record! " Martin shouted.
We're being asked to increase sales by " fifty-five percent " !
Who was it that asked " what price progress? " (Question mark applies to the sentence and the quoted material.)
The news release stated, " We are pleased to announce the appointment of David Jacobson as vice-president of marketing. He will provide strong leadership for our consumer products division. "

Brief and Long Quotations

When quoting a few lines, place quotation marks at the beginning and end of the material.

> As the report on office productivity revealed, " There is a strong relationship between employees' feelings of self-worth and their motivation on the job. "

Long quotations are set off from the rest of the text by being indented and single spaced. No quotation marks are used.

> As the report on office productivity revealed:
>> There is a strong relationship between employees' feelings of self-worth and their motivation on the job. Employees in one plant were given responsibility for setting their own productivity goals and reporting on their progress each week. In every case the employees not only met those goals but exceeded them, often by as much as 35 percent!

Single Quotation Marks

Single quotation marks are used to enclose a quote within a quote.

Examples:

He said, "The letter stated that ' every effort should be made. ' "

"We are instituting ' quality of work life ' here at the plant."

Titles

Quotation marks are used to enclose titles of articles, chapters of books, and titles of many reports and government publications. These titles are set off from the sentence by commas.

Examples:

He used the article, " Labor's Blue-Collar Blues, " for his speech.

The chapter, " Corporate Values and Decision Making, " is excellent.

Please get me a copy of the Labor Department's report, "Women's Job Opportunities in the 1980s. "

I'd like to see Martha's report, " Small Business Appliances. "

Terms and Expressions

Use quotation marks to enclose slang words, technical terms, and other unusual expressions. However, keep such quoted words to a minimum in your writing.

Examples:
Explain the difference between " byte " and " bit. "
I believe his recommendations are a little " off the beam. "
Our new housewares item, called " the little wonder, " has been very successful.
" This office will support the ' Special Olympics ' at our neighborhood school. "
Can you define the term, " signature " as it is used in the printing industry?

Apostrophe

The apostrophe is used to show possession and to form the plural of numbers, symbols, letters, and signs.

Possessive of Singular Nouns

To form the possessive of a singular noun, add an apostrophe and an *s*. In words or names that end in a *z* sound, you can add the apostrophe without the *s* to avoid too many *s* sounds.

the president's opinions
the secretary's desk
Gus's record books
Georgia Burns' report

Possessive of Plural Nouns

To form the possessive of a plural noun ending in *s*, add only the apostrophe. All other types of plural nouns take *'s*.

the managers' staff
the Jones' family business
women's ready to wear
children's sports clothes

Indefinite Pronouns

Indefinite pronouns (*everyone, no one, someone*) require *'s* to form the possessive. However, personal possessive pronouns do not use an apostrophe.

Someone's ID card is here.
It was no one's fault.
That call was **hers.**
Is this **his** book?

Individual and Joint Possession

In hyphenated words, names of organizations and companies, and words showing joint possession, only the last word takes *'s* to show possession. In cases of individual possession, both nouns or pronouns take *'s* or apostrophe only.

Examples:

vice-president's orders	Proctor & Gamble's products
vice-presidents' orders	Montgomery Ward's main store
Margo and Andrew's office (the office belongs to both)	Margo's and Andrew's offices (each one has an office)

Note: When one of the nouns is a possessive pronoun, the other noun is also possessive whether it is a case of joint or individual ownership.

Jack's and **my** assignment (they have the same assignment)	Jack's and **my** assignments (they each have a separate assignment)

Units of Measure as Possessive Adjectives

Words such as *minute, hour, day, week, year, cents, dollars,* and the like require an apostrophe when used as possessive adjectives.

a minute's work	five minutes' work
a day's pay	two weeks' pay
one cent's worth	two cents' worth

Plural Forms of Symbols

Use *'s* to form the plural of letters, numbers, signs, and symbols, and words referred to as words.

Examples:

The higher priced items are marked with blue X's.

Don't use &'s in this letter; put in **and**'s.

Instead of writing 5 and 8, he wrote two 8's.

Hyphens

Use a *hyphen* with compound numbers from twenty-one to ninety-nine and with fractions used as adjectives. There are no spaces before or after the hyphen.

forty - five slides
sixty - two tallies

a three - fifths majority
But: three fifths of the stockholders
(three fifths is a noun)

Prefixes and Suffixes

Always use hyphens with prefixes *ex-*, *self-*, *all-*, and with the suffix *-elect*. Hyphens are also used with all prefixes before proper nouns and adjectives.

self - image
ex - manager
president - elect
all - important
Pan - American games
pro - British

Compound Adjectives

Hyphenate compound adjectives when they precede the noun. However, do not use a hyphen if one of the modifiers is an adverb ending in *—ly*.

well - planned program
government - owned site
a problem - solving sequence
a perfectly typed letter

a program well planned
a site that is government owned
a sequence used in problem solving

To Avoid Confusion

Use hyphens to prevent confusion or awkwardness in words.

Examples:
re - creation (prevents confusion with recreation)
re - educate (avoids awkwardness of reeducation)
sub - subsidiary (avoids awkwardness of subsubsidiary)

Dashes

Use a *dash* to indicate an abrupt break in thought within a sentence. A dash is typed using two hyphens. There is no space before or after.

Examples:

Call John — he'll be back on Thursday — and have him look at this.

Communication — two-way communication — is vital to business.

Use a dash to mean *namely, that is, in other words,* and so on before an explanation.

Examples:

They explained the method to us — we had to record each number.

Many employees share this value — they desire meaningful work.

Parentheses

Use parentheses ( ) to enclose material that is not essential to the meaning of the sentence but adds additional information.

Examples:

Many people feel that etiquette (good manners) is important.

Our survey indicates a declining loss rate (see Figure 3).

If material enclosed in parentheses falls at the end of a sentence, the end mark falls *outside* the closing parenthesis. If the material enclosed is a complete sentence in itself, the end mark falls *within* the parentheses.

Examples:

We make three forecasts. (For complete data, see Appendix A.)

We make three forecasts (for complete data, see Appendix A).

Brackets

Use *brackets* to enclose information within parentheses or within quoted material when the words inserted are not part of the quotation.

Examples:
"Our analysis shows it [the new fabric] to be flame retardant."
Health benefits are explained in the manual (see page 42, Health Benefits [Table 3.3] for a detailed breakdown of coverage).

Ellipses

Ellipsis points (. . .) are used to indicate material that has been omitted from a quotation or quoted material.

Example:
"There are recent indications that the market will remain unstable for some time. I suggest we re-evaluate our present marketing strategy. Research and development should be given more funds."
". . . the market will remain unstable for some time . . . Research and development should be given more funds."
Note: When words at the end of a sentence are omitted, use an end mark plus three dots.

Underscore

Use *underscoring* for any item that would be italicized in print. Underscore the title of books, magazines, movies, plays, newspapers, and other types of periodicals. The first word *a, an, the* is underscored only if it is part of the actual name.

The New York Times	Gone with the Wind (movie)
the Chicago Tribune	World Book Encyclopedia
Forbes	My Fair Lady (play)
The Wall Street Journal	The Insider (corporate magazine)

Foreign Words and Expressions

Underscore foreign words and expressions that have not become part of common usage.

Examples:

He submitted his brief to the court, acting as amicus curiae.

But: The early corporation believed in caveat emptor—"buyer beware!"

Vehicles

Underscore the names of ships, spacecraft, airplanes, and other well-known vehicles.

company yacht: The Yankee Clipper.
space shuttle: Columbia
luxury liner: Star of Bermuda

Words or Expressions

Underscore words used as themselves or expressions you want to emphasize. Such use of the underscore should not be frequent, however.

Examples:

Please define the word partner in your memo.

Because of the firm's record, I recommend we extend credit.

Chapter 17 Capitalization, Abbreviations, Numbers

Style guidelines for capitalization, abbreviations, and numbers are important to good written communications. Study the guidelines in this unit until you are familiar with them. Keep in mind that each company may have its own style rules that may differ slightly from the guidelines given here. In general, however, the style in this section is widely accepted by most organizations and firms.

Capitalization

Capitalize the personal pronoun *I*, the first word in any sentence, and the first word of a direct quotation.

Examples:
When the phone is free, **I** will make the call.
First impressions are important.
I heard her say, "**W**e have seven vacation days this year."

Proper Nouns and Adjectives

Capitalize all proper nouns and adjectives and the names of persons, organizations, business firms, business products, institutions, and government bodies and agencies.

Proper nouns:	New Orleans	*Proper adjectives:*	Canadian
	Washington Square		English

Allison O'Reilly, Roy Neal, Brenda Yu
American Management Association, Women Employed, United Fund
Tandem Computers, American Telephone & Telegraph, Levy & Son
Coca-Cola, Kodak Instamatic, IBM Personal Computer
U.S. Department of Labor, Office of Equal Employment Opportunity
Johns Hopkins Medical Center, Princeton University

Geographical Names and Regions

Capitalize geographical names and regions. However, do not capitalize points of the compass when used simply as directions (north, south, east, west). Also, capitalize earth only when it is used with other planets (Mercury, Mars, Earth); otherwise, it is lowercase.

Examples:
New York, South America, Western Hemisphere, United States
(all cities, townships, countries, states, continents)
Coney Island, Key West, Myrtle Beach
(all islands, peninsulas, straits, beaches)
Arrowhead Lake, Red Sea, Cedar Pond
(all bodies of water)
Rocky Mountains, Pike's Peak, Mount Whitney
(all mountains and mountain chains)
Washington Avenue, Indiana Tollway, Highway 101, Chicago Skyway
(all streets and major thoroughfares)
Yosemite National Park, Grand Canyon, Horicon Flyway
(all parks, forests, canyons, dams)
the South, the Midwest, the North, the Northeast
(all recognized regions of the country)

Capitalize the names of historical events and periods, special events and calendar items.

World War II	World Series
Teapot Dome Scandal	Midwest Video Show
South Sea Bubble	Working Women's Convention
Tuesday	National Book Week
Mothers' Day	New Year's Day
Labor Day	January

Note: Seasons of the year are not capitalized unless personified. The *fall* fashions include fur capes. Last night, *Fall* paid us an early visit.

Nationalities and Religions

Capitalize the names of nationalities and religions. If you capitalize the name of one racial group, capitalize them all. If you lowercase one racial group, lowercase the others as well.

Roman Catholic	Indian	Black *Or* black
Baptist	Australian	White *Or* white

Languages and School Subjects

Capitalize languages and those school subjects that are followed by a number. Do not capitalize general school subjects.

Chemistry 101	chemistry	French, French II
History 402	history	German

Academic Degrees and Titles

Capitalize academic degrees of people. Capitalize titles used as part of people's names. In general, however, titles used after a person's name or without a name are not capitalized (exception: when the title refers to the highest national, state, or church office, such as the President of the United States).

President Newmann of Dunn Company
Barbara Harvey, Ph.D.
Dr. Edward Levi

president of the company
Lou Childers, director

Titles of Persons

Titles of officers in an organization are often capitalized in legal and other documents. Titles and academic degrees should be capitalized when they appear on envelopes, inside addresses, salutations, and closings in correspondence.

Document: According to the terms of this agreement, the Director of Research and the Vice-President of Finance shall report weekly.

Correspondence:

Helen Brown, President
Haydon-Dunlap Corp.
Huntington, Virginia

Dear President Brown:

Sincerely yours,
Louis DeSpain
Vice-President

Documents

Capitalize the first word and all important words (and prepositions five letters and over) in charters, treaties, declarations, laws, and other official documents. However, when the words *charter, act, treaty,* or *law* are used alone, they are not usually capitalized.

Sherman Act	Articles of Incorporation
Uniform Commercial Code	International Treaty of the Sea

Titles of Publications

Capitalize the first word and all important words in the titles of books, chapters, magazines, articles, newspapers, musical compositions, and movies.

Examples:
The Manager in the Modern Organization (book)
"Why GE Won't Get Turned Off" (article)
Beethoven's Eroica Symphony

Religious Terms

Capitalize words referring to the Deity and to sacred texts.

the Creator	the Holy Bible	the Talmud
God	the Lord's Prayer	the Holy Spirit
the Koran	Genesis	the Diamond Sutra

Capitals with Numbers

Capitalize a noun or abbreviation before a number when it designates a formal part of a written work.

Paragraph 4 or Para. 4	Unit 3
Section 19 or Sec. 19	Act V, Scene 2
Chapter 22 or Chapt. 22	Book IV

Abbreviations

The following abbreviations are acceptable in all writing.

A.D. (A.D. 19--)	etc. (and so forth)
B.C. (482 B.C.)	e.g. (for example)
A.M. or a.m. (before noon)	i.e. (that is)
P.M. or p.m. (after noon)	

Note: While it is general practice to use periods with these abbreviations, some also are used without the periods: AM or am, PM or pm.

Company Names

Abbreviations of company names may or may not use periods. Below are some of the more common abbreviations.

IBM
Wm. H. Brown Printers
Gor-Tex, Inc. (incorporated)
Ford Motor Co. (company)
General Motors Corp. (corporation)
Hollingshed, Ltd. (limited partnership)

Note: Be sure to copy a company's name exactly as it is spelled on the firm's letterhead.

Government Agencies

Government agencies also may or may not use periods in their abbreviations. Again, be sure to copy the abbreviations accurately.

HUD (Housing and Urban Development)
DOT (Department of Transportation)
W.H.O. (World Health Organization)

Unnecessary Abbreviations

Avoid using unnecessary abbreviations in your business communications.

Avoid: We would like to set a time on Mon. to meet with you. We suggest the Madison Bldg. on Rush St. if it's convenient.

Better: We would like to set a time on Monday to meet with you. We suggest the Madison Building on Rush Street as a convenient location.

Names and Titles

The following abbreviations are customary before or after a name.

Before the name:	Messrs. (two or more men)	Ms.
	Mesdames (two or more women)	Dr.
	Mrs.	Rev.
	Mr.	

After the name:	Jr. (junior)	A.B.
	Sr. (senior)	M.B.A.
	Esq. (esquire)	Ph.D.

Note: Jr. and Sr. may be preceded by a comma (Jones, Jr.); however, no comma precedes a Roman numeral (Jones III).

Units of Measure

Abbreviations of weights, measurements, and distance are commonly used in statistical or tabular material. They are not generally used in formal writing with the exception of some metric measures.

4 lbs. 7 oz.	45 mi. (miles)	16 mm (millimeters)
16 ft. 4 in.	17 km (kilometers)	20 cm (centimeters)

State, Foreign, and Address Abbreviations

In general, use the postal ZIP Code abbreviations for the states, territories, and Canadian provinces. Many companies also use the address abbreviations suggested by the Postal Service. Note that these abbreviations are capitalized. They do not contain punctuation.

State Abbreviations

Alabama AL
Alaska AK
Arizona AZ
Arkansas AR
California CA
Colorado CO
Connecticut CT
Delaware DE
Florida FL
Georgia GA
Hawaii HI
Idaho ID
Illinois IL
Indiana IN
Iowa IA

Nebraska NE
Nevada NV
New Hampshire NH
New Jersey NJ
New Mexico NM
New York NY
North Carolina NC
North Dakota ND
Ohio OH
Oklahoma OK
Oregon OR
Pennsylvania PA
Rhode Island RI
South Carolina SC
South Dakota SD

Foreign Abbreviations

Guam GU
Puerto Rico PR
Virgin Islands VI

Alberta AB
British Columbia BC
Manitoba MB
New Brunswick NB
Newfoundland NF
Northwest Territories NT
Nova Scotia NS
Ontario ON
Prince Edward Island PE

State Abbreviations

Kansas KS
Kentucky KY
Louisiana LA
Maine ME
Maryland MD
Massachusetts MA
Michigan MI
Minnesota MN
Mississippi MS
Missouri MO
Montana MT

Tennessee TN
Texas TX
Utah UT
Vermont VT
Virginia VA
Washington WA
West Virginia WV
Wisconsin WI
Wyoming WY
Canal Zone CZ
District of Columbia DC

Foreign Abbreviations

Quebec PQ
Saskatchewan SK
Yukon Territory YT
Labrador LB

Common Address Abbreviations

Avenue AVE
Expressway EXPY
Hospital HOSP
Junction JCT
Lakes LKS
Meadows MDWS
Palms PLMS
Parkway PKY
Ridge RDG
Road RD
Shore SH
Square SQ
Terrace TER
Union UN
Village VLG

East E
Heights HTS
Institute INST
Lake LK
Lane LN
North N
Park PK
Plaza PLZ
River RV
Rural R
South S
Station STA
Turnpike TPKE
View VW
West W

Numbers

You will use numbers frequently in your business letters, memos, and reports. The following guidelines should help you express them in a clear and consistent style.

Figures or Words

In general, spell out numbers ten and under; use figures for numbers over ten. Large round numbers (10,000) can be spelled out or written in a combination of words and figures.

Examples:
The letter was eight pages long.
The company laid off almost two thousand workers.
The insurance covers 352 married workers and 198 single workers.
The tanker held over 25 million gallons of oil.

Spell out numbers that begin a sentence. If the sentence contains more than one figure, try to rephrase the sentence so the number does not come first.

Avoid: 43 people attended the conference.

Better: Forty-three people attended the conference.

Avoid: Twelve out of 15 employees preferred the shorter work week.

Better: The shorter work week was preferred by 12 out of 15 employees.

Series

Numbers in a series should be expressed consistently. Use figures if any number in the series is over ten.

Examples:
We bought 24 sheets of music, 7 music stands, and 36 batons.
We need one typewriter, two desks, and five chairs.

Words and Figures Together

If two numbers are part of the same construction, the smaller number is expressed in words. If numbers in a sentence are used in different ways, use words for numbers ten and under and figures for larger numbers.

Examples:
Please get me 250 twenty-cent stamps. But: Make sure we get fourteen 65-cent labels.
Within six years, three of the companies had earned $520,000.

Note: A comma should be placed between two unrelated figures. It is better, however, to revise the sentence to separate them.

In 1983, 420 companies developed high-tech products.
In 1983, a total of 420 companies developed high-tech products.

Addresses

House numbers should be expressed in figures, except for the number *one*. Words are used for numbered street names *one* through *ten*. Use figures for state, interstate, and federal highways.

One South LaSalle Street
1476 Lynn Avenue
15 Second Avenue

U. S. Route 66 (U.S. 66)
Interstate 294 (I-294)
Montana 55

Note: Separate the house number and street name with a hyphen preceded and followed by a space.
17 - 20th Avenue
414 - 110th Street

Dates

When writing dates, use the current style (either month/day/year or day/month/year). Use words or figures (with *d, nd, rd, st,* or *th*) for the day when it occurs alone or when the month is part of a prepositional phrase in a sentence.

Examples:
We received a number of phone calls on January 22, 19--.
Or: We received a number of phone calls on 22 January 19--.

The director discussed the plan on the fifteenth of March.
Or: The director discussed the plan on the 15th of March.

Bills are sent on the second of every month.
Or: Bills are sent on the 2nd of every month.

Centuries and Decades

Use words for centuries and for decades when the century is omitted. The words are not capitalized. Use figures when both decade and century are given.

the nineteenth century *but* 1990s *Or:* 1990's
during the thirties *but* 1930s *Or:* 1930's

Money

Use figures to express sums of money whether foreign or U.S. currency, but use words for small sums of money serving as adjectives.

Examples:

The order cost $4,235.98. It cost £315 and sells for £760.
This ten-dollar pen leaks. They charge a ten-cent fee.

Amounts in even dollars are written without the decimal and zeros. However, if other figures in the sentence use decimals, make sure all amounts of money are consistent.

Examples:

We can get lumber for $6 a foot.
We received two invoices: one for $15.45 and one for $15.00.

Use figures and the word cents for amounts under a dollar. However, if the amount is used with figures over a dollar, use a zero and decimal point before the cents figure.

Examples:

The cassettes cost only 35 cents to produce.
One item cost $1.45, another cost $0.65, and the third cost $2.50.

Percentages

In general, percentages are expressed in figures plus the word *percent*. (However, the symbol % is used in statistical or tabular material.)

Examples:

The company borrowed $44 million at 10 percent interest.
Sales have declined 2.5 percent over the past quarter.

Fractions and Decimals

Mixed fractions and decimals are expressed in figures. A zero is used with decimal fractions not preceded by a whole number. However, simple fractions are expressed in words. If the fraction is used as an adjective, it is hyphenated. If it serves as a noun, it is not hyphenated.

Mixed fractions and decimals	*Simple fractions*
10¼ feet by 12½ feet	one-sixth share of the market
up to 2.25 inches	three-fifths majority
the rate fell 0.15 percent	one tenth of their income
the CPI rose 1.045 percent	one half of the workers

Ages

Express exact ages in figures. Approximate ages can be expressed in words or figures, but be consistent in your usage.

Examples:

At 41, Edgar Thorton is our youngest vice-president.

Our computer is only 2 years and 7 months old.

She is 33, and he is about 40.

He is almost eighty.

Measures

Measurements, weights, and distances are expressed in figures.

Examples:
For this report, use paper that is 8½ by 11 inches.
Each box weighs 75 lbs. 4 oz. (It is common practice to abbreviate pounds and ounces.)
Using air freight, we can cut 376 miles out of the route. (Fractions of a mile are expressed in words: The warehouse is three quarters of a mile from here.)

Temperature and Time

Temperature is expressed in figures with the degree sign, plus the scale being used. Time is expressed in figures when A.M., P.M., or other modifiers are used. With *o'clock,* express time in words.

Examples:

The freezer should be kept at 21° Fahrenheit.

The bank sign recorded 5° Celsius at noon.

We'll arrive at either 5:20 in the evening or 2:15 in the morning.

You have a choice between an 11:35 A.M. or a 2:50 P.M. flight.

You are invited to attend a cocktail hour at five o'clock.
(Time expressed in words is used in more formal correspondence.)

Titles

Official titles and designations are usually expressed in numbers, but you will need to follow the particular organization's style.

First National Bank

1st Federal Savings & Loan

Forty-second Ward

3rd Annual Sports Jamboree

Book Divisions

Generally, major book divisions are expressed in Roman numerals and minor divisions in Arabic figures. However, follow the style used in each book. Page numbers of books are always expressed in figures.

Examples:

Read from Part I, Chapters 2 through 6, to Part III.

Check these names against those on pages 144 and 145.

(Consecutive pages can be expressed either with *and* or *to,* or with a hyphen: pages 344 and 345, pages 344 to 345, pages 344-345.)

Chapter 18 Spelling

To many writers, the English language seems riddled with exceptions to spelling rules. Yet most words conform to specific guidelines, and even the exceptions can be categorized for ready reference. The guidelines in this section will help you in spelling most regular and troublesome words. The section also covers word division and provides a list of frequently misspelled words. Always remember that your best guide to correct spelling is an updated dictionary.

Spelling Guidelines

Prefixes

When a *prefix* is added to a word, the spelling of that word does not change.

Examples:

mis + statement = misstatement
im + material = immaterial
un + needed = unneeded
over + run = overrun
pre + existing = pre-existing
in + flammable = inflammable

Suffixes

When the suffixes *ness* and *ly* are added, the spelling of the word does not change unless the final *y* of a word represents a long *e* sound. Then the *y* changes to *i* before the suffix is added.

No spelling change

wry + ly = wryly
indebted + ness = indebtedness
sincere + ly = sincerely

Final y changed to i + suffix
happy + ness = happiness
steady + ly = steadily
handy + ly = handily
Exception: *busyness* to avoid confusion with *business*

Drop the final *e* if the suffix begins with a vowel. *Retain* the final *e* (1) after *c* or *g* if the suffix begins with *a* or *o* and (2) before adding a suffix that begins with a consonant.

Drop the final e
cope + ing = coping
use + able = usable
(*Exceptions:* saleable or salable)

Retain the final e
courage + ous = courageous
change + able = changeable
manage + ment = management

Words ending in *y* preceded by a consonant change the *y* to *i* before adding a suffix. Words ending in *y* preceded by a vowel do not change.

Change y to i
sunny + est = sunniest
accompany + ment = accompaniment
Exceptions: trying, studying

Retain the y
cloy + ing = cloying
say + ing = saying
boy + ish = boyish

Double the final consonant before a suffix that begins with a vowel if (1) the word has only one syllable or the accent is on the final syllable and (2) if the word ends in a consonant preceded by a vowel.

control + able = controllable
omit + ing = omitting
plan + ing = planning
prefer + ing = preferring
But: preferable
occur + ence = occurrence

For words ending in hard *c* sound, add *k* before suffixes *ing, ed, y.*

panic + ed = panicked
picnic + ing = picnicking
traffic + ed = trafficked
mimic + ing = mimicking

Plurals

The plural of most nouns is formed by adding *s.*

figure	figures	manager	managers
record	records	file	files

For nouns ending in *s, ss, z, sh, ch,* and *x,* add *es* to form the plural.

tax	taxes	kiss	kisses
wish	wishes	buzz	buzzes
watch	watches	gas	gases
address	addresses	fez	fezes

For nouns ending in *y* preceded by a consonant, change the *y* to *i* and add *es.* For nouns ending in *y* preceded by a vowel simply add *s.*

Nouns ending in y preceded by a consonant change y to i, add es		*Nouns ending in y preceded by a vowel add s*	
secretary	secretaries	holiday	holidays
currency	currencies	Wednesday	Wednesdays
category	categories	delay	delays

For nouns ending in *o* preceded by a consonant, add *s* or *es*. If the *o* is preceded by a vowel, add *s*.

Nouns ending in o preceded by a consonant usually add s or es		*Nouns ending in o preceded by a vowel add s*	
potato	potatoes, potatos	radio	radios
hero	heroes	studio	studios
tomato	tomatoes, tomatos	stereo	stereos

Note: All musical terms ending in o add *s* to form the plural.

Many nouns ending in *f* or *fe* simply add *s* to form the plural. However, some nouns change the *f* to *v* and add *s* or *es*.

Add s

chief	chiefs
dwarf	dwarfs

Nouns changing f to v and adding s or es

life	lives	half	halves
knife	knives	thief	thieves
wife	wives	self	selves

Compound nouns written as one word and ending in *s, sh, ch,* or *x* form the plural by adding *es*. In all other cases, the plural is formed by simply adding *s*.

Compound nouns adding es		*Compound nouns adding s*	
lockbox	lockboxes	firefighter	firefighters
toothbrush	toothbrushes	mainframe	mainframes
		cupful	cupfuls

The plural of compounds written as two or more words is formed by adding *s* to the main word. Hyphenated compounds are made plural either by adding *s* to the main word or, if there is no main word, adding *s* to the end of the compound.

Compound nouns of two or more words

editor in chief	editors in chief
notary public	notary publics
vice president	vice presidents

Hyphenated nouns adding s to the main word of compound

president-elect	presidents-elect
ex-governor	ex-governors
son-in-law	sons-in-law
passer-by	passers-by

Hyphenated nouns adding s to the end of compound

trade-in	trade-ins
write-in	write-ins
grown-up	grown-ups

The plural of numbers, letters, words, and symbols is formed by adding apostrophe and *s*.

three 8's	two *'s and three #'s	use x's and o's
use and's	1990's (or 1990s)	yes's and no's

The I and E Rules

Use *i* before *e*, except after *c* for the long *e* sound in a word. Use *e* before *i* when the sound in the word is not long *e*.

i before e (long e sound)

believe	relieve
grievance	retrieve
piece	thief

e before i after c (long e sound)

ceiling	receipt
deceive	receive

Exceptions: neither, leisure, seized

e before i (no long e sound)

freight	weight
neighbor	height
weigh	eight

Frequently Misspelled Words

The following list contains frequently misspelled words used in business communication. Use this list as a reference, but be sure you also have a good dictionary on hand.

A
abbreviate
absence
accommodate
accompanies
accompaniment
accumulate
accuracy
acknowledgment
advantageous
analysis
analyze
apparatus
appreciate
appropriate
argument
arrangement
arrears
ascertain
association
authorize
auxiliary

B
bankruptcy
beneficial
bibliography
bookkeeper
brochure
bulletin

C
calendar
canceled
cancellation
category
changeable
choose
chose
column
commission
commitment
committed
committee
competent
competitor
comptroller
concise
conscience
conscientious
consensus
contingency
correspondence
correspondents
criticize

D
debtor
deferred
depreciation
description
desirable
dilemma
dissatisfied

E
economical
effect
efficiency
embarrassment
emphasize
enforceable
exaggerate
excel
exceptionally
exhibitor
existence
exorbitant
extension

F
facilitate
familiar
feasible
forfeit
forewarn
franchise
fraud
fraudulent
freight
fulfill

G
gauge
grievance
guarantee
guaranty

H
harassment
hindrance
hypothesis

I
illegible
immediately
imperative
implement
inconvenience
indemnity
indispensable
inflationary
initial
installation
initiative
interpretation
interrupt
invoice
itemize
itinerary

J
jeopardize
jeopardy
judgment

K
knowledge
knowledgeable

L
labeled
legitimate
liable
likelihood
livelihood
livable
loose
lose
lucrative

M
maintenance
manageable
mandatory
marketable
measurable
mediator
miscellaneous
misspell
misstatement
municipal

N
necessity
negligible
negotiate
neutral
ninety
ninth
notarize
noticeable

O
objectionable
observant
occasion
occupant
omission
omitted
opinionated
option
overrated

P
pamphlet
parallel
paralysis
parity
particularly
permitted
personnel
pertinent
phenomenon
plausible
possession
practically
precise
preference
preferred
prejudice

Q
quality
quantity
qualitative
quantitative
questionnaire

R
recommend
recommendation
reconciliation
recurrence
reducible
reference
referred
reimburse
remittance
remitted
repetition
respectfully
responsibility
returnable
revenue
routine

S
saleable
schedule
scientific
scrutinize
separate
serviceable
similar
specifically

substantial	transmittal	**W**
supervisor		waive
supersede	**U**	warranty
superficial	unanimous	wholly
superfluous	undoubtedly	withhold
susceptible	unmistakable	
synonymous	unnecessarily	**Y**
		yield
T	**V**	
tariff	vacuum	**Z**
technician	vendor	zealous
tendency	ventilation	
totaling	versatile	
transmit	volumn	

Word Division

Whether you use a typewriter or a word processor, you will need to know how to divide words properly. The guidelines listed below can help you learn the basic rules of word division. As a basic rule, avoid dividing words at the end of more than two or three successive lines. Also, avoid dividing a word at the end of a page or the last word in a paragraph.

Basic Rules

Words are divided only between syllables. As a result, one-syllable words such as *missed, rough, through, while* are never divided.

When a word is divided, there must be more than one letter on the first line and more than two letters with the last part of the word.

sin-cerely *not* sincere-ly
ap-a-thy *not* a-pathy
jew-elry *not* jewel-ry
era-sure *not* e-rasure

Each syllable in word division must contain a vowel; therefore, most contractions cannot be divided.

con-trol *not* con-tr-ol
hy-drau-lic *not* hy-dr-au-lic
couldn't *not* could-n't
isn't *not* is-n't

Final and Double Consonants

If a final consonant preceded by a vowel is doubled before adding a suffix, divide the word *between the two consonants.*

win + ing = win-ning
plan + ing = plan-ning

If the root word ends in a double consonant before the suffix is added, divide the word *between the root word and the suffix.*

tell + ing = tell-ing
assess + ing = assess-ing

Single-letter Syllables

Generally, a single-letter syllable within a word should be left with the first part of the word and not carried over to the second line.

bus-i-ness = busi-ness *not* bus-iness
sep-a-rate = sepa-rate *not* sep-arate
ox-y-gen = oxy-gen *not* ox-ygen

When two single-letter syllables occur together in a word, divide the word *between the single-letter syllables.*

grad-u-a-tion = gradu-ation *not* grad-uation
in-sin-u-a-tion = insinu-ation *not* insin-uation

When the single-letter syllable *a, i,* or *u* is followed by the final syllable *ble, bly,* or *cal,* join the two end syllables and carry them to the next line.

de-pend-a-ble = depend-able *not* dependa-ble
cler-i-cal = cler-ical *not* cleri-cal
in-vinc-i-ble = invinc-ible *not* invinci-ble

Hyphenated Words

Divide hyphenated words and compound hyphenated words *only at the hyphen* that connects them.

clearing-house *not* clear-ing-house
self-assessment *not* self-assess-ment
client-oriented approach *not* client-or-iented approach

Proper Names

Avoid dividing a person's name or any proper name. Separate titles, initials, or degrees from names only when it is unavoidable.

Avoid:		*Preferred:*	
	Mrs. Joan Cunning- ham		Mrs. Joan Cunningham
	Mr. Emmett Mei		Mr. Emmett Mei
	Georgia Watson, Ph.D.		Georgia Watson, Ph.D.

Figures and Abbreviations

In general, avoid dividing figures and abbreviations. If you must separate the parts of an address or a date, however, use the following guidelines.

Dividing addresses

15 Water Street	*not*	15 Water Street
557 West Lockport	*not*	557 West Lock- port
1903 — 71st Avenue	*not*	1903 — 71st Avenue
New York, New York	*not*	New York, New York

Dividing dates

August 20, 19--	*not*	August 20, 19--

Section 7
Automation and the Information Age

Chapter 19: Communication in the Electronic Office

Computers and electronic transmission systems have revolutionized the way we communicate in business. Data, voice, and graphic networks enable business leaders to exchange information and make critical decisions more rapidly than ever before.

Today, one secretary can generate, file, store, process, and retrieve volumes of information that previously would have taken a score of clerks to handle. Over the past thirty-five years, we have witnessed more change in the area of business communication than has occurred during the past several centuries.

Computers and the Human Element

Sophisticated hardware, however, does not alter the fundamentals of communication. The message still originates in the mind of the sender and must be understood by the mind of the receiver. Human operators are responsible for the content, organization, wording, and format of the information sent and received. In fact, because of the speed with which messages can be transmitted, skill in saying precisely and accurately what you mean is even more essential. The guidelines in this handbook for writing effective, accurate, and concise messages can help you make the best use of the communications technology found in today's offices.

Word processing, information processing, telecommunications, and networking have emerged as the dominant technologies in the office and among businesses. These four processes can be combined through various electronic linkages to form the business communication network. Such networks are growing rapidly in this country and in many countries around the world.

Computer Components

Most people are familiar with the *personal computer* or *microcomputer* seen in advertisements for home and business use. But businesses also use *mainframe computers* and *minicomputers* to handle data. Mainframe computers have enough memory and power to store, process, and retrieve all the information in an organization as large as Chase Manhattan Bank or the Social Security Administration. The minicomputer has more memory than a microcomputer but less power than the mainframe.

Businesses may use a combination of these three types of computers. Several terminals can be tied into the mainframe or minicomputer, allowing office staff to work simultaneously with the same information or program. Microcomputers are ideal for individual desk work or as remote terminals with a link to a larger system.

Regardless of size, all computers have five basic parts: input units, output units, a central processing unit or CPU, secondary storage, and memory, as shown in the illustration. The computer and its components are called *hardware*, while the programs used to run the computer are referred to as *software*.

Five Parts of the Computer

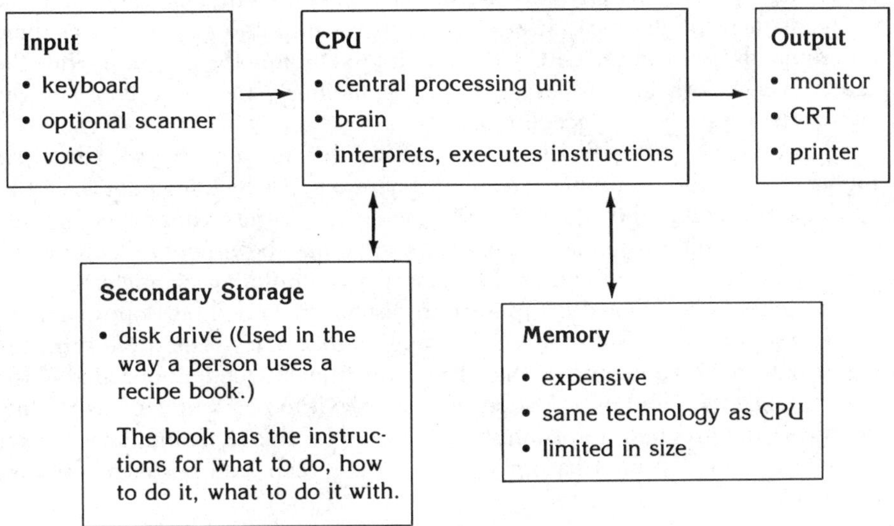

Computer Hardware

The heart of the computer is the central processing unit (CPU). Silicon chips soldered onto printed circuit boards provide the hardware for computer memory and data processing capabilities. The CPU determines how information is handled once it enters the computer.

The computer does not use or understand English. Its basic language consists of electronic impulses called a binary digit or *bit*. A bit is either an "on" or "off" switch. CPU circuits are designed to read groups of these bits in a sequence at almost the speed of light. To combine bits into meaningful commands, they are organized by *bytes* of eight, sixteen, or more bits at a time. A byte, or short sequence of on-off switches, represents about one character or letter.

A *kilobyte* equals 1010 bytes and is the unit of measure for computer memory or storage capacity. When we say a computer has 256 kilobytes (256K) worth of memory, it means that 258,560 bytes or about 2,000,000 characters can be stored in the computer memory before it is saturated. Mainframe computers have thousands of kilobytes or *megabytes* of memory, allowing them to store, process, and retrieve huge quantities of data.

Computer Software

The software program tells the computer what to do. Without a program, the computer is only a sophisticated collection of printed circuits. Programs are recorded on tape cassettes or reels, card decks, floppy diskettes, or hard disks. The CPU reads these programs as a series of electrical impulses and translates them into commands. Some of the CPU's memory is used to store the program while the operator works with it. The larger the CPU memory, the more complex the program the computer can accommodate.

Most likely, you will use a microcomputer in your work. The basic components of a microcomputer are (1) the system unit which includes the CPU, (2) the keyboard, (3) the monitor (video screen), (4) the printer, and (5) the software. The monitor is similar to a TV screen and may be either black and white or color. Black-and-white monitors have sharper resolution of characters.

Programs for personal computers are usually recorded on floppy or hard diskettes and are loaded into the CPU through a *disk drive*. The drive spins the diskette like a record and enables the CPU to read the instructions encoded in the program. Once the program is loaded, you can use it to perform your work. In a word-processing program, for example, you would be able to manipulate text, set margins, move tabs, print what appeared on the screen, and perform countless other functions.

Data Entry and Output

In most business programs, the operator can enter instructions or information into the computer using the keyboard and special function keys which give various commands to the computer contained in the program. For example, if you would like to save the material you have typed into the computer, you would press the "Save text" function key. The computer would either save the text in memory or transfer it to a blank diskette for storage.

The key words in handling data via computer are *input* and *output*. Input refers to the information you enter into the computer through the keyboard or other means. Output is the material displayed on the screen or printer. If you instruct the computer to print out your text on paper, you have output in the form of *hard copy*.

Computers can greatly facilitate information processing. But they are only as useful as the programs that run them. At best, they can extend our capabilities; at worst, they will multiply our mistakes.

Word Processing

Word processing involves the production, editing, and final typing or printing of written material. Despite the sophisticated technology available today, word processing itself is not a new concept. Human beings have been creating and editing text since the first written language appeared several thousand years ago. Only the hardware for the process has changed.

Today, word processing refers to the creation and editing of text on a special typewriter or computer. As data is entered through a keyboard into the word processor, each keystroke is recorded on a magnetic medium—usually a tape or floppy or hard diskette. If you wish to change the text, you can erase the material and record over it, much as you would do with a cassette tape in a tape recorder.

Word processors make the creation and revision of material much easier than is possible with an ordinary typewriter. You can delete, rearrange, reword, or duplicate sentences, paragraphs, even whole pages of text simply by pressing the right function key on the keyboard. Once all the corrections have been made, you can print out the material on a microprinter attached to the word-processing machine. Many industrial printers can type documents at hundreds or even thousands of characters per second. In some offices, photocopiers are attached to the system and can make copies of the finished document as a final step in the process. Software word-processing programs even let the operator set an automatic search for misspelled words, improper syntax, and grammatical errors. The computer will proofread the final text, as shown in the illustration.

Word-processing programs are invaluable when an office must produce a mass mailing to customers. The computer can personalize each letter by inserting the customer's name in the salutation. It can also "merge" names and addresses with various form letters, producing hundreds of copies in a few hours. These features of small business computers have enabled even single-proprietor companies to take part in direct-mail selling.

Managers and analysts who must write lengthy proposals, reports, and memos—often with graphics to illustrate the text—appreciate the capabilities of word processors. In the past, corrections and revisions to the text would have meant retyping the entire document or redrawing any graphic illustrations. By recording the document on the word processor, changes can be inserted easily, and only the revised material needs to be proofread.

Word processing not only makes the writer's job easier, it improves the speed and efficiency of business communications. Software programmers are working to make their word-processing packages more sophisticated and powerful with each version. For example, programs now exist that alert the writer to clichés, stereotyped phrasing, jargon, and lengthy or unclear sentences in the text. In addition, the program will suggest alternative phrasing or terms. The computer, far from restricting communication, may preserve the art of good writing!

When IBM first introduced automated word processing in the early 1960s, only a few firms were able to afford the investment of time and money to install the systems and train their staff. Today, a wide range of businesses and individuals can purchase the hardware and software needed to do word processing on their own. In fact, it is estimated that by the late 1980s, the market for word-processing equipment and software will reach over $5 billion a year.

Information Processing

According to some industry experts we have moved from the Atomic Age into the Information Age. Information processing involves the manipulation of data by electronic means to collect, organize, record, and store information for decision-making purposes. For example, a hospital may use information processing to record diagnoses and recommend treatment for each patient, handle the constant flow of insurance forms, and keep track of billing. Retail stores use computerized checkout counters to help them maintain proper inventory levels on each item in the store. Scanners or "electronic eyes" built into the countertop at the cashier's station "read" coded inventory numbers off each item and relay the information to the computer. The item is then automatically deducted from the inventory list. The store manager, by reading the computer printout, will know which products need to be reordered and which ones should be discontinued.

Information processing can be used to create electronic files, replacing the bulky file cabinets and drawers that exist in most offices. File data are recorded on computer disks and backup copies are made to guard against the possible loss of information. Data can be retrieved easily by inserting the proper disk in the computer and calling up the file name. The files can be updated and revised as often as necessary.

Information processing is so vital a part of the current business scene that it has spawned many companies whose sole product is information—supplying it, creating it, and managing it for other businesses at a subscription or per project fee. For example, a company may sell demographic information about various consumer groups to retail firms. Such data can help these firms target their products more carefully, resulting in greater returns on sales and higher profits.

The Information Age is likely to prove as large a source of new industries and jobs as did the Industrial Revolution over 150 years ago.

Telecommunications

In telecommunications, information that has been created, collected, and stored through word processing and information processing is sent electronically from one location to another. This method transmits data rapidly and avoids the slower, more costly systems of company mail, the U.S. Postal Service, and private mail carriers.

Computers in one location are linked through telephone lines and special communications hardware to computers in another location or several locations. Both sender and receiver must have a telecommunications link in order to transmit and receive information. Any type of data that can be created on the computer screen—graphics, maps, diagrams, charts, figures, text—can be sent from one site to another. Nor is distance a problem. Messages can be transmitted from one coast to the other or from continent to continent via cable or satellite relays.

Telecommunications also allow companies to set up electronic teleconferencing. Instead of business people gathering at one central location for a meeting, the meeting can come to them. Video pictures can be relayed to several locations and telephone links transmit the sound to each smaller "conference." Individuals can discuss a project as if they were present in the same room even though they are actually hundreds, even thousands, of miles apart.

Telecommunications may soon be possible through fiber optic cables (small bundles of cables that can carry millions of bits of information); through communications satellites; and even through laser technology. It appears that in many ways the office of the future is happening today!

Networking

A network is a system of different types of office equipment linked together electronically. A network can refer to an in-house company system of computers, terminals, typewriters, printers, and copy machines or to a system that links several companies. Office equipment may be connected by phone lines, cables, or broadcast channels.

Networks can save considerable time and money and increase the ease and speed of communication. For example, tying in data processing files with word processing makes it possible for managers to use file data when writing reports. More than one terminal can be connected to a main computer, which allows several people to use the same data for their work. Using the same program to drive several terminals reduces the cost of operating the computer equipment. Likewise, integrating different machines into the same system eliminates the need to invest in higher-priced equipment. For example, typewriters compatible with computers could be used as letter-quality printers. The company would not have to buy a more expensive printer.

Specific benefits of an integrated communication network include:

1. Every key employee can have word-processing and data-processing capability along with access to central information banks.
2. Electronic mail and phone message service can be provided to all employees.
3. Every employee can have scheduling management—automatic notice of meetings, appointments, agendas, directories and so on.
4. Central filing systems can be established that save, cross-reference, sort, update, index, and maintain each employee's data as part of general office files.
5. Computer terminals can be located in employees' homes or other field locations and tied into the office computer. Employees would be able to work at remote sites without needing to commute every day to a central office.

Electronic communications from word processing to networks opens up new possibilities and potentials for the business communicator that did not exist even ten years ago. With such expanded capabilities, however, each person must develop skills of analysis, organization, and facility with language to manage the available information. There is still no substitute for the skilled human communicator.

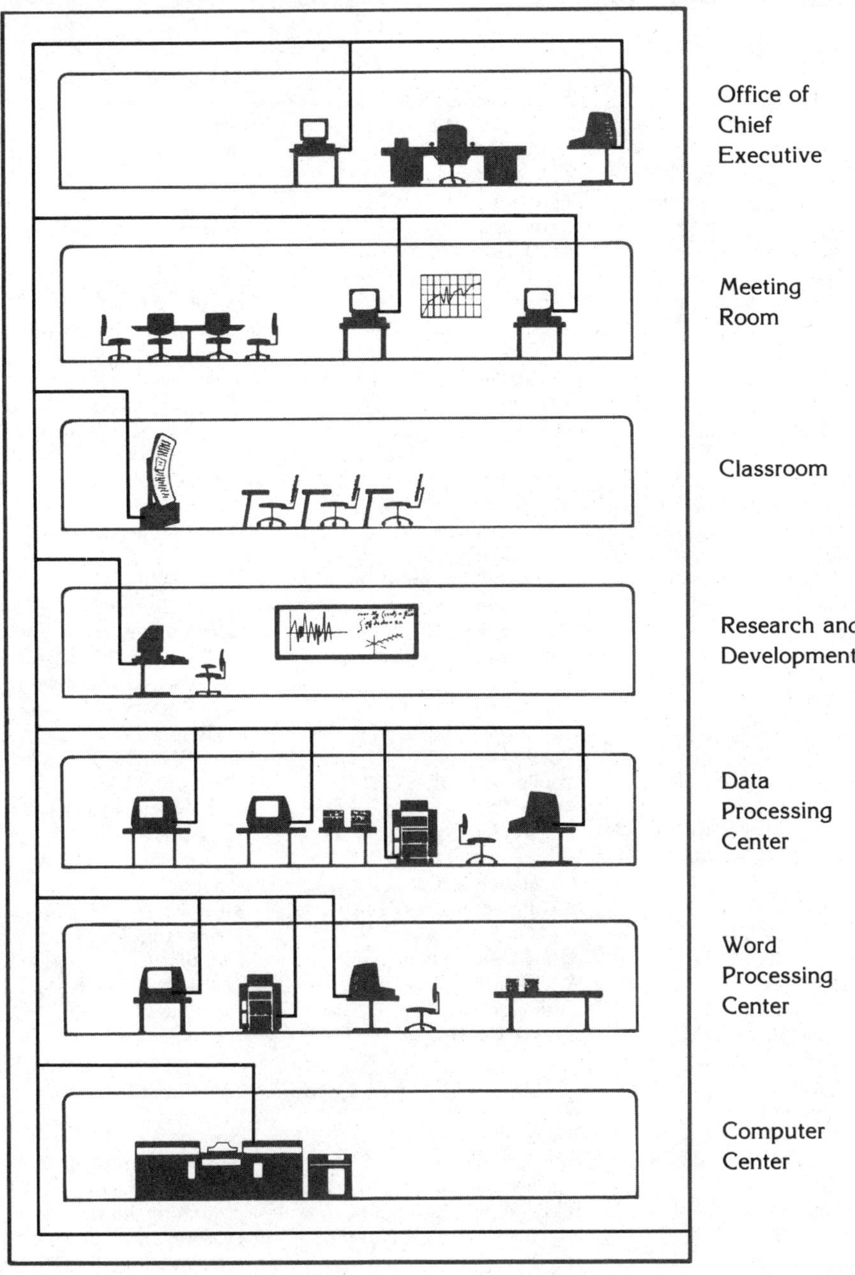

Artist's rendering of what a typical wired office might look like with a variety of equipment attached to the same cable.

Index